Westmoreland County, Virginia

Deeds and Wills

1761–1768

Deed Book 14

Abstracted by
Michael R. Marshall

Heritage Books
2023

HERITAGE BOOKS
AN IMPRINT OF HERITAGE BOOKS, INC.

Books, CDs, and more—Worldwide

For our listing of thousands of titles see our website
at
www.HeritageBooks.com

Published 2023 by
HERITAGE BOOKS, INC.
Publishing Division
5810 Ruatan Street
Berwyn Heights, MD 20740

International Standard Book Number
Paperbound: 978-0-7884-2957-6

INTRODUCTION

Deed and will books can contain land transactions, mortgages, leases, bills of sale, powers of attorney, marriage contracts, estate settlements, and much more information of genealogical interest. They are a must for researching your family history.

The volume contains entries from Westmoreland County Deed and Will Book No.14, 1761-1768 beginning on page 1 and ending on page 571 for Courts held March 31, 1761 through September 27, 1768.

An every-name index adds to the value of this work.

Notes with parenthesis "[ ]" contain additional information or clarification.

Spelling of names and places were cross-checked against the following publications for accuracy.

- Colonial Lands and Roads of Westmoreland County, Virginia; [Edward J. White] 2020
- Lands and Lesser Gentry of Eastern Westmoreland County, Virginia 1650-1840s, [Edward J. White] 2014
- Historical Atlas of Westmoreland County, Virginia; [David Wolfe Eaton] 1942

Page 1.
John Walker Will
In the name of God Amen, I John Walker of the Parish of Cople and County of Westmoreland being in health and sound and perfect memory do make this my last will and testament in manner and form following.
Item I give and bequeath to my loving wife Ann Walker the use of my estate during her natural life or widowhood and in case my wife should marry after my decease my will is she have of my estate what the law allows and the residue of my estate to me divided equally among my three children' vizt; William Walker, James Walker and Elizabeth Walker.
Item I give and bequeath to my loving son William Walker, the land & plantation whereon I now live to him and the male heirs of his body and for want of heirs to my son James Walker and the male heirs of his body and for want of heirs to my daughter Elizabeth Walker and her heirs.
Lastly, I appoint my loving wife Ann Walker and my loving son William Walker and my loving cousin John Baley [Bailey] whole and sole executors of this my last will & testament. In witness whereof I have hereunto set my hand and seal this 25th day of September 1760.
Peter Hemming John Walker (his mark)
Elizabeth Baley [Bailey]
John Baley [Bailey]
Westmoreland Sct. At a court held for the said county the 31st day of March 1761, this will of John Walker, deceased was presented into court and sworn to by Ann Walker and John Baley two of his executors therein named, the same being also proved by the oaths of Peter Hemming and Elizabeth Baley two of the witnesses thereto is admitted to record and on motion of the executors and their performing what the law in such case require certificate is granted them for obtaining a probate thereon in due form.
Recorded the 9th day of April 1761 Test: George Lee CCW

Page 2.
Samuel Courtney's Will
In the name of God Amen, this 18th day of July 1759, I Samuel Courtney of the County of Westmoreland being sick and weak but in perfect sound mind and memory do make and ordain and appoint this my last will and testament in manner and form following.
Item I give and bequeath to my godson Samuel Courtney 500 pounds of tobacco for use of his schooling. Also, I give to my godson Thomas Garner 500 pounds of like tobacco to be put to the same use.
Item I give to my brother James Courtney one shilling sterling.
Item I give unto Samuel Joe 5 pounds to be paid by my executors hereafter named.
My desire is that the rest of my estate should be equally divided between my brother Leonard Courtney and Jeremiah Courtney and my sister Rosamond Garner to them and their heirs and I do hereby nominate and appoint my brothers Leonard Courtney and Jeremiah Courtney executors of this my last will and testament.
In witness whereof I have hereunto set my hand and seal in presence of
Rodham Pritchett Samuel Courtney (his mark)
Henry Self
Westmoreland Sct. At a Court held for the said county the 31st day of March 1761 this will of Samuel Courtney, deceased was presented into court and sworn by Jeremiah Courtney and Leonard Courtney the executors therein named, the same being also proved by the oaths of all the witnesses thereto is admitted to record and on motion of the said executors and their performing what the law and each case requires certificate is granted for them of obtaining a probate thereof in due form.
Recorded the ninth day of April 1761 Test: George Lee CCW

Page 3.

Robert Todd Will

In the name of God Amen, I Robert Todd of the County of Westmoreland and Parish of Cople in Virginia being sick and weak of body but of perfect memory do make this my last will and testament in manner and form following.

Item I give and bequeath to Richard Caddeen of the Parish of Cople and County aforesaid all my estate whatsoever here in Virginia, to him and his heirs.

I also appoint Richard Caddeen my whole and sole executor of this my last will and testament.

January 18, 1761 Robert Todd (his mark)

Robert Middleton

Stephen Crane

Westmoreland Sct. At a Court held for the said County the 31st day of March 1761 this last will and testament of Robert Todd, deceased was presented into Court and sworn to by Richard Caddeen executor therein named, the same being also proved by the oath of the witnesses thereto is admitted to record and on motion of the executor and his performing what the law in such cases require, certificate is granted him for obtaining a probate thereof in due form.

Recorded the ninth day of April 1761 Test: George Lee CCW

Page 3.

Thomas Chancellor's Will

In the name of God Amen, I Thomas Chancellor of the County of Westmoreland being very sick and weak but of sound and perfect memory do constitute make and appoint this to be my last will and testament in manner and form following.

I give and bequeath unto my wife Katherine Chancellor the place whereon I now live during her life as widow, and Negroes; Will, Litte, and Ned.

I give and bequeath unto my son John Chancellor all my land after my wife's decease and Negro Moses.

I give and bequeath unto my daughter Katherine Chancellor: Negro boy Ben.

I give and bequeath unto my daughter Grace Chancellor, Negro boy Dick.

I give and bequeath unto my daughter Rebeccah Chancellor, Negro girl Frank and feather bed and furniture.

I give and bequeath unto my son Thomas Chancellor, Negro boy James, and the horse colt that he now lays claim to, and a feather bed and furniture.

I give and bequeath unto my daughter Sarah Chancellor, Negro girl Marey and a feather bed and furniture.

The remaining part of my estate that is not already given to be equally divided after my wife's decease.

I do constitute and appoint my loving wife Katherine Chancellor and my son John Chancellor to be my executors of this my last will and testament. In witness whereof I have hereunto set my hand and affixed my seal this 19th day of November 1760.

Signed sealed and acknowledge in the presence of us Thomas Chancellor

John Omohundro, Jr.

William Wroe

Augustine Weedon

Westmoreland Sct. At a Court held for the said county the 31st day of March 1761 this last will of Thomas Chancellor, deceased was presented into Court and sworn to by John Chancellor one of the executors therein named, the same being proved by the oath of all the witnesses thereto is admitted to record, and on motion of the said executor and his performing what the law in such cases require, certificate is granted him for obtaining a probate thereof in due form.

Recorded the ninth day of April 1761 Test: George Lee CCW

Page 4.

Samuel Johnson's Will

In the name of God Amen, the 22nd day of December 1760, I Samuel Johnson, Sr., the Parish of Washington in County of Westmoreland, planter being sick and weak in body but of perfect mind and memory do make and ordain this my last will and testament.

Imprimis, I give and bequeath unto my beloved wife Ann Johnson all my estate, real and personal with the profits, privileges and uses thereto belonging during her natural life to her own proper use and pleasure without any molestation; and that such of my estate as is not given as legacies in the said will that she may dispose of the same as she thinks proper. That no division be made nor legacies paid until my said wife's decease except she think proper to bestow Mary Binks hereafter mentioned her legacy if married.

Item I give and bequeath unto my granddaughter Ann Johnson, Negro man Harry.

Item I give and bequeath unto my two granddaughters, Margaret Johnson and Mary Johnson each of them 20 pounds cask to be paid by my executors after the death of my beloved wife which said money to be raised out of the work of my slaves, and one cow and calf to each.

Item I give and bequeath unto Mary Binks, daughter of Thomas Binks, deceased two young Negroes, Ben and Bett to her in the heirs of her body; and for want of such heirs then to return to my grandson Samuel Johnson and his heirs. I likewise given to the said Mary Binks one bed and furniture and one young horse called Spanker.

Item I give and bequest to my grandson Samuel Johnson the following slaves; Mozingo, Jack, Ned, Jane and her children, Jude and her children, except Bett given as above, to him and his heirs and for want of heirs then the said slaves to return and be equally divided between my granddaughters above mentioned and Mary Binks or their heirs.

Item it is my will and pleasure that my executor hereafter mentioned during the minority of my grandson and after the death of my wife, take unto himself the full and absolute care of my said grandson and his estate into his possession as my executor to receive the profits of the said estate without being liable. It being my desire no inventory nor appraisement be made of my estate or any parcel thereof but to be disposed of by my executors according to the tenure of this my last will and testament.

In further it is my desire that my said grandson be kept at school until he arrives to the year 18; and that he not be interested with any part of his estate till he arrives at the age of 21 years.

I do hereby constitute make and ordain my beloved wife and William Smith executors of this my last will and testament. In witness whereof I have hereunto set my hand and seal the day and year above written

Signed sealed and delivered in the presence of us Samuel Johnson (his mark)
John Higdon
Joseph Butler
Thomas Williams

Westmoreland Sct. At a court held for the said County the 31st day of March 1760 one this last will and testament of Samuel Johnson, deceased was presented into Court by Ann Johnson his executrix who made oath thereto and being sworn by the oath of John Higdon and Joseph Butler two of the witnesses thereto is admitted to record and on motion of the executrix and her performing what the law in such cases require, certificate is granted her for obtaining a probate thereon in due form.

Recorded the ninth day of April 1761 Test: George Lee CCW

Page 7.

Thomas Vivion Will

I Thomas Vivion of the County of Westmoreland do make and ordain this my last will and testament in manner and form followeth.

Imprimis, I give and bequeath to my son Charles Vivion my land and plantation lying in King George County on Rappahannock River.

Item I give and bequeath to my son Francis Vivion the land and plantation whereon I now live together with all my lands in Westmoreland County.

Item I give to my daughter Jane Vivion that I had with my late wife before marriage the sum of 500 pounds current money of Virginia, to be raised by my executors out of my estate as hereinafter directed, and paid to her on her arriving to the age or date of marriage.

Item I give to my daughter Mary Vivion the sum of 500 pounds current money of Virginia to be raised by my executors out of my estate as hereinafter directed him paid to her of her arriving to age or day of marriage.

Item I give to my daughter Jane Vivion Negro girl Lucy with all her increase; I also give her a young horse, saddle and bridle.
Item I give to my daughter Mary Vivion Negro girl Rachael with all her increase; I also give her a young horse, saddle and bridle.
Item in case either or both of the Negro girls herein given to my two daughters should die before my daughters come to age or marry my will and desire is that other Negro girls of equal value be allotted to them out of my estate.
Item my will and desire is that in case either my daughters Jane Vivion and Mary Vivion should die before they come to age or marry that my other daughters possessed and enjoyed all the estate herein given to the one dying.
Item my will and desire is that my executors hereafter named receive all the money and that they put the same into good hands with what money I may have by me together with the sales of my household furniture and the yearly profits of my estate and interest, allowing my two daughters Jane Vivion and Mary Vivion to be maintained out of the profits of my lands and Negroes with my two sons until such time as my executors may have raised the sums herein granted to my said to daughters Jane Vivion and Mary Vivion and afterwards I desire that my two daughters be maintained out of the interest of the monies given them.
Item I give my daughter Frances Brooking a gold ring of the value of 20 shillings.
Item I give to my daughter Margaret Pratt a gold ring of the value of 20 shillings.
Item I give to my son Charles Vivion and my son Francis Vivion all and every part of the remainder of my estate of what kind soever, and desire the same may be equally divided between them.
Item my will and desire is that my two daughters Jane Vivion and Mary Vivion be under the care and direction of Mrs. Elizabeth Jett and Mrs. Dianna Goodloe until they come to age.
I desire that my estate be not appraised.
Lastly, I nominate and appoint my friends Thomas Jett, Mr. John Orr, and Mr. Peter Daniel guardians to my two sons Charles Vivion and Francis Vivion until they come to age as also executors of this my last will and testament.
In witness whereof I have hereunto set my hand and seal this 10th day of September 1760
Signed sealed and acknowledged in presence of. Thomas Vivion
Thomas Jett
John Jarvis
Westmoreland Sct. At a court held for the said County the 28th day of April 1761 this will of Thomas Vivion, deceased was presented into Court and sworn by Thomas Jett and Peter Daniel two of the executors therein named, the same being proved by the oath of the witnesses thereto is admitted to record in upon motion of the said executors and their performing what the law in such cases require, certificate is granted them for obtaining a probate thereof in due form.
Recorded the 30th day of April 1761 Test: George Lee CCW

Page 8.
Thom to Jarvis Lease
This indenture made the 10th day of December 1760 between Alexander Thom, tailor of the Parish of Washington and County of Westmoreland of one part and Field Jarvis. Witnesseth that Alexander Thom in consideration of five shillings current money of Virginia, does bargain and sell to Field Jarvis a parcel of land containing 64 acres lying in the Parish of Washington in County of Westmoreland. Beginning at a marked locust standing on the north side of a small run that falls into the head of Popes Creek and divides this land and the land of William Kimber and extending up the land of George Seyward, Northeast 140 pole; to a marked oak standing in John Foxall's line, then along said line West Northwest 140 pole to another oak, thence South Southwest to a white oak standing on the north side of the aforesaid run 18 poles; finally, down the run to the first beginning. To have and to hold the said tract of land for the term of one whole year from thence next ensuing yielding and paying and ear of Indian corn at the expiration of the term if demanded to the intent and purpose that by the statute for transferring uses and possession the said Field Jarvis may be in actual possession of the said tract of land and premises. In witness whereof the said Alexander Thom has to this present indenture set his hand and seal the day and month and year first above written.

Sealed and delivered in the presence of us Alexander Thom
James Hore
Francis Williams
John Jarvis
Joseph Butler
John Tancil
Westmoreland Sct. At a Court held for the said County the 28th day of April 1761 Alexander Thom came into court and personally acknowledged this lease for land by him passed to Field Jarvis and ordered to be recorded.
Recorded the first day of May 1761 Test: George Lee CCW

Page 10.
Thom to Jarvis Release
This indenture made the 11th day of December 1760 between Alexander Thom, tailor the Parish of Washington of the one part and Field Jarvis, planter of the parish and county aforesaid of the other part. Witnesseth the said Alexander Thom in consideration of 70 pounds current money of Virginia has confirmed and release unto Field Jarvis in his actual possession now being by virtue of a bargain and sale to him paid by indenture bearing date the day next before the date of these presents and by the force of the statute for transferring uses into possessions all that tract of land containing 64 acres situated in the Parish of Washington and the County of Westmoreland. [Boundaries the same as above lease]. In witness whereof the said Alexander Thom hath to this present indenture set his hand and seal the day month and year first above written.
Sealed and delivered in presence of Alexander Thom
James Hore
Francis Williams
John Jarvis
Joseph Butler
John Tancil
Westmoreland Sct. At a court held for the said County the 28th day of April 1761 Alexander Thom came into Court and personally acknowledged this release for land indented by him passed to Field Jarvis and ordered to be recorded.
Recorded the 1st day of May 1761 Test: George Lee CCW

Page 11.
John Lowe Verbal Will
John Lowe of Cople Parish in Westmoreland County now deceased, departed this life on the 6th day of March 1761, did on the 5th day of March 1761 declare that what is hereafter mentioned was his last will and testament and requested us to go before a magistrate to have the same put in writing.
Imprimis, that he left all his estate to his wife after his debts were paid, during her widowhood or till her children came of age, but if she marries before they came to age, the whole estate to be divided according to law and if she continues a widow, to the children as come to age that she should have the estate also be divided according to law.
Item he desired that George [Gerrard] Hutt and Bradley Garner to be his executors.
Signed by us as witnesses the 7th day of March 1761 before Richard Jackson
John Lathrum
John Carter
Westmoreland Sct. At a Court held for the said County the 28th day of April 1761 this verbal will of John Lowe, deceased was presented into court and proved by the oath of the witnesses thereto and ordered to be recorded.
Recorded the first day of May 1761 Test: George Lee CCW

Page 12. Crabb to Crabb to Crabb Bond
Know all men by these presents that I John Crabb of Westmoreland County and Cople Parish am held and firmly do stand bound and indebted to Osmond Crabb of the aforesaid county and parish

in the full and penal sum of 500 pounds current money of Virginia I bind myself by these presents. Sealed with my seal and dated the 5th day of November 1760.
The condition of the above obligation is if the above bounden John Crabb do well and truly stand and abide by the determination and judgement of Mr. James Baley, Jeremiah Middleton and John Baley or any two of them arbitrators indifferently chosen and elected as well on part and behalf of the above bound John Crabb as on the part of the above named Osmond Crabb to arbitrate, judge, settle and determine all differences in relation to the lands in dispute between them now, as always that the said award, arbitrament be made and done and put in writing within ten days after the date of these presents and ready to be delivered to either of them or such of them that shall come and require the same of them.
Sealed and delivered in the presence of us John Crabb
Abraham Garner
William Rice
Matthew Partridge
Westmoreland County, At the special request of Mr. John Crabb and Osmond Crabb, we whose names are underwritten being appointed by the said parties to settle and adjust the differences between them in relation to a lease passed from John Crabb to Osmond Crabb and Jane Crabb his wife during the life of Osmond Crabb and Jane Crabb his wife have a right to lease or rent the said land or any part thereof they complying with the said lease.
Given under our hands this 8th day of November 1760
James Baley
John Baley
Westmoreland Sct. At a court held for the said county the 28th day of April 1761 This bond together with the report thereon between John Crabb and Osmond Crabb was by mutual consent of both parties ordered to be recorded
Recorded the first day of May 1761 Test: George Lee CCW

Page 13.
Burditt Ashton's Will
In the name of God Amen, this 7th day of March 1760, I Burditt Ashton of Washington Parish and County of Westmoreland being sick and weak but of perfect disposing sense and memory do make and ordain this my last will and testament in manner and form following:
Item give and bequeath my whole estate real and personal to my nephew Burditt Ashton, son of Charles Ashton and Sarah Ashton his wife but if he dies before the age of 21 years or without heirs of his body then I give the whole estate to my brother Charles Ashton during his life, and I also desire that his wife Sarah Ashton after his death may have the use of the same during her natural life, and if my nephew Burditt Ashton dies without heirs as aforesaid then my desire is that my nephew Lawrence Ashton enjoy the same to him and his heirs forever but not to be possessed or have the use thereof during the life of his father and mother. It is also my desire that if my nephew Burditt Ashton died without heirs as aforesaid that my nephew John Ashton and the lands, I hold on the head of Mattox Creek to him and his heirs forever, I do hereby ordain and appoint my brother Charles Ashton my whole and sole executor of this my last will and testament. In witness whereof I have hereunto set my hand and seal the day and year aforesaid.
Sealed and published for Burditt Ashton, Senior
Richard Bernard
Lawrence Butler
William Berryman
Codicil to the within will, it is my desire my estate may not be inventoried nor praised. Witness my hand and seal the day and year within written.
Witness to the codicil Burditt Ashton, Senior
Richard Bernard
Lawrence Butler
William Berryman
Westmoreland Sct. At a court held for the said County the 29th day of July 1761 this last will and testament and the codicil therein of Burditt Ashton, deceased was presented into Court by Charles

Ashton his executor therein named who made oath thereto and being proved by the oath of Lawrence Butler and William Berryman two of the witnesses thereto was ordered to be continued for further proof. And now at a court held for the county aforesaid the 26th day of May 1761, the said will and codicil more fully proved by the oath of Richard Bernard a witness thereto and ordered to be recorded.
Recorded the 25th day of June 1761 Test: George Lee CCW

Page 15.
Blair & Grays Exchange Deed
This indenture made the 23rd day of May 1761 between James Blair the County of Westmoreland, merchant of the one part and Francis Gray the same county, Gent., of the other part. Whereas James Blair is possessed of a tract of land containing 140 acres lying in the Parish of Washington and County of Westmoreland in fee simple and whereas Francis Gray is possessed in fee simple of a tract of land in the same parish and county; and whereas James Blair and Francis Gray are minded and willing to exchange the lands and tenements; i.e. Francis Gray shall have the lands and tenements whereof James Blair possesses and James Blair shall have 270 acres out of the tract of land that Francis Gray is possessed. Now this indenture witnesseth that in consideration and in pursuance of the said exchange James Blair by these presents doth exchange and release unto Francis Gray the before mentioned 140 acres bounded as follows: beginning at the head of Rozier's Creek and running down the several meanders to a spanish oak on the bank near a house in which Job Sims formerly lived, thence North 20° West to the road, thence West 3° South to a gate formerly belonging to the said Sims: thence South 42° North to a water oak, thence South 58° West to a small hickory, thence to a large white oak standing in the South West line and along the same to the beginning' and all houses, outhouses, gardens, orchards, woods, ways, waters, profits, commodities and appurtenances whatsoever to the same belonging or in any way appertaining and the dwelling house in which Mrs. Sarah Strother now lives and 5 acres of land next adjoining and surrounding the same which are part of the said 140 acres.
This indenture further witnesseth that in consideration and in pursuance of the said exchange that Francis Gray hath exchanged and released unto James Blair the said 270 acres of a larger tract and is bounded as follows: At a place known by the name of "Round Hills" beginning at a stump near the head of a branch adjoining to the land of James Blair, thence along Blair's line to the land of Henry Washington's, thence along Washington's line to the land of Richard Bernard, thence along Bernard's line to the land of Francis Gray, thence along Gray's line to the beginning containing 135 acres;
Also another piece of land whereon Thomas Taylor now lives, beginning at the mouth of a small branch running into a swamp, known by the name of Ralph's Gutt, running up the branch westerly including a spring called Prices[?], and up the said branch to the head spring of the same, thence up the valley to James Butler's line, thence to William Tyler's road, thence to James Blair's line, thence to a small branch, thence down the branch to the beginning;
Also another parcel of land beginning at James Blair's corner, thence to Ralph's Branch at the road the leads to Rozier's Creek running South 80° East to a spanish oak, then South 71° east to an oak, thence North 78° East to a spanish oak, thence North 35° East to a spanish oak, thence to a slash, thence up the slash North 43° East to a turkey oak, thence North 35° East to a spanish oak, thence North 18° East to a hickory, thence North 58° East to a turkey oak, thence North 57° East to a sweet gum, thence to William Tyler's line, thence along Tyler's and Blair's line to the beginning , the two above pieces of land containing 200 acres.
In witness whereof the said James Blair and Francis Gray have interchangeably set their hands and seals the day and year aforesaid.
Signed sealed & Acknowledged in presence of us James Blair
John Higdon Francis Gray
Butler Baker
John Hilton
Westmoreland, Sct. At a court held for the said county the 26th day of May 1761 this deed of exchange for land indented between James Blair and Francis Gray was presented into court and proved by all the witnesses thereto and ordered to be recorded.

Recorded the 9th day of July 1761 Test: George Lee CCW

Page 18.

Simpson to Williams Lease

This indenture made the 25th day of May 1761 between Joseph Simpson, clerk of the Parish of Lunenburg and the county of Richmond of one part and Francis Williams of the Parish of Washington of the other part. Witnesseth that Joseph Simpson in consideration of 5 shillings current money of Virginia has sold by these presents to Francis Williams, two tracts of land containing 400 acres lying in the Parish of Washington which tracts of land he the said Joseph Simpson purchased of Edward Knowles. To have and to hold from the day of the date hereof for and during the full term of one year from thence next ensuing yielding and paying yearly the rent of one ear of Indian corn if demanded to the intent and purpose and of the statute for transferring uses into possession, the said Francis Williams may be in actual possession to be better enabled to accept and grant and release of the reversion and inheritance thereof to him. In witness whereof Joseph Simpson hath to this present indenture set his hand and seal the day month and year first above written.

Sealed and delivered in the presence of Joseph Simpson

[none listed]

Westmoreland Sct. At a court held for the said county the 26th day of May 1761, Joseph Simpson, clerk, came into court and personally acknowledged this lease for land indented by him passed to Francis Williams and ordered to be recorded.

Recorded the 9th day of July 1761 Test: George Lee CCW

Page 19.

Simpson to Williams Release

This indenture made the 26th day of May 1761 between Joseph Simpson, clerk and Mary Simpson his wife of the Parish of Lunenburg and the county of Richmond of one part and Francis Williams of the Parish of Washington of the other part. Witnesseth that Joseph Simpson in consideration of 130 pounds current money of Virginia has sold and released by these presents unto Francis Williams, in his actual possession by virtue of a bargain and sale made by indenture bearing date the day next before the date of these presents and by force of the statue for transferring uses into possession all those two several tracts containing by estimation 400 acres lying in the Parish of Washington in the county aforesaid that the said Joseph Simpson purchased of Edward Knowles.

In witness whereof the said Joseph Simpson and Mary Simpson his wife to this indenture have interchangeably set their hands and seals the day month and year first above written.

Sealed and delivered in the presence of Joseph Simpson

[none listed]

Westmoreland Sct. At a court held for the said county the 26th day of Mary 1761, Joseph Simpson, clerk came into court and personally acknowledged this release, together with the receipt thereon endorsed for land indented by him passed to Francis Williams and ordered to be recorded

Recorded the 9th of July 1761 Test: George Lee CCW

Page 22.

Gerard McKenney's Will

In the name of God Amen, I Gerard McKenney of the Parish of Cople and County of Westmoreland being very weak and sick but in sound judgment do ordain this my last will and testament.

I give and bequeath unto my beloved wife Letias Mckenney all my estate during as long as she lives a widow and after her death of my wife, I desire all my children to have an equal share of my estate.

I do appoint my wife Letias McKenney and my son Gerard McKenney my whole and sole executors.

Signed and Sealed December Gerard McKenney

The 15th day 1760

This last will and testament of Gerard McKenney, deceased was presented into court and sworn to by the executors therein named, the same being proved by the oaths of the witnesses thereto were

admitted to record. And upon motion of the said executors and their performing what the law in such cases require, certificate is granted them for obtaining a probate thereof in due form.
Recorded 9th July 1761 Test: George Lee CCW

Page 22.
William Redman Will
In the name of God Amen, I William Redman of Cople Parish and County of Westmoreland being sick and weak but in perfect sense and memory do make this my last will and testament in manner and form following:
Item I give and bequeath to my daughter Winifred Redman and the heirs of her body my Negro girl Hannah and her increase. If my daughter should die without heirs of her body, I give the Negro and her increase to be equally divided between by children.
Item I give and bequeath to my two sons John Redman and William Redman and my two daughters Lettice Redman and Winifred Redman my two Negroes Cesar and Jenny and the increase of her body.
Item I give and bequeath to my four children John Redman, Lettice Redman, Winifred Redman and William Redman and their heirs all my moveable estate of what nature or kind soever to be equally divided.
Item I give and bequeath to my beloved wife my horse and her saddle and it is my desire that my wife should have and keep my whole estate so long as she shall keep single.
Item I give and bequeath to my son John Redman, one sorrell mare colt.
It is my will and desire that my whole estate be undivided till my son William arrives to the age of 18 years.
Lastly, I do appoint my loving wife Frances Redman and my son John Redman executors of this my last will and testament. In witness whereof I have hereunto set my hand and affixed my seal this 27th day of November 1760.
Signed sealed published in presence of us William Redman
Francis Callis
John Butler
Westmoreland Sct. At a court held for the said county the 26th day of May 1761 this last will and testament of William Redman, deceased, was presented into court and sworn to by Frances Redman and John Redman, the executrix and executor therein named, the same being proved by the oath of the witnesses thereto is admitted to record. And upon motion of the executors and their performing what the law in such cases require, certificate is granted them for obtaining a probate thereof in due form.
Recorded the 9th July 1761 Test: George Lee CCW

Page 24.
Rachel Mullins Will
In the name of God Amen, I Rachael Mullins of the Parish of Cople and County of Westmoreland being sick and weak of body but of good in perfect sense and memory do make and ordain this to be my last will and testament.
Imprimis, I given to my son Peter Mullins one shilling current money of Virginia.
Item I give unto John Barber 100 pounds of tobacco to pay for year schooling.
Item I given to my executor hereafter named 150 pounds tobacco to pay for my funeral expenses; in my desire is to have as much plank out of my house left as well make my coffin.
Item I given to my daughter Rachael Mullins all the remainder of my estate of what kind or nature soever to her and her heirs forever.
I do hereby constitute and appoint Samuel Rust to be executor of this my last will and testament. In witness whereof I have hereunto set my hand and seal the 2nd day of January 1761.
Sealed signed and declared in the presence of us Rachael Mullins (her mark)
Rodham Pritchett
Peter Rust
Moxley Rust
Westmoreland Sct. At a Court held for the said County the 26th day of May 1760 one this last will of

Rachael Mullins, deceased was presented into Court and sworn to by Samuel Rust her executor therein named, the same being proved by the oath of Rodham Pritchett and Peter Rust two of the witnesses thereto was ordered to be recorded and on motion of the said executor and his performing what the law on such cases require, certificate is granted him for obtaining a probate thereof in due form.
Recorded the 9th July 1761 Test: George Lee CCW

Page 25.
William Settle's Will
I [William Settle] being weak in body but in proper senses and memory.
I give unto my wife Sarah Settle all that I have in this world, cattle, hogs, mare, beds and all my house goods both indoors and out, corner in tobacco, I give during her life and then to fall to my son Joel Settle into his heirs.
Given under my hand this first day of October 1760 this is my last will and testament.
Witnesses William Settle (his mark)
Andrew Harrison
Joel Settle
Joseph Settle (his mark)
Westmoreland Sct. At a Court held for the said County the 26th day of May 1761 this last will and testament of William Settle, deceased was presented into Court by Sarah Settle his relict, and proved by the oath of Andrew Harrison, one of the witnesses thereto and ordered to be recorded and on the motion of the said Sarah Settle in her performing all such things as the law in such cases require administration of all and singular the goods and chattels of the said deceased with the will annexed is in due form granted her.
Recorded the ninth day of July 1761 Test: George Lee CCW

Page 26.
Courney's Renunciation of Will
Westmoreland County, Sct. I Dorcas Courtney, spinster of the Parish of Cople in the County aforesaid do declared by these presents that I will not accept, receive or take any legacy or legacies that is or may be given me or bequeathed by my deceased husband Samuel Courtney by his last will and testament and do hereby renounce all benefit and advantage which I may or could claim by such last will and do further pray that this worshipful court order may such part as the law directs when no children are procreated as this is the now case before your worships and all this I do certified under my hand and seal this 27th day of June 1761.
Signed and sealed in presence of us Dorcas Courtney
John Newton
Vincent Cox
Westmoreland Sct. At a Court held for the said County the 30th day of June 1761 this renunciation of Dorcas Courtney the will of her late husband Samuel Courtney, deceased was presented into Court and proved by the oath of John Newton, Gent., One of the witnesses thereto and ordered to be recorded.
Recorded the ninth day of July 1761 Test: George Lee CCW

Page 26.
Charles Rose's Will
In the name of God, this is the last will and testament of Charles Rose of the Parish of Cople, clerk.
I give to my son Robert Rose, Negro boy Little Frank and £40.
I give to my son John Rose, mullato boy Joe.
I give to my son Alexander Rose, the boy named Jack.
I give to my daughter Catherine Rose, Negro girl Iris and one bed and furniture.
I give to my daughter Molly Rose, mullato girl Willy and one bed and furniture.
After my debts are paid and the above legacies are delivered I give and bequeath the use of all the rest of my slaves and personal estate whatsoever to my beloved wife during her widowhood and after my wife's marriage or death I give all the said slaves given to my wife as aforesaid together

with their increase to my daughters, Catherine Rose, and Molly Rose forever and I give all the rest of my personal estate so given to my wife as aforesaid at her marriage or death to my daughters Catherine Rose and Molly Rose and to my sons John Rose and Alexander Rose equally to be divided.

I appoint my wife Catherine Rose, my brother Alexander Rose and my nephew John Rose executors of this my last will and guardians to my children.

In witness whereof I have hereunto set my hand and seal this 27th day of March 1760.

Signed sealed and declared in presence of Charles Rose

Francis Lafon

John Self

Alexander Rose

Westmoreland Sct. At a court held for the said County the 30th day of June 1761 this last will and testament of the Rev. Charles Rose, deceased was presented into Court by Catherine Rose his relict and executrix thereon named who made oath thereto and the same being proved by the oath of Alexander Rose, Gent., And John Self two of the witnesses thereto was admitted to record and on motion of the said executrix and her performing what the law in such cases require, certificate is granted her for obtaining a probate thereof in due form.

Recorded the ninth day of July 1761 Test: George Lee CCW

Page 27.

Edward's Wife to Grisgsby Privy Examination

To James Hamilton, Francis Peyton, Aneas Campbell and George Hart of the County of Loudoun, Gent. Whereas Benjamin Edwards of the aforesaid County of Loudoun and Jane Edwards his wife by their deed bearing date the 21st day of April 1760, conveyed unto Aaron Grigsby of the County of King George the fee simple estate of 100 acres of land situated in the Parish of Washington in County of Westmoreland. And whereas the said Jane Edwards cannot conveniently travel to our court to make acknowledgment of the said conveyance. Therefore, we do give unto you or any two of you to receive the acknowledgment which the Jane Edwards shall be willing to make. Witness George Lee, clerk of our said County Court of Westmoreland 18th day of February 1761.

Loudoun Sct. By virtue of a writ directed to us the subscribers have taken the privy examination of Mrs. Jane Edwards apart from her husband Mr. Benjamin Edwards and the said Jane Edwards declares that she freely and willingly without persuasion acquits her right of dower in the lands and premises sold to Aaron Grigsby by deed of lease and release and bearing date the 20th and 21st days of April 1760.

Westmoreland Sct. At a court held for the said county the 30th day of June 1761 this commission for the privy examination Jane Edwards the wife of Benjamin Edwards for relinquishment of her right of dower and inheritance of in and to the lands conveyed to Aaron Grigsby is ordered to be recorded.

Recorded the 9th of July 1761 Test: George Lee CCW

Page 29.

Thomas Williams Will

In the name of God Amen, I Thomas Williams of the Parish of Cople and County of Westmoreland being sick in body but of good and sound memory do make constitute and ordain and declare this my last will and testament in manner and form following.

Item I give and bequeath unto my son Elisha Williams and a new suit of blue cloth.

I give to my son Daniel Williams all my land and Negro girl Luce and her increase

After the death of my wife the rest of my temporal estate after her decease to be equally divided amongst my three children.

Elizabeth Williams executrix.

As witness my hand and seal this 20th day of May 1761 Thomas Williams (his mark)

Witnesses; Francis Gilbert, Thomas Metheny

Westmoreland Sct. At a Court held for the said County the 30th day of June 1761 this last Will and Testament of Thomas Williams, deceased was presented into court by the executrix therein named and proved by the witnesses thereto and ordered to be recorded.

Recorded the 10th of July 1761 Test: George Lee CCW

Page 30.
Frances Rust Will
In the name of God Amen, I Frances Rust of the County of Westmoreland and Parish of Cople being weak but of perfect mind and memory do make this my last will and testament.
I give and bequeath to my son Robert Middleton my book called "The explanation of the New Testament."
Item I give to my daughter Rachel Cox one cow and calf.
Item give to my son Benedict Rust two cows and calves, two ewes, two sows, and the feather bed and furniture called mine, and a young mare called Fancy.
Item I give to my two daughters Frances Shearman and Molly Rust all the rest of my estate before not given to be equally divided between them;
in my will and desire is that what provisions I have now by me to be for the use of the family now on the plantation.
I do appoint my son Robert Middleton and Daniel Tebbs my executors of this my last will and testament. As witness my hand this 23rd day of July 1759
Sealed and delivered in presence of Frances Rust
George Rust
Michael Gilbert
Francis Gilbert
Samuel Rust
Westmoreland Sct. At a Court held for the said County the 30th day of June 1761 this last will and testament of Frances Rust, deceased was presented into Court and sworn to by Robert Middleton her executor therein the same being proved by the oaths of George Rust and Francis Gilbert two of the witnesses thereto was admitted to record and upon motion of the said executor and his performing what the law is such cases require, certificate is granted him for obtaining a probate thereof in due form.
Recorded the 10th day of July 1761 Test: George Lee CCW

Page 31.
Linton to Simpson Indenture
This Indenture made this 28th day of February 1761 between John Linton and Mary Ann Linton his wife of the County of Westmoreland of the one part and Joseph Simpson, clerk of the county of Richmond of the other part. Witnesseth that whereas John Linton and Mary Ann Linton his wife in consideration of 160 pounds lawful money of Virginia has sold unto Joseph Simpson all the lands I have in Westmoreland being by estimation 166 acres excepting ½ acre for a burying place. In witness whereof the parties to these presents have interchangeably set their hands and seals the day and year first mentioned.
Sealed and delivered in the presence of John Linton
Daniel McKenney Mary Ann Linton (her mark)
Peter McClanahan
William Moore
John Singer (his mark)
James Baley (his mark)
Robert Tidwell (his mark)
Richard Thompson
George Simpson
Westmoreland Sct. At a court held for the said county the 30th day of June 1761 this deed of feoffment indented, together with the livery of seizen and receipt thereon endorsed passed from John Linton and Mary Ann his wife to Joseph Simpson was at May court last, proved by the oath of Richard Thompson and George Simpson two of the witnesses thereto and continued for further proof and now at this court the same was fully proved by the oath of Peter McClanahan a witness thereto, and ordered to be recorded.
Recorded the 10th July 1761 Test: George Lee CCW

Page 34.
Walker to Short Indenture
This indenture made this 28th of June 1761 between Richard Walker of the County of Westmoreland and Parish of Cople of the one part and John Short of the same parish and county of the other part. Witnesseth that Richard Walker in consideration of 60 pounds current money of Virginia has sold to John Short a tract of land containing 83 acres being the half of a tract given by the William Walker, deceased bearing date the 26th day of June 1733 to his two sons, John Walker and Richard Walker and according to a division made by Mr. William Garland, surveyor between the two sons. To have and to hold the said messuage of 83 acres of land being on the main branch of Yeocomico River in the Parish of Cople and County of Westmoreland. In witness whereof the said Richard Walker hath hereunto set his hand and seal the day and year first mentioned.
Signed sealed & delivered in presence of Richard Walker
[no names listed]
Westmoreland Sct. At a court held for the said county the 30th day of June 1761 Richard Walker came into court and personally acknowledged this deed of feoffment for land by him passed (the wife of Richard Walker being first privy examined and thereto consenting) together with the livery of seizen and the receipt thereon endorsed this deed for land by him passed to John Short to be his proper act and deed and ordered to be recorded
Recorded the 13th day of July 1761 Test: George Lee CCW

Page 37.
Abraham Garner's Will
In the name of God Amen, I Abraham Garner of the Parish of Cople and County of Westmoreland, planter being sick and weak of body to make and appoint this my last will and testament in manner and form following.
Item I give and bequeath to my daughter Frances Garner daughter of Sarah Garner all my lands not conveyed to Richard Lee, Esq., and in case of her death before she comes to age, then I give the above bequeath to my daughter Martha Garner and so on in succession to my daughter Lettice Garner and Rachel Garner, daughters of Sarah Garner.
I order my executors to carry on and defend my suits with Robert Carter, Esq., which expense is to be bore out of my estate.
Lastly, I constitute and appoint my friends Richard Lee, Esq., Willoughby Newton, and Bradley Garner to be my executors of this my last will and testament. In witness whereof I have hereunto set my hand and affixed my seal this 21st day of February 1761.
Signed sealed published in presence of Abraham Garner
Leroy Hipkins, John Crabb
Matthew Partridge, Gerard Crabb (his mark)
Westmoreland Sct. At a Court held for the said County the 30th day of June 1761 this last will and testament of Abraham Garner, deceased was presented into court and sworn to by Bradley Garner one of the executors therein named the same being proved by the oath of Leroy Hipkins and John Crabb two of the witnesses thereto was admitted to record, and upon motion of the said executor and his performing what the law in such cases require, certificate is granted him for obtaining a probate thereof in due form.
Recorded the 13th day of July 1761 Test: George Lee CCW

Page 38.
Downton to Bernard Indenture
This indenture made the 26th day of July 1761 between Lawrence Downton the Parish of Washington in County of Westmoreland, planter of the one part and William Bernard, attorneys-at-law of the other part. Witnesseth that Lawrence Downton in consideration of 50 pounds has sold to William Bernard a parcel of land that the said Lawrence Downton now liveth lying and being in the parish and county aforesaid upon Attopin Dam or the main branch of Rozier's Creek, lying South of and adjoining to a tract of land belonging to William Bernard and containing by estimation 100 acres, which tract descended to the said Lawrence Downton in fee simple upon the death of

Nicholas Downton his father who died intestate. In witness whereof the said Lawrence Downton have hereunto set his hand and seal this day and year first above written.
Lawrence Downton
Westmoreland Sct. At a Court held for the said County the 28th day of July 1761 this deed indented for land together with the receipt thereon passed from Lawrence Downton to William Bernard, Gent., was acknowledged by the said Downton and ordered to be recorded.
recorded 7 August 1761 Test: George Lee CCW

Page 40.
White to White Indenture
This indenture made the 20th day of May 1761 between James White, the elder and Thomas White, son of the said James White of the Parish of Washington and County of Westmoreland of the one part and James White, the younger, likewise son of the said James White, the elder of the parish and county aforesaid of the other part. Witnesseth that whereas James White, the elder being possessed and having an estate in fee simple in a certain tract of land lying upon the south side of Attopin Dam in the parish and county aforesaid containing 270 acres and having several sons as well as the said Thomas White and James White, parties to these presents, the said James White, the elder in order to make provision for his said sons as they respectively come to age did allot to his several sons by particular marked trees and lines a dividend of his said tract of land and gave up to them possession thereof minding the same in his will which he always kept by him and which he assured the said sons he never modify, and whereas among other divisions and allotments the said James White, the elder for the provision and advancement of his son the said Thomas White party to these presents, upwards of 20 years ago did mark out for him a part of his said tract containing 75 acres or thereabouts and gave him possession thereof and according to the said Thomas White entered upon and hath had the possession of the said 75 acres ever since. Witnesseth that the said James White, the elder as well for the natural love and affection which he hath to his son James White, the younger as to comply with his promise to his son, the said Thomas White and the said Thomas White for and in consideration of 15 pounds paid before the execution of this indenture has sold the said 75 acres of land where he now lives on to James White, the younger. To have and to hold the said 75 acres of land upon condition nevertheless that the said Thomas White shall hold use occupy and possess the said tract or dividend of land during his natural life. In witness whereof the said James White, the elder and Thomas White have hereunto set their hands and seals the day and year aforesaid.
Signed sealed and delivered in presence of James White, Sr. (his mark)
Lawrence Downton Thomas White
John White
Gideon Smith
Joseph Smith
Lawrence Weedon
Westmoreland Sct. At a Court held for the said County the 28th day of July 1761 this deed indented for land passed from James White, the elder and Thomas White to James White, the younger was proved by the oath of Gideon Smith, Lawrence Downton and John White in the receipt endorsed thereto was proved by the oath of John White witnesses thereof and ordered to be recorded.
Recorded the 18th day of August 1761 Test: George Lee CCW

Page 42.
White to Middleton Indenture
This indenture made this 28th day of July 1761 between Zachariah White of the Parish of Lunenburg in the County of Richmond and Seleashea White, his wife of the one part and Robert Middleton of the Parish of Cople in the County of Westmoreland of the other part. Witnesseth that whereas Thomas Walker grandfather to the aforesaid Seleashea White, late of the Parish of Cople in the County of Westmoreland, deceased by virtue of a deed passed to him by Robert Middleton, late of the parish and county aforesaid, deceased dated the 25th day of August 1686 was seized at his death of 150 acres of land lying in the parish and county aforesaid and bounded as followeth; beginning at a red oak by a path being a corner and beginning tree of the said Robert Middleton,

from thence extending South 22° East 20 poles to a corner red oak on a branch, from thence North 40° East 170 poles to a hickory corner tree of Richard Dunahew, from thence South 75° East 48 poles to a red oak corner tree of Richard Dunahew and George Lamkin, from thence South 32° East 27 poles to a red oak of George Lamkin, from thence South 45° West bordering South East on the land of Francis Clay 232 poles to a red oak corner tree of the said Clay and Robert Middleton, from thence extending West 132 poles to a red oak standing in being in the said Robert Middleton's line, from thence along the said Robert Middleton's line North 45° East 140 poles to the beginning tree which said 150 acres of land the said Thomas Walker gave and bequeathed to his son Benjamin Walker, father of the said Seleashea White as by his last will and testament dated the 26th day of January 1710 [1715/16] and that Benjamin Walker departed this life without making any will whereby the aforesaid 150 acres of land descended to the three daughters of the said Benjamin Walker, to wit; Seleashea Walker, Mary Jeffries Walker and Alice Walker. In witness whereof the parties aforesaid have to these presents interchangeably set their hands and seals the day and year first mentioned. Zachariah White
Seleashea White

Westmoreland Sct. At a Court held for the said County the 28th day of July 1761 Zachariah White and Seleashea White his wife (she being first privy examined thereto consenting) acknowledged this deed of feoffment for land indented by them passed to Robert Middleton and ordered to be recorded.
Recorded the 18th day of August 1761 Test: George Lee CCW

Page 45.
Rust's Wife to Wright Privy Examination
To Willoughby Newton, Richard Lee and John Newton of the County of Westmoreland, Gent., Greetings. Whereas John Rust and Sarah Rust his wife by their indenture of feoffment bearing date the 29th day of January 1761 have conveyed unto Francis Wright of the county aforesaid the fee simple estate of 200 acres of land lying in the Parish of Cople and county aforesaid and whereas Sarah cannot conveniently travel to court to make acknowledgment of the said convenience. Therefore, we do give you or any two of you power to receive the acknowledgment which the said Sarah Rust shall be willing to make personally before you. Witness George Lee, clerk of our said court the 18th day of July 1761.
Westmoreland Sct. By virtue of a commission from the County Court of Westmoreland to us bearing date the 18th day of July 1761 we have examined Sarah Rust the wife of John Rust touching her willingness to relinquish her right of dower to 200 acres of land sold by her husband John Rust to Francis Wright by deed bearing date the 29th day of January 1761, which right of dower she voluntarily and freely of her own will relinquished and is desirous and willing it should be recorded in Westmoreland court. Given under our hands and seals this 18th day of July 1761.
Richard Lee
John Newton
Westmoreland Sct. At a Court held for the said County the 28th day of July 1761 this commission for the privy examination of Sarah Rust the wife of John Rust for relinquishing in land by her said husband sold and conveyed to Francis Wright being returned that she was thereto consenting is admitted to record her right of dower and inheritance
Recorded the 18th day of August 1761 Test: George Lee CCW

Page 47.
Spencer Ariss Will
In the name of God Amen, I Spencer Ariss of the Parish of Cople in the County of Westmoreland being sick and weak but of sound and perfect disposing mind and memory do make this my last will and testament in manner and form following.
Imprimis, I give and devise to my dear wife Sarah Ariss, one half of my whole estate both real and personal after my just debts are paid for and during her natural life upon condition that she remains single and after her death I give the same to my daughter Elizabeth Ariss and the heirs of her body lawfully begotten but if my daughter should die without such heirs then I give the same to my brother John Ariss and his heirs forever; but if my wife should marry after my decease I then revoke

the legacy I have before given her and I devise to her in lieu thereof one third part of my whole estate for and during her natural life and after her decease I give the same to my daughter Elizabeth Ariss and the heirs of her body and for want of such heirs to my brother John Ariss.
Item I give and bequeath all the rest of my lands and Negroes and to my daughter Elizabeth Ariss and for want of such heirs to my brother John Ariss.
Item I give and bequeath unto my daughter Elizabeth Ariss all the rest of my personal estate of what nature and kind soever.
Item give my said daughter should die as aforesaid without issue and my brother John Ariss should be possessed of the estate aforesaid, I do direct and order that out of the same he do pay to my nephew John Ariss Callis one third part of the value the Negroes he shall become so possessed of but in case my nephew should die before he arrives to the age of 21 years then the bequest to him to be void.
Item upon the said contingency of my daughter Elizabeth Ariss dying without issue and my brother John Ariss becoming possessed of the estate given to him as aforesaid I give and bequeath to my sister Sorrell also one third part of the value of the said Negroes.
Item I do direct and order that my estate given as aforesaid to my said daughter Elizabeth Ariss to be kept together by my executors to my daughter arrives to the age of 21 years or is married whichever is first in whatever profits shall be made on the same give more than sufficient for the maintenance of my daughter be laid out in the purchase of slaves for her.
Item I do nominate and appoint my dear wife Sarah Ariss, my brother John Ariss, and my good friends William Booth and John Washington, Gent., Executors of this my last will and testament.
Signed sealed published and declared to be my last will and testament this 23rd day of November 1760

Witnesses Spencer Ariss
Richard Parker
Joseph Stone
Robert Dick

Westmoreland Sct. At a court held for the said County the 28th day of July 1760 one this last will and testament of Spencer Ariss, deceased was presented into Court and sworn to by John Ariss one of the executors therein named the same being proved by the oath of all the witnesses thereto was admitted to record and on motion of the said executors and his performing what the law in such case requires certificate is granted him for obtaining a probate thereof in due form.
Recorded the 24th day of August 1761 Test: George Lee CCW

Page 48.
<u>Robert Tidwell's Will</u>
In the name of God Amen, I Robert Tidwell of Cople Parish in Westmoreland County being weak of body but of sound and perfect sense and memory to make and ordain and declare this to be my last will and testament in manner and form following this 27th day of September 1757.
Item I give and bequeath to Hannah Tidwell all the land whereon I now live together with the lands I purchased of Peter Dunkin during her natural life and after her death I give and bequeath the said lands to my son John Tidwell.
Item I give and bequeath to my son William Carr Tidwell all my lands in Machodoc Neck and in case he should die without heir I give my said lands to my daughter Elizabeth Tidwell.
I give and bequeath to son John Tidwell the following Negroes; Judith, George and Lucy and I give the first child (with its increase) that shall be born of either Negro woman to my granddaughter Hannah Tidwell.
Item I give and bequeath to my son William Carr Tidwell the following Negroes; Jack, Jean and the wench called Plumbers Judy.
Item I give and bequeath to my good daughter Elizabeth Tidwell the following Negroes; Daniel, Lett, James, Nell, Kesiah, Frank and a child called Tom Brown and in case he should die without heirs then I give the three Negroes already given him to my son John and Elizabeth to be equally divided.
I give and bequeath to my loving wife her choice of all my Negroes for to choose out two which she is to have the use of during her natural life and after her decease to return to the child to whom they

shall happen to belong.
I desire my executors may purchase a negro fellow with what money I have in the house which is about 46 pounds and if that sum should not be sufficient, my will is and desire is that there shall be money raised out of my crops to make up the sum and that I give and bequeath the said negro fellow to my son William Carr Tidwell and should he die without heirs then to my son John Tidwell.
I order that my son William Carr Tidwell shall pay to my executors the money that they shall advance out of my crops to pay for the Negro fellow I desired.
Item I give to John Justiss my fustian coat, ticken waist coat, bear skin coat, cambelt waistcoat, two pair of cloth breeches, hall shoes and stockings and one fine shirt and I desire that he may have allowed out of my estate working clothes for next year suitable for one of his employments.
I give and bequeath to Catharine Jenkins one cow and calf, and a bed and furniture.
If my daughter Elizabeth Tidwell choose to give Catharine Jenkins the Negro girl Frank, I give her the said Negro girl to the said Catharine together with the increase, but in such case, then Catharine shall not have the cow and calf and bed and furniture already given her.
Item I give to my loving wife Hannah Tidwell the use of all my stocks of horses, cattle, hogs, sheep, etc. and the use of all my household goods & furniture together with everything else upon my plantation during her natural life and after her death my will and desire is that they be equally divided between my three children; John Tidwell, William Carr Tidwell and Elizabeth Tidwell.
Item I give and bequeath to my daughter Elizabeth Tidwell my riding horse called Jockey after the death of my wife.
I order my estate not to be appraised.
Lastly, I ordain, constitute, and appoint my sons John Tidwell and William Carr Tidwell, executors of this my last will and testament. In witness whereof I have hereunto set my hand and seal agreeing and declaring the within three sides to be & contain my last will and testament the day & year first above written.
Signed sealed and delivered in presence of Robert Tidwell (his mark)
Joseph Lane
Stephen Baley (his mark)
John Justiss
Westmoreland Sct. At a court held for the said county the 28th day of July 1761 this will of Robert Tidwell, deceased was presented into court and sworn to my William Carr Tidwell one of the executors therein named the same being proved by all the witnesses thereto was admitted to record, and upon motion of the said executor and his performing what the law in such cases require, certificate is granted him for obtaining a probate thereof in due form.
Recorded the 24th August 1761 Test: George Lee CCW

Page 51.
Christopher Marmaduke's Will
In the name of God Amen, I Christopher Marmaduke of the County of Westmoreland in the Parish of Cople being weak and sickly of body but of perfect sense and sound memory do make and ordain this my last will and testament in manner and form following.
Item I give and bequeath unto my son Christopher Marmaduke my plantation whereon I now live with all the land thereunto belonging to have and to hold during his natural life and after his decease I give the said plantation to my grandson Vincent Marmaduke son of my said son Christopher Marmaduke and to his heirs forever.
Item I give and bequeath to my son Christopher Marmaduke my two Negroes, James and Nan and her future increase upon condition that he the said Christopher Marmaduke do pay to my son Daniel Marmaduke 25 pounds current money when he has possession of the said Negroes I left him.
Item I lend to my daughter Esther Robinson my Negro girl Sarah during her natural life and after her decease give and bequeath the said Negro to my two granddaughters Hannah Holland and Elizabeth Holland to be equally divided between them.
Item I lend to my daughter Jemima Sandy by Negro girl Hannah for and during her natural life and after her decease I give and bequeath the said Negro and her increase to my grandson Thomas Sandy.

Item I also give and bequeath to my daughter Jemima Sandy one sow and six shoats, and two large killable barrows.
Item I give and bequeath to my son Daniel Marmaduke one bed and furniture the same being where I now lie on, with everything belonging to it.
Item I also give and bequeath to my son Daniel Marmaduke my best suit of wearing clothes and all the rest of my clothes I give and bequeath to my son John Marmaduke.
Item my will and desire is that my still and worm shall be sold and all my large casks to the highest bidder for money and the said money to be equally divided amongst all my children.
Item I give and bequeath to my son Christopher Marmaduke all my small casks, also three cows and calves, my mare and colt, one bed and furniture the same being that which he now lies on.
Item I give and bequeath to Margaret Sanford and my granddaughter Elizabeth Marmaduke one small bed the same having an osnaburg tick and all the furniture thereupon to belonging.
Item I give and bequeath to my daughter Jemima Sandy one cow and calf.
Item I give and bequeath to my grandson Vincent Marmaduke my Negro boy Jack to be delivered to him when he comes to age of 21 years and not before.
Item and all the rest of my estate herein not given or otherwise bequeath it is my will and desire that it shall be equally divided amongst all my children namely; Christopher Marmaduke, Jean Marmaduke, John Marmaduke, Daniel Marmaduke, Esther Robinson, William Marmaduke: and Jemima Sandy.
Item and lastly, I appoint and ordain my two sons Christopher Marmaduke and Daniel Marmaduke my whole and sole executors of this my last will and testament. In confirmation whereof I have hereunto set my hand and affixed my seal this 20th day of January 1761.
Signed sealed and delivered in presence of us Christopher Marmaduke
Augustine Sanford
Sarah Marmaduke (her mark)
Mary Marmaduke (her mark)
Westmoreland Sct. At a court held for the said County the 28th day of July 1760 one this last will and testament of Christopher Marmaduke, deceased was presented into Court and sworn to by Christopher Marmaduke one of the executors therein named same being proved by the oath of Augustine Sanford and Sarah Marmaduke two of the witnesses thereto was admitted to record and upon motion of the said executor in his performing what the law in such cases require, certificate is granted him for obtaining a probate thereof in due form.
Recorded 24 August 1761 Test: George Lee CCW

Page 54.
Edward Baxter's Will
In the name of God Amen, I Edward Baxter of Westmoreland County, planter being sick and weak of body but of perfect memory and judgment do now make this my last will and testament as follows.
In the first place I appoint George Monroe son of William Monroe, deceased my executor.
I give unto the said George Monroe, Negro girl Sall and her increase.
I give unto Patrick Connelly all my wearing clothes and 40 shillings cash.
Likewise, to George Monroe's daughter Mary Monroe 20 shillings to make her a ring.
The said George Monroe is to have the remainder part of my estate appraised and equally divided between my two brothers George Baxter and Thomas Baxter.
The said George Monroe is to look over the plantation while a crop is finished and then divided.
In witness whereof I have signed and sealed this is my last will and testament the 16th day June 1761.
Witness Edward Baxter (his mark)
John Rice (his mark)
Patrick Connelly (his mark)
Westmoreland Sct. At a court held for the said County the 28th day of July 1761 this last will and testament of Edward Baxter, deceased was presented into Court by George Monroe the executor therein named, whereupon George Baxter appeared and contested proof of the said will upon examination of several witnesses and Patrick Connelly one of the subscribing witnesses to the said

will agreeing to relinquish the legacies to him therein bequeath, the said will was admitted to proof, whereupon the same was sworn to by the said executor and proved by the oath of both the witnesses thereto and ordered to be recorded. And upon motion of the said executor and his performing what the law is such cases require, certificate is granted him for obtaining a probate thereof in due form.
Recorded 24th August 1761 Test: George Lee CCW

Page 55.
Simpson's Wife to Williams Privy Examination
To Traverse Tarpley, and William Peachey of the County of Richmond, Gent.
Whereas Joseph Simpson, clerk of the County of Richmond and Mary Simpson his wife by their deed bearing date the 25th and 26th days of May 1761, conveyed unto Francis Williams of the County of Westmoreland the fee simple estate of 400 acres of land situated in the Parish of Washington in County of Westmoreland. And whereas the said Mary Simpson cannot conveniently travel to our court to make acknowledgment of the said conveyance. Therefore, we do give unto you or any two of you to receive the acknowledgment which the Mary Simpson shall be willing to make. Witness George Lee, clerk of our said County Court of Westmoreland 26th day of June 1761.
Richmond Sct. By virtue of the dedimus hereunto annexed me have taken the [privy] examination of Mary Simpson apart from her husband Joseph Simpson and the said Mary Simpson declares that she freely and voluntarily acknowledged the deeds in the said dedimus and without the persuasions or threats of her husband. Given under our hands and seals this 24th day of August 1761.
Traverse Tarpley
William Peachey
Westmoreland Sct. At a court held for the said county the 25th day of August 1761 this commission for the privy examination Mary Simpson the wife of the Rev. Joseph Simpson for relinquishment of her right of dower and inheritance of in and to the lands conveyed to Francis Williams is ordered to be recorded.
Recorded the 16th day of September 1761 Test: George Lee CCW

Page 56.
Sarah Ariss Renunciation of Will
To all to whom these presents shall come know ye that I Sarah Ariss of the Parish of Cople in the County of Westmoreland, widow of Spencer Ariss, lately of the said parish and county, Gent., deceased not been satisfied with the provisions made for me by the said Spencer Ariss in his will lately recorded record of the said County of Westmoreland do hereby disclaim any right or title I may have under the said will to any part or parcel of the estate of the said Spencer Ariss either real or personal, in I do declare I will not accept of the legacies to me by the said will given or any part thereof. In witness whereof I have hereunto set my hand and seal this 15th day of August 1761.
Signed sealed in the presence of us.
Augustine Washington Sarah Ariss
Alexander Moxley
Westmoreland Sct. At a Court held for the said County the 25th day of August 1761 this renunciation of Sarah Ariss to her late husband Spencer Ariss' Will was presented into Court and proved by the witnesses thereto and ordered to be recorded.
Recorded the 14th day of September 1761 Test: George Lee CCW

Page 57.
Gray to Blair Indenture
This indenture made the 17th day of August 1761 between Francis Gray the Parish of Washington and County of Westmoreland of the one part and James Blair of the parish and county aforesaid of the other part.
Witnesseth that the said Francis Gray in consideration of 305 pounds 15 shillings and 5 pence current money of Virginia has sold to James Blair a tract of land in the Parish of Washington in

County aforesaid containing by estimation 300 acres; beginning at the mouth of a gut called "Ralph's Gutt on Rozier's Creek, from thence easterly to a marked locust, thence to a marked white oak, thence to a small locust marked, thence to a marked red oak, thence to a willow, thence to a willow marked for a corner, thence to a marked sweet gum, thence to a marked sassafras, thence to a marked white oaks, then to a marked beech, thence to a beech marked for a corner, thence up a branch to the main road by the Round Hill Church, thence down the main road to John Chancellor's line, thence to Augustine Weedon's line, thence down and over Rozier's Creek to the first beginning. In witness whereof the said Francis Gray has hereunto set his hand and seal the 17th day of August 1761.

Signed sealed and delivered in the presence of Francis Gray

Gabriel Johnston
John Hilton
Butler Baker
Samuel Smith
Thomas Taylor

Westmoreland Sct. At a court held for said County the 25th day of August 1761 this deed indented for land together with the endorsement thereon passed from Francis Gray to James Blair, Gent., was proved by the oath of Gabriel Johnston, John Hilton and Butler Baker three of the witnesses thereto and ordered to be recorded.

Recorded the 15th day of September 1761 Test: George Lee CCW

Page 59.

Shadrick to Spark Assignment of Lease

Know all men by these presents that by an indenture of lease bearing date the 24th day of February 1746 made between Robert Vaulx, Gent., of the County of Westmoreland on the one part and Thomas Shadrick, tailor of the said county of the other part. He the said Robert Vaulx for the consideration therein mentioned did demise grant and to farm let unto the said Thomas Shadrick, his wife Mary Shadrick, and his son Job Shadrick for and during their natural lives he certain plantation of land lying in the County of Westmoreland in Parish of Washington containing 150 acres; to have and to hold paying the yearly rent of 630 pounds of crop tobacco. Now these presents witnesseth that Thomas Shadrick, his wife Mary Shadrick, and his son Job Shadrick jointly and severally, for and in consideration of the sum of 21 pounds 10 shillings lawful money of Virginia has sold and assigned over unto Alexander Spark the said plantation of land after the 1st day of January 1761, and also the right and title of the estate term of years to come. In witness whereof we have hereunto set our hands and seals this 13th day of February 1761.

Richard Muse Thomas Shadrick (his mark)
Daniel Muse Mary Shadrick (her mark)
Edward Muse Job Shadrick (his mark)

Westmoreland Sct. At a Court held for the said County the 25th day of August 1761 this assignment of the lease from Thomas Shadrick, Mary Shadrick his wife and Job Shadrick his son passed to Alexander Spark was proved by the oath of all the witnesses thereto and ordered to be recorded.

Recorded 16 September 1761. Test: George Lee CCW

Page 61.

Massey to Weedon Indenture

This indenture made the 12th day of September 1760 between John Massey the County of Westmoreland of the one part and John Weedon of the same county of the other part. Witnesseth that John Massey in consideration of 30 pounds current money of Virginia has sold to John Weedon a tract of land lying in the Parish of Washington and County of Westmoreland containing by estimation 50 acres being the half part of 100 acres which the said John Massey purchased of John Ashton, Jr., as by deed bearing date the 21st day of May 1760, which land descended to the said John Ashton from his father Burditt Ashton, Sr., Gent., as his eldest son and bounded as follows; beginning at a sassafras post near the South corner of the land which was left to the said John Massey by his father, from thence along a line of posts to a mulberry post and small sweet gum standing on the north side of Attopin Dam and joining easterly to the land of the said John Weedon and from thence joining northerly to the land of Samuel Dishman and so on to the beginning. In witness whereof the said John Massey has hereunto set his hand and seal the day and year aforesaid.

Signed sealed and delivered in the presence of John Massey
William Berryman
Thomas Clark
Gideon Smith
Thomas Arrowsmith [spelled Arrasmith in record]
John Bryant

Westmoreland Sct. At a Court held for the said County the 25th day of August 1761 this deed indented for land passed from John Massey to John Weedon was at March court last proved by the oath of William Berryman, Gent., And Thomas Arrowsmith two of the witnesses thereto and lodged for further proof now at this court the same was fully proved by the oath of Gideon Smith a witness thereto and ordered to be recorded.

Recorded the 16th day of September 1761 Test: George Lee CCW

Page 63.

Carter to Perry Lease

This indenture made the 1st day of January 1761 between Robert Carter of Westmoreland County of the one part and Roderick Perry of the other part. Witnesseth that Robert Carter in consideration of the rents and covenants hereafter mentioned has demised and to farm let unto Roderick Perry 144 acres of land being in the Parish of Cople and County of Westmoreland on the branch of Nominy River being part of a tract of 1000 acres and called Brent's Tract and bounded as followeth; beginning at the letter "J" a stake near the road, thence South 60° West to "H" the head of a branch that divides Lot No. 2, thence down the said branch to "K", thence South 72° East 205 poles to the division between Lot No. 3, to "L" thence North 15° East 126 poles to "N" a stake in the back line of Brent's patent, thence West by North 249 poles to the letter "O", corner red oak, thence North 46° West 15 poles to "P" a stake by a road, thence up the road to the beginning. To have and to hold during the term of 21 years yielding and paying yearly and every year from the date of these presents the sum of 5 pounds 2 shillings and 9 pence current money of Virginia to the said Robert Carter at his house in the City of Williamsburg. And the said Roderick Perry doth covenant and agree by these presents that he shall within three years after the date of these presents build on the said premises a good dwelling house, 16 ft.² and a house 32' x 20' as good as the common tobacco houses, and plant 50 apple trees and 50 peach trees and the same enclose with a lawful fence. In witness whereof the said Robert Carter and Roderick Perry have hereunto interchangeably set their hands and seals the day and year first above written.

Sealed and delivered in the presence of us Robert Carter
William Dunbar Roderick Perry
Thomas Delozier
James Brown

Westmoreland Sct. At a Court held for the said County the 25th day of August 1761 this lease for land indented passed from the Hon. Robert Carter, Esq., to Roderick Perry was proved by the oath of all the witnesses thereto and ordered to be recorded.

Recorded the 16th September 1761 Test: George Lee CCW

Page 67.

Carter to Brown Lease

This indenture made the 1st day of January 1761 between Robert Carter of Westmoreland County of the one part and James Brown, weaver of the other part. Witnesseth that Robert Carter in consideration of the rents and covenants hereafter mentioned has demised and to farm let unto James Brown 119 acres of land being in the Parish of Cople and County of Westmoreland on the branch of Nominy River being part of a tract of 500 acres and called the Metcalf Tract and bounded as followeth; beginning at a red oak on the north branch of Nominy River, thence North by East 228 poles to a red oak thence east by South 75 poles to a small pine in a bottom, thence South 9° West

200 poles to a Spanish oak on the north branch of Nominy River, thence up the said branch to the beginning.

To have and to hold during the term of 21 years yielding and paying yearly and every year from the date of these presents the sum of 5 pounds and 3 shillings current money of Virginia to the said Robert Carter at his house in the city of Williamsburg. And the said James Brown doth covenant and agree by these presents that he shall within three years after the date of these presents build on the said premises a good dwelling house, 16' x 20' and a house 32' x 20' as good as the common tobacco houses, and plant 50 apple trees and 50 peach trees and the same enclose with a lawful fence. In witness whereof the said Robert Carter and James Brown have hereunto interchangeably set their hands and seals the day and year first above written.

Sealed and delivered in the presence of us Robert Carter
William Dunbar James Brown
Thomas Delozier
David Mitchell

Westmoreland Sct. At a Court held for the said County the 25th day of August 1761 this lease for land indented passed from the Hon. Robert Carter, Esq., to James Brown was proved by the oath of all the witnesses thereto and ordered to be recorded.
Recorded the 17th September 1761 Test: George Lee CCW

Page 70.

Carter to Dunbar Lease

This indenture made the 1st day of January 1761 between Robert Carter of Westmoreland County of the one part and William Dunbar of the other part. Witnesseth that Robert Carter in consideration of the rents and covenants hereafter mentioned has demised and to farm let unto William Dunbar 168 acres of land being in the Parish of Cople and County of Westmoreland on the branch of Nominy River being part of a tract of 1000 acres and called Brent's Tract and bounded as followeth; beginning at the letter "B" a stake near the road, thence to "C" the head of the spring branch, thence down the branch to letter "D", the mouth of the said branch, thence down the next branch of Nominy River to "G" where the said branch forks, thence up the said branch to "H", westerly to the head, thence North 60° East 20 poles to the letter "J" a stake near the road, thence up the said road to the beginning.

To have and to hold during the term of 21 years yielding and paying yearly and every year from the date of these presents the sum of 7 pounds, 4 shillings and 6 pence current money of Virginia to the said Robert Carter at his house in the city of Williamsburg. And the said William Dunbar doth covenant and agree by these presents that he shall within three years after the date of these presents build on the said premises a good dwelling house, 16' x 20' and a house 32' x 20' as good as the common tobacco houses, and plant 50 apple trees and 50 peach trees and the same enclose with a lawful fence. In witness whereof the said Robert Carter and William Dunbar have hereunto interchangeably set their hands and seals the day and year first above written.

Sealed and delivered in the presence of us Robert Carter
Thomas Delozier William Dunbar
David Mitchell
James Brown

Westmoreland Sct. At a Court held for the said County the 25th day of August 1761 this lease for land indented passed from the Hon. Robert Carter, Esq., to William Dunbar was proved by the oath of all the witnesses thereto and ordered to be recorded.
Recorded the 17th September 1761 Test: George Lee CCW

Page 73.

Carter to Mitchell Lease

This indenture made the 1st day of January 1761 between Robert Carter of Westmoreland County of the one part and David Mitchell of the other part. Witnesseth that Robert Carter in consideration of the rents and covenants hereafter mentioned has demised and to farm let unto David Mitchell 61 ½ acres of land being in the Parish of Cople and County of Westmoreland on the branches of Nominy River being part of a tract of 500 acres and called the Metcalf Tract and bounded as followeth; beginning at a small cedar on the back line of Metcalf's patent, thence West by North 95 poles near Poor Jack's old field and corner of Metcalf's patent, thence South by West 114 poles to a white oak, thence East by a stake in an old field, thence North by East 114 poles to the beginning.

To have and to hold during the term of 21 years yielding and paying yearly and every year from the date of these presents the sum of 3 pounds, 7 shillings and seven pence current money of Virginia to the said Robert Carter at his house in the city of Williamsburg. And the said David Mitchell doth covenant and agree by these presents that he shall within three years after the date of these presents build on the said premises a good dwelling house, 16 ft.² and a house 24' x 16' as good as the common tobacco houses, and plant 50 apple trees and 50 peach trees and the same enclose with a lawful fence. In witness whereof the said Robert Carter and David Mitchell have hereunto interchangeably set their hands and seals the day and year first above written.

Sealed and delivered in the presence of us Robert Carter
William Dunbar David Mitchell
Thomas Delozier
James Brown

Westmoreland Sct. At a Court held for the said County the 25th day of August 1761 this lease for land indented passed from the Hon. Robert Carter, Esq., to David Mitchell was proved by the oath of all the witnesses thereto and ordered to be recorded.
Recorded the 17th September 1761 Test: George Lee CCW

Page 76.

Carter to Delozier

This indenture made the 1st day of January 1761 between Robert Carter of Westmoreland County of the one part and Thomas Delozier of the other part. Witnesseth that Robert Carter in consideration of the rents and covenants hereafter mentioned has demised and to farm let unto Thomas Delozier 148 acres of land being in the Parish of Cople and County of Westmoreland on the branch of Nominy River being part of a tract of 1000 acres and called Brent's Tract and bounded as followeth; beginning at the letter "C" in the beginning line of Brent's patent 118 poles from the West branch of Nominy River, thence North 72° West 205 poles to "K" on a branch, thence down the said branch to the mouth to "G" thence down the West branch of Nominy River with marked trees to the letter "H" a white oak near the marsh, thence to the beginning.

To have and to hold during the term of 21 years yielding and paying yearly and every year from the date of these presents the sum of 5 pounds, 2 shillings and 9 pence current money of Virginia to the said Robert Carter at his house in the city of Williamsburg. And the said Thomas Delozier doth covenant and agree by these presents that he shall within three years after the date of these presents build on the said premises a good dwelling house, 16' x 20' and a house 32' x 20' as good as the common tobacco houses, and plant 50 apple trees and 50 peach trees and the same enclose with a lawful fence. In witness whereof the said Robert Carter and William Dunbar have hereunto interchangeably set their hands and seals the day and year first above written.

Sealed and delivered in the presence of us Robert Carter
James Brown Thomas Delozier
David Mitchell
Roderick Perry

Westmoreland Sct. At a Court held for the said County the 25th day of August 1761 this lease for land indented passed from the Hon. Robert Carter, Esq., to Thomas Delozier was proved by the oath of all the witnesses thereto and ordered to be recorded.
Recorded the 24th September 1761 Test: George Lee CCW

Page 79.

Degge to Sanford Lease

This indenture made the 1st day of April 1761 between Ziperus Degge of the County of Gloucester of the one part and Augustine Sanford of the County of Westmoreland of the other part. Witnesseth that Ziperus Degge in consideration of the yearly rents and covenants has demised and to farm let unto Augustine Sanford a tract of land lying in the Parish of Cople and County of Westmoreland containing 200 acres called "Dias". To have and to hold the said tract of land during the natural life of Ziperus Degge, yielding and paying every year starting after the 25th day of March 1763, the yearly rent of 1,030 pounds of neat crop tobacco in one hogshead upon the 25th day of March in every year. In witness whereof the said Ziperus Degge have hereunto set his hand and seal the day month and year first above written.

Signed sealed and delivered in presence of us Ziperus Degge
John Marmaduke
Willoughby Sanford
James Washington

Westmoreland Sct. At a Court held for the said County the 25th day of August 1761, Ziperus Degge came into Court and personally acknowledged this lease for land indented by him passed (Mary Degge the wife of the said Ziperus Degge being first privy examined and relinquishing all her right of dower and thirds therein) to Augustine Sanford and ordered to be recorded.

Recorded the 25th day of September 1761 Test: George Lee CCW

Page 81.

Degge to Sanford Lease

Know all men by these presents that I Mary Degge of the County of Westmoreland am held and stand firmly bound and indebted to Augustine Sanford of the County aforesaid in the full and just sum of 100 pounds current money of Virginia by these presents. Sealed with my seal and dated this 26th day of August 1761. Whereas Robert Sanford my former husband by his last will and testament gave and devised to me a certain piece of land called "Dias" containing 200 acres during my natural life and my now present husband Ziperus Degge has leased to my son Augustine Sanford the above land for and during his life which said lease bearing date the 1st day of April 1761, and I do by these presents give up my whole right and title of the said land and plantation with all the profits thereon belonging to him my said son Augustine Sanford his heirs and assigns in do warrant the same to him from the claim of one or any other person whatsoever, he his heirs or assigns yielding and paying to me the yearly rent of 500 pounds of tobacco after the decease of my husband Ziperus Degge in case I should be the longest liver. Now the condition of the above obligation is such that if the above bound Mary Degge do stand to and abide by the above articles and agreement in every respect and save harmless and indemnify the said Augustine Sanford his heirs or assigns from all encumbrances whatsoever, the above obligation is to be void and of non-effect, otherwise to stand and remain in full force power and virtue.

Signed sealed and delivered in presence of us Mary Degge
Francis Randall
Hannah Ann Randall

Westmoreland Sct. At a court continued and held for the county the 26th day of August 1761 Mary Degge came into Court and personally acknowledged this bond by her passed to Augustine Sanford to be her proper act and deed and ordered to be recorded.

Recorded the 25th day of September 1761 Test: George Lee CCW

Page 82.

Pritchett to Cox Deed

This indenture made this 24th day of October 1761 between Rodham Pritchett of Cople Parish in Westmoreland County of one part and Fleet Cox of the same parish and county of the other part. Witnesseth that the said Rodham Pritchett in consideration of 70 pounds current money of Virginia has sold to Fleet Cox all that tract of land which I bought of William Self containing 40 acres lying in the parish and county aforesaid and is bounded as followeth; beginning at a small walnut tree standing in the line of Presley Cox and extending along the said Coxe's line to the main road that leads to Yeocomico Church and thence down the said road to the land of Thomas Self, deceased and then along the said Self's line to the land of Thomas Bennett, Jr., and along the said Bennett's line to the beginning. In witness whereof the parties to these presents have interchangeably set their hands and seals the day and year first above written.

Signed sealed and delivered in the presence of Rodham Pritchett
William Cox

Thomas Claytor
John Alverson
Stephen Self (his mark)
At a Court held for Westmoreland County the 26th day of January 1762 this deed of feoffment together with the memorandum of livery and seizen and receipt endorsed were acknowledged by Rodham Pritchett party thereto and ordered to be recorded.
Test: James Davenport CCW

Page 86.
Jonathan Newmarch's Will
In the name of God Amen, I Jonathan Newmarch of the County of Westmoreland and Parish of Cople being very sick and weak of body but of perfect sense and memory do make and publish this my last will and testament.
Imprimis, I bequeath unto my son Thomas Newmarch one large high bedstead and bed, one pair of sheets, one blanket and counterpane thereto belonging, also one walnut tree desk, one bay horse name Roger, and one cow and calf, his first choice of the whole.
Item I give unto my son Jonathan Newmarch one bed and bedstead, one pair of blankets, one pair of sheets and a counterpane thereto belonging, one bed and bedstead upstairs with one pair of blankets and a rug belonging to the same, also one cow and calf his next choice of the whole.
Item I give to my grandson William Brown my young gray horse.
Item I give to Dorothy Tingle a bedstead, bolster, one pair sheets and pair of blankets belonging thereto, also one pair of wool and one pair cotton cards, one spinning wheel, two barrels of corn and two young hogs about 18-month-old each.
Item I give unto Joseph Connet a young heifer with calf.
Lastly, my will and desire is that all the residue of my estate (not already given) horses, hogs, cattle, sheep, geese, ducks, fowls, household furniture and the remaining time of two servants, Ephraim Dobson and Francis Dobson, not yet expired, be equally divided together with my crop of tobacco and corn, after the discharge of my lawful debts and funeral charges, betwixt my two sons Thomas Newmarch and Jonathan Newmarch and my grandson William Brown, and if my said grandson should die before he is of age or without heir them the said part of my estate bequeath to him is to descend upon my daughter Elizabeth Brown if she should survive him.
I appoint my son Thomas Newmarch and my son-in-law James Brown executors of this my last will and testament. In witness whereof I have hereunto set my hand and seal this 13th day of November 1761.
In the presence of   Jonathan Newmarch (his mark)
Richard Moxley
Alexander Spark, Sr.
John Sandy
Alexander Spark
Richard Moxley
John Sandy (his mark)
At a Court held for Westmoreland County the 26th day of January 1762 this will was proved according to law by the oath of Alexander Spark and Richard Moxley witnesses thereto and ordered to be recorded and on the motion of Thomas Newmarch and James Brown the executors named in the said will who made oath according to law and together with Edward Sanford and Joseph Stone their securities entered into and acknowledged their bond with condition as the law directs, certificate is granted to them for obtaining a probate thereof in due form.
Test: James Davenport CCW

Page 87.
James Naughty Will
In the name of God Amen, I James Naughty of Washington Parish in the County of Westmoreland being sick of body but of perfect memory and mind do make this my last will and testament in manner as followeth:
Item I give to my daughter Mary Gerrard two Negro girls Frank and Winny already in her

possession during her natural life and 5 pounds current money, and after her decease I leave Negro girl Frank to my granddaughter Ann Gerrard and Negro girl Winny to my granddaughter Elizabeth Gerrard and that to be their part of my estate.
Item I give to Martha Brown: one crop hogshead of good and lawful tobacco, and one bay mare called Peggy.
Item I give to John Briges [Bridges] one dark bay mare, three years old and my saddle and all my wearing apparel and my long gun.
Item I give to Mary Brown, one heifer with her first calf.
Item I give to my son John Naughty, one heifer with her first calf.
Item I give to my son John Naughty all the lands belonging to me together with nine Negroes; Tom, Dick, Nan, Sucky, Lett, Pegg, Bett, Sam and Little Tom and all my stocks and household furniture of every sort and kind soever and in case of none such to descend to my grandson James Gerrard.
My will and desire is that my son John Naughty be my whole and sole executor to this my last will and testament. In witness whereof I have hereunto set my hand and seal this 22nd day of August 1761. James Naughty
Test:
George Payne
Joseph Eidson
Christopher Mothershead
At a court held for Westmoreland County the 26th day of January 1762 this last will and testament of James Naughty, deceased was proved accordance to law by the oaths of George Payne, Joseph Eidson and Christopher Mothershead the witnesses thereto and ordered to be recorded. And on the motion of John Naughty, the executor named in the said will who made oath according to law and together with George Payne and Christopher Mothershead his securities entered and acknowledged their bond with condition as the law directs, certificate is granted him for obtaining a probate thereof in due form.
Test: James Davenport CCW

Page 89.
<u>William Self Will</u>
In the name of God Amen, I William Self of Cople Parish and Westmoreland County being in perfect health and sound memory do make and ordain this to be my last will and testament in manner and form following:
My will and desire is to be buried at the plantation whereon I now live.
Item I give to my son William Self that end of my land where he now lives adjoining to Col. Richard Lee's land as far as the valley to the near spring during his natural life and after his death I give the land to my grandson Peter Self, and for want of such heirs to fall to his brother William Self.
Item I give to my grandson Peter Self all the rest of my land to him and his heirs and if no heirs to his brother William Self. And my desire is that the piece of ground by the road that is now woods should not be cleared by any body till my grandson Peter Self comes to the age of 21 years.
Item I give to my grandson Peter Self a large iron spit, a large dripping pan and a brass cask belongs to the dripping pan, and iron pott rack, and a pair of small stilliards and for want of heirs to his brother William Self.
Item I give to my son William Self half the cask and the other half to Stephen Self.
Item I give to my daughter Susannah Self my large looking glass.
Item I give one cow and calf to be for the use of Benjamin Hail's children.
Item I give to my daughters Becky Self and Lettice Self all the rest of my moveable estate before not given after my wife's death and if one should die without heir her part should fall to the other.
Item my desire is that Stephen Self should live on my plantation to raise and take care in bringing up my children until the first of my grandchildren comes of age and takes the land for which Stephen Self is to pay no rent.
Item my son Abraham Self is to have one year schooling and one young mare or horse and saddle which he thinks proper.
I do constitute and appoint my friend Mr. Fleet Cox and Stephen Self my executors of this my last will. In witness whereof I have hereunto set my hand and seal this 10th day of March 1761.

Sealed and delivered in presence of William Self (his mark)
Daniel Tebbs
Benedict Middleton
Daniel Tebbs, Jr.
At a court held for Westmoreland county the 26th day of January 1762 this last will and testament of William Self, deceased was proved according to the law by the oaths of Daniel Tebbs and Benedict Middleton witnesses thereto and ordered to be recorded; and Fleet Cox, one of the executors named in the will personally appeared and refused to take upon himself the burthen of the execution thereof. And on the motion of Stephen Self the other executor named in the said will who made oath according to law and together with Rodham Mitchell his security ordered into and acknowledged his bond with condition as the law directs, certificate is granted him for obtaining a probate thereof in due form.
Test: James Davenport CCW

Page 90.
Norman Dunn's Nuncupative Will
Westmoreland: December 6th, 1761, Memorandum that on the [blank] day of November last, I heard Norman Dunn tell Anne Anderson, wife of William Anderson of this county that as she had took such a great trouble on her in taking care of him in his sickness that if he lived to get over it he would send her satisfaction and that if he departed this life in his present sickness, he then in the presence of me freely gave her his horse as a satisfaction but with the reserve that if any one came from where he lived in Carolina and paid her for the trouble and expense she had been and with him and his sickness she must deliver the horse to them that made or offered such satisfaction.
John Hornsby
Westmoreland Sct. This day came John Hornsby before me and made oath that the above writing. Certified under my hand this eighth day of December 1760. John Newton
At a court held for Westmoreland County the 26th day of January 1762 this writing purporting the nuncupative will of Norman Dunn, deceased was proved by the oath of John Hornsby the witness thereto and ordered to be recorded. And on motion of William Anderson who made oath according to law and together with Richard Henry Lee his security entered into and acknowledged bond with condition as the law directs, certificate is granted him for obtaining letters of administration of the said decedent's estate of the said will annexed in due form.
Test: James Davenport CCW

Page 91.
George Lee's Will
In the name of God Amen, I George Lee of the Parish of Cople in the County of Westmoreland, Gent., being sick and weak but of perfect mind memory do make this my last will and testament in manner and form following.
First, I desire I may be buried very decently but without any pomp in my garden as near to my wife as possible.
Item I desire that all my just debts punctually paid and as soon as may be after my decease.
Item I give and devise unto my eldest son George Fairfax Lee and to his heirs forever, besides the tract of land I live on which is entailed on him; the three several tracts or parcels of land which I hold in fee simple adjoining to the said entailed land, one of which tracts I have an escheat deed, for another I bought of Henry Garner, and the third is known by the name of the Burnt House tract which was held by the late President Hon. Thomas Lee, Esq. in which was conveyed to me by the Hon. Philip Ludwell Lee, Esq. agreeable to the will of his father on this condition, nevertheless that my said son George Fairfax Lee suffer the Negroes herein after given to my two sons Lancelot Lee and William Lee, and the increase, the said Negroes to work on his land aforesaid with his own Negroes until the said Lancelot Lee arrives to the age of 21 years when a division of slaves given to my two sons Lancelot Lee and William Lee is to be made in the said Lancelot Lee is to possess with his dividend of same and after my son Lancelot Lee arrives to the age of 21 years said George Fairfax Lee also permit my said son William Lee's slaves work on the said lands with his own until the said William Lee arrives to the age of 21 years and until all my said sons arrived to their

respective ages they are to be suitably maintained and educated discretion of my executors hereafter named out of the profits of the whole of the Negroes as well as those of my son George Fairfax Lee's as of my said other two sons working on the said land and what profits remain over and above what are to be applied as aforesaid to be to use of my said son George Fairfax Lee and his heirs forever. But if my said son George Fairfax Lee should refuse to let my sons Lancelot Lee and William Lee slaves work on his lands as aforesaid or should after they have worked on the same refused to suffer my executors apply the profits as is before directed, I then revoke the devise of the three tracts or parcels of land which I held in fee simple in which I have given to my said son George Fairfax Lee on the condition aforesaid and do devise the same unto my son Lancelot Lee his heirs also upon the condition that he the said Lancelot Lee the shall suffer my said son William Lee's Negroes to work on the same land until my said son William Lee comes to the age of 21 years and permit him to receive the profits of his said Negroes during the whole time, but if my said son Lancelot Lee should refuse to permit the same and I give the three tracts or parcels of land unto my son William Lee.

Item I give and devise unto my son Lancelot Lee and his heirs forever one half of a tract of land as I believe in Loudoun County containing 1900 acres which tract of land was granted by deed from the proprietors office bearing date the 1st day of July 1741 to Miss Ann Fairfax and Sarah Fairfax jointly and afterwards the joint tenancy was severed by deed executed by the said Ann Fairfax and Sarah Fairfax since which the said Ann Fairfax whom I intermarried hath by joint deed with me recorded in the general Court conveyed her half part to Richard Lee, Esq. in trust to the use of me and my heirs in fee.

Item I give and devise unto Lancelot Lee and his heirs forever a tract containing 570 acres in Frederick County which was granted to Lawrence Washington, Gent., deceased and by him devised to his will the said Ann Fairfax who after her intermarriage with me executed a deed for the same with several other tracts of land the said Richard Lee in trust for the use of me and my heirs. But if my son Lancelot Lee should die under age without issue, I give all the said lands herein before devised to him to my son William Lee and his heirs forever.

Item I give and devise unto my son William Lee and his heirs forever a tract of land containing 1840 acres lying in Loudoun County on the north side of Elk Run of Cub Run granted to Ann Fairfax by proprietor's deed bearing date the 12th day of June 1741; also, a tract of land containing 1400 acres lying in Loudoun County on the branches Bull Run and the Broad Run of Potomack. Also granted to the said Ann Fairfax by proprietors deed bearing date the 16th day of June 1741; also a tract of land containing 303 acres lying on or near the branches of Goose Creek, granted by proprietor's deed to the said Lawrence Washington and by him devised to his widow the said Ann Fairfax of which said several tracts or parcels of land said Ann Fairfax jointly with me after intermarried conveyed to the said Richard Lee in trust the use of me and my heirs as by a deed of record in the secretary's office of this colony may more fully appear, but if my said son William Lee should die under age without issue the said several tracts or parcels of land to my son Lancelot Lee his heirs forever.

Item I give and devise unto my two sons Lancelot Lee and William Lee and their heirs 22 slaves following; Lancho, Sambo, Juba, Tom, George, Alice, Judy's girl Kate, Marcus, Man, Frank, Nell, Lucy, Harry, Sam, Glasgow, Okery, Judy, the last six are Nell's children, Abraham, Judy, Graham, Will, Joe, (Judy's child Cesar at home & Kate) be equally divided when Lancelot Lee shall arrive to the age of 21 years, but if either my said two sons die before they arrive to the age of 21 years without issue then I give the slaves to the survivor.

Item following 34 slaves; Dick, Nan, Winny, Jenny, Alice, Juba, Phillis, the two last Nan's children, Moll, Sue, Flora, Pegg, Jenny's children, Cesar, Jacob, George, Nan, Jem, Cesar, Winney's children, Will, Harry, Bess, Letty, Kate, Ralph, Aborella, Daniel, Natt,, the six last Betty's children, Okery, Moll, Phillis, Ben, Prue, Dinah, Moll and Harry, the five last Phillis' children; being entailed they decend to my son George Fairfax Lee and it is my will he have them.

Item if it should so happen that my son George Fairfax Lee should die without issue by which means his entailed estate both land and Negroes will descend to my son Lancelot Lee and in such case, I revoke the several bequeaths to him the said Lancelot Lee made of the lands and slaves aforesaid and do devise the same to my son William Lee.

Item I give and bequeath to my dear daughter Elizabeth Lee 1000 pounds current money of

Virginia to be paid to her by my executors when she arrives to the age of 21 years or is married which ever should first happen upon condition she relinquish all right or title she may have a claim to Negro wench Judy's Alice, which I bought of one Minor and formerly promised to give to my daughter Elizabeth Lee, but if my said daughter refuses to make such relinquishment of her right to the said Negro Alice and her increase I then revoke the legacy of 1000 pounds and give her only 800 pounds current money in lieu thereof.
Item I give unto my good friend Richard Henry Lee my Maunton gun.
Item I given to my son George Fairfax Lee 100 head of neat cattle in such other staff as my executor shall think necessary for his plantations. I also give him the quilt worked by his mother, all his mother's and my books, my grandfather's picture, and my father's picture set in gold, the mourning ring I expect from England for his mother, all the plate in the house, Col. Fairfax's snuff box and George's mothers stone buttons set in gold which are in the snuff box.
Item I give to my daughter Elizabeth Lee the mourning ring which I wore for her late mother as also the great bible and common prayer book which were her mothers.
Item I give to my son Lancelot Lee a seal set in gold with the family coat of arms cut thereon which was given to me by my friend Col. Richard Lee.
Item I desire that my chariot and chariot horses and all my blooded horses, mares and colts may be sold but that in order to have them sold to the greatest advantage the time and place of sale be first advertised in the Virginia Gazette.
Item I desire that all my household furniture and other personal estate except what is specifically given by this my will and except such stocks as my executors shall think proper to keep for the use of my said son's plantations may be sold for the most that can be got for them.
Item I give to my son William Lee, two guineas to purchase him a mourning ring for his mother.
Item such stocks as my executors shall think proper to be kept for my sons Lancelot Lee and William Lee and all the rest of my personal estate after my debts and legacies are paid, I give to my sons Lancelot Lee and William Lee equally divided when Lancelot Lee arrives to the age of 21 years.
Item It is my earnest will and desire that my executors as soon after my death will send my son George Fairfax Lee to England to the care of my friend Mr. James Russell to receive his education there.
Item if my executors think they can have my two sons Lancelot Lee and William Lee well educated cheaper in England than in Virginia, I do give them the power of sending them.
Item as I do impower my friends Col. George William Fairfax, Col. Richard Henry Lee, Col. Richard Lee, Mr. Bryant Fairfax and Capt. John Turberville whom I hereby appoint guardians to all my children to lease out or sell any of the back lands that are herein before given to my two sons Lancelot Lee and William Lee before they arrive to the age of 21 years, and whatever sum or sums of money arise from the sale of such lands or any part thereof, I desire may be put out at interest on good security and that the same be paid to each son that the land so sold is devised at age 21 years.
Item I desire my daughter Elizabeth Lee may be suitably maintained out of my estate until she arrives to the age of 21 years or is married.
Item I request of my executors that they will not put the wench called Home House Kate, to the hoe or to any hard labor, but to keep her whilst it is necessary to wait on and take care of my children, and when there shall be no need of such service, that she be kept to making the negros clothes or such like business.
I likewise request of my executors that they never permit any other kind or sort of tobacco than sweet scented to be tended on the Old House plantation or the lower plantation under the hill and that they ship all my tobacco and do not sell them in this country and I recommend it to them to consign such tobacco to my friend Mr. James Russell as long as he continues in the tobacco trade.
I also desire that the goods, cloths and tools wanted for the use of the negros and plantation may be yearly set for to England and none purchased in this country.
Lastly, I do nominate and appoint my good friends Richard Henry Lee, Richard Lee and John Turberville executors of this my last will and testament. In witness whereof I the said George Lee have to this my last will and testament set my hand and seal this 13th day of September 1761.
Signed sealed and published In presence of us George Lee

William Lee
George Turberville
Martha Turberville
Richard Parker
At a court held for Westmoreland County the 26th day of January 1762 This will was proved according to law by the oaths of George Turberville and Richard Parker witnesses thereto and ordained to be recorded and on the motion of Richard Henry Lee, Richard Lee and John Turberville, Gent., the executors named in the said will who made oath according to law and together with John Augustine Washington, Richard Parker and Francis Lightfoot Lee their securities entered into and acknowledged their bond with condition as the law directs, certificate is granted them for obtaining a probate thereof in due form.
Test: James Davenport CCW

Page 98.
Lambert to Tuberville Indenture
This indenture made the 16th day of October 1761 between William Lambert of the Parish of Cople and County of Westmoreland and Elizabeth Lambert his wife of the one part and John Turberville of the aforesaid parish and county of the other part. Witnesseth that William Lambert and Elizabeth Lambert his wife in consideration of 160 pounds current money of Virginia has sold to John Turberville a tract in Parish of Cople and County of Westmoreland between Flood's Creek and South West Creek branches of Nominy bounded as followeth; beginning at a corner on a point at the mouth of South West Creek on Nominy River extending down the said river North 75° East 40 poles to the mouth of Flood's Creek, thence up the creek and crossing a cove South 85° East 32 poles and South 38° East 5 poles, South 42° East 25 poles to the mouth of a gut that divides this land from the land of the aforesaid John Turberville, thence extending up the same water course to the road that leads to Machodoc which was formerly called the Machodoc Old Path, thence along a line of marked trees North 86° West 17 poles to a white oak, thence South 83°West 14 poles to another white oak, thence South 73° West 32-1/2 poles to a large white oak and North 72° West 8 poles to another white oak and North 45° West 4 poles to a white oak at a branch of South West Creek, thence down the several meanders of the branch and gut to the head of the creek and along the several turnings thereof to the beginning including 80 acres and 2 rods of land, being part of a patent for 300 acres formerly granted to John Tasker bearing date the 18th day of October 1650 which afterwards became the right and inheritance of Richard Kenner in fee who together with Elizabeth Kenner his wife sold the land to Peter Dunkin by deed bearing date the 6th day of October 1665 and afterwards patented by the said Peter Dunkin in his own name the 2nd day of July 1669 for 140 acres, whereof part of this is a moiety or half part which by several conveyances became the estate of George South the elder, deceased who by his last will and testament bearing date the 1st day of February 1698 bequeath the lands to be equally divided between his two sons, George South and John South and should they die without issue to fall to his two daughters, Tamer South and Joan South and the two sons dying without issue the land descended to the two daughters. And afterwards the land was divided by Tamer South and Joan South and for bounds of the division thereof appointed a swamp and several trees in and about the same by them marked as a dividing line between them. The aforesaid Joan South married Thomas Lambert whom she had two sons William Lambert and Thomas Lambert and after her death the said 80 acres and 2 rods of land being the moiety of 140 acres the aforesaid George South, the elder purchased of Thomas Youell bearing date the 31st day of October 1683 became vested in William Lambert, son and heir at law of Joan South and party to these presents. In witness whereof the parties to these presents have hereunto set their hands and seals.
Signed sealed and delivered in presence of
Thomas Lambert
George Turberville
James Bellflower
Peter Harding
John Avent (his mark)

William Lambert
Elizabeth Lambert

Elizabeth Lambert's commission for privy examination by Willoughby Newton and Richard Lee,

27th day of October 1761
At a court held for Westmoreland County the 26th day of January 1762 this indenture of feoffment together with the commission annexed for taking the acknowledgement and privy examination of Elizabeth Lambert wife of William Lambert and a certificate of the execution thereof ordered to be recorded.
Test: James Davenport CCW

Page 103.
Peter Rust's Will
In the name of God Amen, I Peter Rust the Westmoreland county and Parish of Cople do make and ordain this to be my last will and testament.
Give and bequeath to Daniel Lamkin all my right and title of 712 acres of land I bought of George Eskridge now in Loudoun County on Tuscarora Run and for want of heirs to fall to my four sons, Richard Rust, James Rust, John Rust and Peter Rust into their heirs.
Item I give to my son Richard Rust 125 acres of land in Bull Neck after the death of his mother.
Item I give all the remainder of my land In Bull Neck to my son Samuel Rust including the land I bought of Craddock Butler.
Item I give to my son James Rust my land in the place called Frog Hall and two Negroes, Loudoun and Abraham after the death of his mother.
Item I give to my beloved wife Elizabeth Rust the use of 100 acres of land joining to my dwelling house during her widowhood.
Item I give all my land called Sandy Point which I purchased of Samuel Ball to my son Samuel Rust.
Item I give to my son John Rust all the land I have at the mill with said mill and appurtenances after the death of his mother.
Item I give to my son John Rust two Negroes, Harry and Dick after the death of his mother.
Item I give to my son Peter Rust all the land I hold on the eastern shore in Dorsit County [Dorchester County, Maryland] and Negro man Peg.
Item I give all the rest of my Negroes not before given be equally divided among my four daughters. Mary Rust, Martha Rust, Hannah Rust, and Elizabeth Rust after the widowhood of their mother.
Item I give all this tract of land that I now live on to my son Samuel Rust, only the reserve mentioned above to my wife.
Item I give to my beloved wife the use of the land and Negroes mentioned above whether it be for life or widowhood to use and bring it my children.
Item I give all the rest of my estate before not given to be equally divided between my wife and children before named and I appoint my son Samuel Rust in my son John Rust my executors of this my last will and testament. In witness whereof I have hereunto set my hand and seal this ninth day of November 1761.
Signed sealed and delivered in presence of us Peter Rust
Daniel Tebbs
Jeremiah Courtney
Valentine Garner (his mark)
At a court held for Westmoreland County this 26th day of January 1762 this last will and testament of Peter Rust, deceased was proved according to law by the oath of Daniel Tebbs, Jeremiah Courtney and Valentine Garner the witnesses thereto, and ordered to be recorded, and on the motion of Samuel Rust one of the executors named in the said will who made oaths according to law and together with Daniel Tebbs and George Rust his securities entered into and acknowledged bond with condition as the law directs, certificate is granted him for obtaining a probate thereof in due form, liberty being reserved to John Rust the other executor (and is an infant) to join in the probate when he shall attain the age of 21 years.

Page 105.
William Dunbar's Will
In the name of God Amen, the 11th day of November 1761 I William Dunbar of the County of Westmoreland and colony of Virginia being in perfect and sound memory do make and ordain this

my last will and testament in manner and form following.
Item my will and desire is that all such Negroes in servants as I am now possessed with shall and may be kept and employed on the plantation which I leased of Robert Carter, Esq. during the said lease, also my will and desire is that my estate of what nature or kind soever should be equally divided between my three children Molly Dunbar, James Dunbar and William Dunbar and in case Mrs. James Eskridge should want to make use of any of the stock during her widowhood is that she may not be debarred from it, also my desire is that much of the stock as my executors hereafter named shall think the plantation and the hands can maintain should be upon the same and further my will and desire is that Fleet Cox, Peter Presley Cox and George Rust be executors of this my last will and testament. In witness whereof I have here unto set my hand and seal the day and year first above written.
Signed sealed and delivered in presence of William Dunbar
George Rust
John Murray
Richard Eskridge
At a court held for Westmoreland County the 23rd day of February 1762 this will was proved according to law by the oath of Richard Eskridge in witness thereto and the same having been proved at the last court by the oath of John Murray another witness thereto is ordain to be recorded and on motion of George Rust one of the executors named in the will who according to law and together with Thomas Bennett, Jr., his security entered into and acknowledged bond with conditioned as the law directs, certificate is granted him for obtaining a probate thereof in due form, liberty being reserved to Fleet Cox and Peter Presley Cox the other executors named in the said will to join in the probate thereof when they shall think fit.
Test: James Davenport CCW

Page 106.
Berryman & Wife to Triplett Indenture
This indenture made the 20th day of June 1761 between James Berryman and Sarah Berryman his wife in the Parish of Washington and County of Westmoreland the one part and John Triplett of the Parish of Hanover in County of King George of the other part. Witnesseth that James Berryman in consideration of 70 pounds current money of Virginia has sold John Triplett two tracts of land containing 600 acres being on the head of Weedon's Dam in Westmoreland County part of the aforesaid land being formerly purchased of John Triplett of King George County and the other part from the executors of George Blackmore by Francis Settle, and Francis Settle and Sarah Settle his wife sold and conveyed unto John Martin by deed dated 11 day of November 1755 and by John Martin and Mary Ann Martin his wife of Westmoreland sold and conveyed unto the said James Berryman by deed dated 15 to July 1759. As witness whereof the said James Berryman and Sarah Berryman his wife have hereunto set their hands and seals this day year first above written.
Sealed and delivered in the presence of James Berryman
John Jett Sarah Berryman
James Triplett
William Triplett
At a court held for Westmoreland County the 23rd day of February 1762 this indenture and the receipt endorsed were proved by the oath of John Jett, James Triplett and William Triplett the witnesses thereto in the memorandum of livery and seizen also endorsed was proved by the oath of the said John Jett and James Triplett together with the said indenture and receipt ordered to be recorded
Test: James Davenport CCW

Page 108.
Chilton to Moxley Indenture
This indenture made the 14th day of October 1761 between Thomas Chilton of the Parish of Cople and County of Westmoreland of the one part and Richard Moxley of the Parish of Washington and county aforesaid of the other part. Witnesseth that Thomas Chilton in consideration of 70 pounds current money has sold to Richard Moxley a tract containing 160 acres lying in the Parish of Cople

and County of Westmoreland, bounded as follows; beginning at a corner marked white oak at the fork of a great swamp running easterly dividing the land of Edward Moxley up the said swamp to a corner tree dividing the land of David Moxley, thence northerly by a line of marked trees to the main road, and thence to extend to the cross road, and then North West up the main road to a corner tree dividing the land between William Taylor, deceased and John Washington, thence running southerly by a line of marked trees dividing the land of John Washington to the head of a great swamp, thence down the said swamp still dividing the land of the said John Washington to the first mentioned white oak; it being a parcel of land that William Moxley, Sr., gave to his grandson Richard Omohundro by deed of gift bearing date May 28th 1713. In witness whereof the party first above mentioned have to these presents interchangeably set his hand and affixed his seal the day and year first above written.

Signed sealed and delivered in the presence of Thomas Chilton
Thomas Chilton, Jr.
Leroy Hipkins
Daniel Moxley

At a court held for Westmoreland County the 23rd day of February 1762 this indenture together with the memorandum of livery and seizen and receipt endorsed were acknowledged by Thomas Chilton and ordered to be recorded.
Test: James Davenport CCW

Page 111.
White to White Indenture
This indenture made the 20th day of February 1762 between John White, Joseph Smith and Janey Smith his wife, and Woffendall Kendall and Susannah Kendall his wife of the Parish of Washington and county of Washington of the one part and Samuel White, planter of the aforesaid parish and county of the other part. Witnesseth that John White, Joseph Smith and Woffendall Kendall in consideration of 15 shillings current money of Virginia have sold unto Samuel White a tract of land lying in Washington Parish and County of Westmoreland containing 100 acres bounded as followeth: beginning at a marked white oak standing on the forest road as leads from Washington's Mill to the ridge road a corner of Thomas Peach's, running thence southerly to the mouth of a branch called the First Fork, thence down the meanders of Weedon's Dam to a line of Augustine Weedon, from thence along Weedon's line and Chancellor's line westerly to the said road, thence up the said road to the first beginning tree. In witness whereof John White, Joseph Smith and Woffendall Kendall and their wives have hereunto set their hands and seals this 20th day of February 1762.

Signed sealed and delivered in the presence of us	John White
Lawrence Downton	Joseph Smith
Lawrence Weedon	Janey Smith
Alvin Mothershead (his mark)	Woffendall Kendall
Thomas Peach	Susannah Kendall

At a court held for Westmoreland County the 23rd day of February 1762 this deed of feoffment together with the memorandum of livery and seizen and receipt endorsed were proved by the oaths of Alvin Mothershead, Lawrence Downton and Lawrence Weedon, the witnesses thereto and ordered to be recorded.
Test: James Davenport CCW

Page 114.
Knowles to Oldham Indenture
This Indenture made the 22nd day of October 1761 between Edward Knowles and Martha Knowles his wife of the province of North Carolina of the one part and Capt. Samuel Oldham of the Parish of Washington and County of Westmoreland in the colony of Virginia, Gent., of the other part. Witnesseth that Edward Knowles in consideration of 35 pounds current money of Virginia has sold to Samuel Oldham has sold all the tract lying and being part in Westmoreland County and part in King George County containing 95 acres and bounded as follows; beginning at a marked white oak close on the head of Storke's Dam extending south 36° Westerly 79 poles to a marked white oak

corner by the road, thence North 68° Westerly 49 poles to a spanish oak corner line to the land of Edward Taylor, thence North 40° West 101 poles to a hickory corner tree of the land of the said Taylor: thence North 21-1/4° West 24 poles to a dead hickory corner in the line of the land of William Balthrop, thence North 67° East 120 poles to a dead oak corner between this land and the land of Charles Weedon, thence South 27-1/4° East to the beginning. In witness whereof Edward Knowles have hereunto set his hand and seal this 22nd day of October 1761.

Signed sealed and delivered in presence of us Edward Knowles (his mark)
Lawrence Weedon
Archibald Betty
Robert Wilkinson
Gabriel Johnston

At a court continued and held for Westmoreland County the 24th day of February 1762 this indenture of bargain and sale was proved by the oaths of Gabriel Johnston and Archibald Betty witnesses thereto and the receipt endorsed was also proved by the oath of Gabriel Johnston the witness thereto and the said indenture having been proved by the oath of one other of the witnesses thereto is together with the said receipt ordered to be recorded.

Page 116.
Sarah White's Will

In the name of God Amen, this 26th day of November 1761, I Sarah White of Westmoreland County being very sick and weak but of perfect sense and memory do make and ordain this to be my last will and testament in manner and form as follows.

Item I give and bequeath all my estate, Negroes, stock and household furniture to be equally divided between my son John White and my daughter Jenny Smith and my daughter Susanna White.

Item I give and bequeath all my remaining clothes to my daughter Margaret Mothershead.

In witness whereof I have hereunto set my hand and seal.

Test: Samuel White,
John White Sarah White (her mark)

At a court continued and held for Westmoreland County the 24th day of February 1762 this will was proved according to law by the oaths of Samuel White and John White witnesses thereto and ordered to be recorded and on the motion of the said John White who made oath according to law and together with Samuel White and John Balthrop his securities entered into and acknowledged bond with condition as law directs, certificate is granted him for obtaining letters of administration of the estate of the said Sarah White with the said will and asked in due form.

Test: James Davenport CCW

Page 117.
John Baker's Will

In the name of God Amen, this 27th day of November 1761 I John Baker of the Parish of Cople in the County of Westmoreland being very sick and weak in body. [the following is one long sentence] I give and bequeath to my loving wife Elizabeth Baker this tract of land for her life and then to my son William Baker and one still, I give my son William Baker and one bed and I give to my son William Baker and one large gun to William Baker in the little John, I give to my son John Baker, and my riding horse, I give to my loving wife Elizabeth Baker and one young horse colt, I give to my son William Baker one breeding mare, I give to my daughter Ann Baker and the first colt to my son John Baker that she shall bring and one suit of clothes I give to my son William Baker and the remainder part of my estate I give to my loving wife and children to be equally divided between them one bed and furniture I give to my son John Baker and one bed and furniture I give to my daughter Ann Baker.

Test: John Baker
John Hutt
Simon Rice
John Rice

At a court held for Westmoreland County the 30th day of March 1762 this will was proved according to law by the oath of John Hutt and Simon Rice witnesses thereto and ordered to be recorded and on motion of Elizabeth Baker, widow and relict of the said deceased who made oath according to law and together with Gerrard Hutt and Nathaniel Jackson her securities entered into and acknowledged bond with condition as the law directs, certificate is granted her for obtaining letters of administration of the estate of the said John Baker with the said will and next in due form.

Page 118.
Elizabeth Nash's Will
In the name of God Amen, I Elizabeth Nash of the County of Westmoreland and Parish of Cople being engaged but of perfect sense and memory.
Item I give to my daughter Ann Nash one cow and calf
Item I give to my son John Nash one feather bed and furniture
Item I give to my son Thomas Brown one Shilling
Item I give to my son Nathaniel Nash one Shilling,
Item I give to my daughter Elizabeth Bragg one Shilling
Item I give to my son William Nash one Shilling
Item I give to my son Jeremiah Nash all the rest of my estate
Item I desire my son Jeremiah Nash my executor.
Gerrard Hutt, Jr. Elizabeth Nash (her mark)
Osmond Crabb
At a court held for Westmoreland County the 30th day of March 1762 this will was proved according to law by the oaths of Gerrard Hutt, Jr. and Osmond Crabb the witnesses thereto and is ordered to be recorded and on the motion of Jeremiah Nash the executors named in the said will who made oath according to law and together with George Duncan and Osmond Crabb his securities entered into and acknowledged bond with condition as the law directs, certificate is granted him for obtaining a probate thereof in due form.
Test: James Davenport CCW

Page 119.
Stephen Smith's Will
In the name of God Amen, I Stephen Smith, Sr., of Westmoreland County in the Parish of Cople being sick and weak of body but of sound and perfect memory do make this my last will and testament.
Item I give to my well-beloved son Robert Smith, one cow big with calf.
Item I will that my well-beloved son Samuel Smith have two years schooling out of my estate and when according to the opinion of my executors he be big enough to go to a trade my will is that he should be bound to his uncle George Banister.
Item my will is that my wife and children keep together on my plantation as long as they can contrive to subsist well on the same and if any of the elder children should go away and leave the rest they shall not carry away any part of my estate, and my will is when they can live on the said place no longer that then my executors set up my land to public auction for ready money and them that is of age to take their parts of the same and they that are underage their money to be laid up by my executors and made to be bound out to whom my executors think proper.
Lastly, I appoint my beloved brother Samuel Smith and my loving friend James Baley and my loving wife Ann Smith whole and sole executors of this my last will and testament. In witness whereof I have hereunto set my hand and seal this 22nd day of November 1761
Test Stephen Smith
Daniel Baley
Peter McClanahan
John Baley
At a court held for Westmoreland County the 30th day of March 1762 this will was proved according to law by the oath of Peter McClanahan and John Bailey witnesses thereto and ordered to be recorded and on the motion of Ann Smith, James Baley and Samuel Smith the executors named in the said will who made or oath according to law and together with William Creswick, John Baley and James Baley, Sr., their securities entered into and acknowledged bond with condition as

the law directs, certificate is granted them for obtaining a probate thereof in due form.
Test: James Davenport CCW

Page 120.
Harding & White to Middleton Bond
Know all men by these presents that we Peter Harding and the Parish of Cople and County of Westmoreland and Zachariah White of the Parish of Lunenburg and county of Richmond are firmly bond unto Robert Middleton of the Parish of Cople and County of Westmoreland in the penal sum of 200 pounds current money of Virginia to which payment will well and truly to be made by these presents, sealed with our seals and dated this 7th September 1761. The condition of the above obligation is whereas the above bound Peter Harding and Mary Jeffries Harding his wife, daughter and one of the co-heirs of Benjamin Walker late of the County of Westmoreland, deceased have sold unto Robert Middleton all their right and title to a tract of land containing 150 acres lying in the County of Westmoreland and Parish of Cople which formerly belonged to Thomas Walker grandfather to the said Mary Jeffries Harding and from him descended to this three daughters Seleashea Walker, Mary Jeffries Walker and Alice Walker as co-heirs of Benjamin Walker and that the said Mary Jeffries Harding is not yet of full age to pass a conveyance unto Robert Middleton for her part of the said land, now so it is that if they Peter Harding and Mary Jeffries Harding his wife shall when required to acknowledged lawful deeds for the making over and conveying all the right and title of the 150 acres of land then the above obligation to be void and of none effect, otherwise to stand and remain in full force power and virtue.
Signed sealed and delivered on presence of 	Peter Harding
David Boyd 	Zachariah White
Francis Randall
John Eidson
At a court held for Westmoreland county this 30th day of March 1762, this bond for the performance of covenants was proved by the oaths of David Boyd and Francis Randall witnesses to the same and ordered to be recorded.
Test: James Davenport CCW

Page 122.
Robert Moore Will
In the name of God Amen, I Robert Moore of the County of Westmoreland being very sick and weak but of sound and perfect memory to make my last will and testament in manner and form as follows.
Item my will is that my loving wife Elizabeth Moore have the use of my whole estate during her natural life or widowhood.
Item my will is that after the death of marriage of my beloved wife, I give the plantation I now possess of to my beloved son John Moore and his heirs and for want of such heirs, to my son Robin Moore.
Item I give to my son John Moore my bay mare and gun.
Item my will is that when my son John Moore arrives to the age of 21 years if he be possessed of my estate that he then shall equally divide all the negroes and other moveable estate amongst the rest of my children and himself.
Item I give to my loving daughter Eleanor Moore one chest.
Lastly, I appoint my well-beloved wife Elizabeth Moore and my loving son John Moore the whole and sole executors of this my last will and testament. As witness my hand and seal this 5th day of December 1761.
Test 	Robert Moore (his mark)
Daniel Baley
John Baley
William Creswick
At a court held for Westmoreland County the 30th day of March 1762, This will was proved according to law by the oaths of John Baley and William Creswick, witnesses thereto and ordered to be recorded, and on the motion of Elizabeth Moore the executrix named in the same will who

made oath according to law and together with James Baley, Sr. and John Baley her securities entered into and acknowledged with condition as the law directs, certificate is granted her for obtaining a probate thereof in due form, liberty being reserved to John Moore an infant, the executor in the said will also named to join in the probate thereof when he shall attain to the age of 21 years.
Test: James Davenport CCW

Page 123.
John Davis Will
In the name of God Amen, I John Davis of the Parish of Cople and County of Westmoreland being very sick and weak of body but of sound mind and memory do make this my last will and testament in manner and form following.
Item I give and bequeath unto my son William Davis and his heirs all my land and plantation whereon I live and in failure of such heirs to the heir at law.
Item all the remainder of my estate, I leave to be equally divided between my loving wife Jane Davis and all my children.
Item I appoint my beloved wife and William Porter and George White my executors and hereto set my hand and seal this 17th day of January 1754. John Davis (his mark)
William Lawson
Elizabeth White (her mark)
Mary White (her mark)
At a court held for Westmoreland County the 30th day of March 1762 this will was proved by the oaths of Zachariah White and Mary White, witnesses thereto and ordered to be recorded and on the motion of Jane Davis, widow and relict of the said John Davis and one of the executors named in the said will who made oath according to the law and together with Samuel Smith and John Baley, her securities entered into and acknowledged bond with condition as the law directs, certificate is granted her for obtaining a probate thereof in due for.
Test: James Davenport CCW

Page 124.
Bulger & Wife to Wright
This indenture made 30th day of March 1762 between Edmund Bulger of the Parish of Lunenburg in the County of Richmond, planter, and Jane Bulger his wife and Thomas Wright of the said parish and county, planter and Elizabeth Wright his wife of the one part and Gerrard Davis of the Parish of Cople in the County of Westmoreland, planter of the other part. Witnesseth that in consideration of five shillings paid to Edmund Bulger and Thomas Wright has given granted bargained sold released by these presents unto Gerrard Davis all manner of dower and right and title what soever to a parcel of land situated in Cople Parish and county aforesaid containing by estimation 150 acres which is given by the will of John Wright late of the said parish and county, deceased to his son John Wright, deceased former husband of the said Jane Bulger and father to the said Thomas Wright party to these presents in fee tail, which said Thomas Wright hath since by deed bearing date the 13th day of April last past sold the same to Gerrard Davis. In witness whereof the parties to these presence have hereunto set their hands and seals the day and year first above written.
Sealed and delivered in the presence of us Edmund Bulger
Francis Callis Jane Bulger (her mark)
Joseph Stone Thomas Wright
Richard Moxley Elizabeth Wright (her mark)
At a court held for Westmoreland County the 30th day of March 1762this deed was acknowledged by the parties thereto and ordered to be recorded.
Test: James Davenport CCW

Page 125.
Michael Branham's Will
In the name of God Amen, the 3rd day of December 1761 Michael Branham of the County of Westmoreland being sick and weak in body but of perfect sense and memory do make and ordain

this my last will and testament in manner and form following.
Item I give to my son Barnaby Branham all my shoemaking tools.
Item I give and bequeath to my loving wife Rosana Branham all and singular the remaining part of my estate in whose ever hands the same may be found for and during her natural lives, provided she don't marry, otherwise for and during the time she lives a widow and after her decease or at the day of her marriage, the same to be equally divided between my six children; Ignatius Branham, Barnaby Branham, Joseph Branham, William Branham, Elizabeth Branham and Rosannah Branham.
Item I leave my loving wife Rosannah Branham full and whole the executrix of this my last will and testament. In witness whereof I have hereunto set my hand and seal the day and month and year first above written.
Signed sealed and acknowledged in the presence of us Michael Branham (his mark)
E. Norwood
Robert Lang
Henry Self
At a court held for Westmoreland County the 27th day of April 1762 this last will and testament of Michael Branham, deceased was proved according to law by the oath of Robert Lang, [xxxxxxx] witnesses thereto and ordered to be recorded and on motion of Rosannah Branham the executrix named therein who made oath according to law, and together with John Brown and Robert Lang her securities entered into and acknowledged bond with condition as the law directs, certificate is granted her for obtaining a probate therein due form.
Test: James Davenport CCW

Page 126.
Augustine Washington's Will
In the name of God Amen, I Augustine Washington of Washington County and colony of Virginia being bound on a voyage to Great Britain and intending to settle my temporal affairs in case of mortality do make this my last will and testament.
Imprimis, I will that all my just debts be discharged by my executor or executors hereafter named as soon as conveniently may be and for this purpose I desire my outstanding debts to be collected in and applied in the first place to the payment of my said debts.
Secondly, my will is that if my outstanding debts are not sufficient to discharge those who from me, my executors to dispose of such part of my personal estate (Negroes excepted) as shall seem to them sufficient for this purpose, but if it shall be found that my outstanding debts together with such part of my personal estate as my said executors shall think, fit to dispose of, are not sufficient to them I have directed them to be applied, then and the third place I empower my executors and it is my desire that they should take or borrow money upon interest to set aside such sums as shall be unpaid from the aforesaid funds and that they put under mortgage's such part of my estate for the whole if they think proper as a security for the repayment thereof.
Item I give and devise to my son William Augustine Washington all my lands as well in this country as elsewhere (except as is hereafter excepted) to him and his heirs forever.
Item I give to my said son William Augustine Washington and his heirs 30 Negro slaves which number I desire may be made up and delivered to him at the age of 21 years or marriage in the following manner; first my will is that all those Negroes to make up I shall have a right after the death of Mrs. Ann Lee wife to Col. George Lee late of this County by virtue of a remainder limited in the will of my deceased brother Lawrence Washington to be delivered to my said son in part of the number above devised to him, secondly that the residue of the number be made up to him at the discretion of my executors out of such Negroes or their increase as I am now in possession of, further my will is that if the said Ann Lee shall be living at my sons arrival to the age of 21 years that he then have it in his choice to wait for those Negroes on remainder as aforesaid or have the said number made up to him by my executors out of such Negroes as shall then be on my several plantations.
Item I give to my three daughters Betty Washington, Nancy Washington and Jane Washington each 1000 pounds current money be paid and satisfied to each of them upon their arrival the eldest to the age of 21 years or marriage in the following manner.

First, I desire that my Negroes remaining after delivery of the number devise to my son aforesaid be justly appraised and an equal division thereof made between my said three daughters and that the said Negroes according to such valuation should go in part to discharge the portions above given to them.
Secondly, I desire that my stock of horses, cattle, sheep and hogs in my household furniture be either appraised in the manner as the Negroes and above directed and delivered to my daughters according to such valuation or that my executors sell the same and apply the money or so much thereof as to make up the variance of the portions devised to my said daughters.
Thirdly, I desire that the surplus of the profits of my whole estate after maintenance of my wife, son, and three daughters be also applied in the discharge of so much of the money devised to my said daughters as the same quality divided amongst them shall amount to, and; Fourthly, if the said residue of my Negroes, stocks and furniture together with the surplus of the profits of my estate to be insufficient for the payment of my said daughters portions I then empower my said executors to sell and dispose of and to make absolute deeds of conveyance of my interest and estate in the share I hold in all the ironworks both in this colony and in the province of Maryland devised to me in the will of my said deceased brother and to apply as much of the money arising thereby as shall make up the sums devised to my daughters aforesaid and the residue thereof I give and to my son William Augustine Washington to be in the hands of my executors till he arrives to the age of 21 years.
Item if it should happen that my beloved wife being at this time ensient with a son, give and devise to such son and his heirs forever all my lands in the county of Hampshire together with 10 Negroes and 500 pounds current money which said Negroes and the monies are to be delivered to him and raised at his age of 21 years in the following manner. First, as I have already devised to my son William Augustine Washington 30 Negroes and directed in what manner they are to be delivered to him my will and desire is that my executors take from the number devise to him five Negroes at their discretion which said five Negroes I give unto such son and his heirs forever. Secondly, out of the residue of my Negroes devise to my daughters I desire my executors take five other Negroes which I also given to such son and his heirs forever in my will is that the valuation of the said five Negroes be deducted from the portion before devised to my daughters and further my will is touching the 500 pounds devise to such son, that the said sum be raised together with the daughters portions out of the profits of my plate in the sale of my share in the said iron works in that at the same be insufficient for raising the whole that my said daughters and son lose so much of the sums devise to them in proportion to such deficiency but if my said wife shall be pregnant with a daughter, my will is and I give and devise unto such daughter 1000 pounds to be raised out of the residue of my Negroes, stocks, furniture, profits and sale of ironworks as is directed before for the raising of my other daughters proportions if the same shall be sufficient for such purpose, but if it should prove insufficient in my will is that each daughter lose proportionately and further my will is that it either of my daughters born or such child as may wife may be ensient with, die under the age of 21 years unburied the sum of money devise to such child be equally divided among the survivors.
Item I give unto my beloved wife such maintenance for herself and children out of my whole estate during her widowhood as she shall think consistent with the circumstances of my estate having respect to the raising the portions of my said daughters, but if my said wife shall again Mary, I give and devise to her during her life my dwelling plantation and 10 grown Negroes at the discretion of my executors hereafter named with liberty notwithstanding to my wife to take and to her number of Negroes all or any of my house servants which said Negroes the allotted to my wife after her death together with their increase, I devise to my son William Augustine Washington in part of the number before devised to him.
Item I empower my executors hereafter named to make a conveyance or conveyances of certain lands taken up in my name by my deceased brother Lawrence Washington to such uses and to such purposes and persons as in his will is directed.
Item I appoint my beloved wife sole executrix of this my last will and testament during her widowhood, but if she marry again my will is that her executorship immediately terminate and that she account with my other executors hereafter named for the surplus of the profits of my estate after a sufficient allowance for the maintenance of my family.

Lastly, upon the marriage of my said wife or her demise I appoint my esteemed friends Fielding Lewis, Richard Henry Lee and my brothers George Washington and John Washington executors of this my last will and testament. In witness whereof I have hereunto set my hand and seal this 18th day of September 1758

Signed sealed published and declared in the presence of Augustine Washington

William Booth
Samuel Washington
John Ariss
Edward Ransdell

Be it known for that whereas, since the making and executing of my will bearing date 18 September 1758, my wife has been delivered of a son, I do by these presents confirm unto my said son George Washington all and singular the bequeaths in my said will devise to the son my wife might be at that time be pregnant with, with the following alterations and additions. Imprimis, it is my will and desire that if my executors in my said will mentioned shall think it more for the interest of my said son George Washington to sell the lands given him in the colony of Hampshire, I do hereby give them full power and authority to do so and I also desire the money arising from the sale of the said land be either put out to interest or other lands purchased in lieu thereof.

Item whereas my wife has 300 acres of land joining to 100 acres I bought of Capt. William Aylett's estate (which said 100 acres of land I give to my son George Washington and his heirs forever, and desire is that she make over the said 300 acres to my son George Washington, and if it should be in tail, I do hereby expressly order and direct his brother William Augustine Washington to make my said son George Washington a title to the same at the age of 21, and in case he neglects or refuses to do so, I then in that case give to my son George Washington and his heirs forever the 30 Negroes I gave to my said son William in my will.

Item to prevent any doubts that may arise on that part of my will where I have directed the sale of my share of ironworks in the scholarly and in the province of Maryland, I do hereby desire my executors named in my will as soon as conveniently they can after my decease provided they shall think proper so to do, to sell and dispose of and I hereby empower them to make absolute deeds and conveyance of my interest and estate in the share I hold of all ironworks in this County and in the province of Maryland and the money arising from the sale I would have applied in the first place towards the payment of my debts and the legacies given in my will.

Item whereas I gave in my will aforesaid to my son William Augustine Washington, Old Moll and her descendants be included among those slaves been in possession of Col. George Lee in right of his wife since deceased I do hereby give Hannah the daughter of Frances being granddaughter to Old Moll aforesaid to my daughter Betty Washington and her heirs forever; which said slave is to be valued in her part of the Negroes and my son William Augustine Washington to have another of equal value allotted him in lieu thereof.

Item I desire my daughter Nancy Washington have Jemima and her part of the Negroes.

Item if either of my daughters shall die before they arrive of 21 or marry I desire their fortune may be equally divided among all my children, if my youngest son should die under age I leave his Negroes and cash to be divided equally among my three daughters and his lands I leave to his brother William Augustine Washington and his heirs forever and if my son William Augustine Washington should die before he arrives to the age of 21 years I give his lands to his brother George Washington and his heirs forever and 20 of his Negroes so as to make my son George Washington's number 30 to him and his heirs forever, the rest of my son William Augustine Washington's estate I direct to be equally divided between my three daughters.

Item it is my will and desire that if my two sons die before they arrive to the age of 21 years irrespectively then on their both so dying, I give the hundred acres of land before mentioned to have been bought by me from the estate of William Aylett to the heir male of Mr. William Booth by his present wife, my sister-in-law, and to his heirs forever, and it is my will and desire that my three daughters should convey to the said heir of William Booth and to his heirs forever the 300 acres mentioned to be adjoin to the said 100 acres and belonging to my wife in descent from her grandfather Col. Ashton; provided the said heir pay to my said daughters 600 pounds current money and if my said daughters refuse so to do, in that case I desire Mrs. Booth's heir aforesaid may be paid 100 pounds current money by each of my said daughters to be deducted out of their

respective fortunes.
Item if all my children should dye before they arrive to the age of 21, or marry and have heirs as the case may be, should both these contingencies happen, then I give all my lands in Washington Parish, Westmoreland County to my brother George Washington and his heirs forever and to my brother John Augustine Washington I give one full third part of my Negroes and personal state and the remaining two thirds of my Negroes and personal estate to be divided equally between my brothers Samuel Washington, Charles Washington: the children of my sister Lewis: and the children of my sister-in-law Mrs. Booth.
Item I give to each of my executors named in my will a mourning ring of 20 shillings value.
Item I leave it discretionary in my executors to lend my son William Augustine Washington to Britain for his education, or not as they shall think proper.
Item by son George Washington I recommend to the care of his uncle, my brother George Washington for his education.
Item I give to Mrs. William Booth of Cople Parish a mourning ring of 30 shillings value.
Signed sealed published and declared to be the codicil to my will before mentioned, the 16th day of February 1762
Signed sealed and published in the presence of us Augustine Washington
Ann Lee
Anne Allerton
Archibald Campbell
At a count held for Westmoreland County the 25th day of May 1762 this will was proved according to law by the oath of William Booth and Edward Ransdell witnesses thereto and the codicil annexed was also proved by the oath of Ann Lee, Ann Allerton and Archibald Campbell: the witnesses thereto and together with the said will ordered to be recorded, and on motion of Ann Washington widow and executrix named in the said will who made oath according to law and together with William Booth, Edward Ransdell and William Pierce her securities entered into and acknowledged bond with condition as the law directs, certificate is granted for obtaining a probate thereof in due form.
Test: James Davenport CCW

Page 132.
Harrison to Harrison's Deed
I Joshua Harrison of the parish of Cameron and the county of Fairfax of my own free will, natural love, and affection and for other good and sufficient causes me thereunto moving have given by these presents unto my two brothers Samuel Harrison and Daniel Harrison and to their heirs forever the whole track of land made over to me by deed bearing date the [blank] 1758. In witness whereof I have hereunto interchangeably set my hand and affixed my seal this 17 day of May 1762.
Signed sealed and delivered in presence of Joshua Harrison
Samuel Harrison
William Harrison
Jeremiah Harrison
John Harrison, Jr.
John Hornsby
At a court held for Westmoreland County the 25th day of May 1762 this indenture was proved by the oath of Samuel Harrison, William Harrison, John Harrison, Jr., and John Hornsby witnesses thereto and ordered to be recorded
Test: James Davenport CCW

Page 133.
Peter Presley Cox's Will
In the name of God Amen, I Peter Presley Cox of the County of Westmoreland being in perfect sense and memory but weak in body do make this my last will and testament.
First, I give to my godson Richard Wright, one Negro girl named Mugg to him and his heirs, forever.
Item I give and bequeath to my god-daughter Molly Cox, one Negro girl named Frank to her and her heirs.

Item I leave to Jane Muffet's daughter Sally Muffet, one Negro girl named Patt, to her and the heirs of her body and for want of such heirs I give the said Negro girl to my brother Fleet Cox.
Item I leave to Jane Muffet's daughter Nancy Muffet one Negro girl named Beck to her and her heirs and for want of such heirs I give the Negro girl to my brother Fleet Cox.
Item I leave to Jane Muffet the use of Negro man named Lymas during her natural life.
Item I give and bequeath to my brother William Cox Negro boy named Isaac to him and his heirs forever.
Item I give to Jane Muffet 20 pounds worth of household furniture and stock.
Item I give to my brother Fleet Cox all the rest of my estate not before given to him and his heirs pay to Jane Muffet's to daughters Sally Muffet and Nancy Muffet 50 pounds current money a piece when they come to the age of 18 years or marry and my brother Fleet Cox or his heirs is to board and clothe the said two daughters until they come to the age of 18 years or marry.
I do appoint my brother Fleet Cox executor of this my last will and testament. As witness my hand and seal this sixth day of June 1762.
Richard Holliday Peter Presley Cox
Absalom Holliday
George Holliday
At a court held for Westmoreland County the 29th day of June 1762 this will was proved according to law by the oath of Richard Holliday and Absalom Holliday witnesses thereto and ordered to be recorded and on motion of Fleet Cox the executors named in the said will who made oath according to law and together with Willoughby Newton and Francis Lightfoot Lee his securities entered into and acknowledged bond with condition as the law directs, certificate is granted him for obtaining a probate thereof in due form.
Test: James Davenport CCW

Page 134.
George Bannister's Will
In the name of God Amen, I George Banisterof the Parish of Cople and County of Westmoreland being sick and weak of body but of sound and perfect memory do make this my last will and testament in manner and form following.
Item I will that my sister Ann Smith have satisfaction for her trouble of May and my sickness.
Item I will that my sister's son Robert Smith may have my bearskin coat and a serge waist coat, and a fine felt hatt.
Item I give to my brother-in-law John Baley, a serge coat, a pair of breaches idem, a pair of shoes, and a white linen shirt.
Item I give and bequeath to my loving sister Ann Smith two pair of yarn hose.
Item I will that the rest of my estate be equally divided between my two sisters, Ann Smith and Elizabeth Baley.
Lastly, I appoint John Baley, Robert Smith and Mr. Francis Wright my executors of this my last will and testament. In witness whereof I have hereunto set my hand and seal this 24th day of May 1762
Sealed and delivered in the presence of us George Banister
James Baley
James Baley, Jr.
Stephen Baley
At a court held for Westmoreland County the 29th day of June 1762 this will was proved according to law by the oath of James Baley, Sr. and Stephen Baley, witnesses thereto and ordered to be recorded, and on the motion of John Baley and Robert Smith two of the executors named in the said will who made oath according to law together with James Baley and Francis Wright their securities entered into and acknowledged bond with condition as the law directs, certificate is granted them for obtaining a probate thereof in due form.
Test: James Davenport CCW

Page 135.
Peter Lamkin's Will
In the name of God Amen, I Peter Lamkin of the Parish of Cople and County of Westmoreland

being sick and weak of body but of good and perfect memory do make and ordain this to be my last will and testament.
Item I give unto my son Matthew Lamkin my plantation whereon I now lives and all the land adjoining to it that I bought of my cousin Lamkin: a mill and 15 acres of land I bought of Samuel Rust, one Negro man Cooper, and the horse called Diamond provided he will make a good and lawful [deed] to my son Peter Lamkin 100 acres of land that was given and entailed on me by my fathers will.
Item I give to my son George Lamkin, the land I bought of Benjamin Rust.
Item I give to my son Peter Lamkin all the land I bought of George Cox and 100 acres adjoining to it that my father gave me by his will, and if Matthew Lamkin refuses to make a good and lawful right [deed] to his brother Peter Lamkin for the 100 acres of land before mentioned my will is that my son Peter Lamkin and his heirs should have the mill and the 15 acres of land and the Negro man that was mentioned for Matthew Lamkin in lieu of the 100 acres of land.
Item I give to my son James Lamkin all the lands I bought of William Rust.
My will is that after my debts and legacies are paid off that all the remainder of my estate be it real or personal to be equally divided between my loving wife Ann Lamkin and all my children.
I do hereby constitute and appoint my loving wife Ann Lamkin and my son Matthew Lamkin and my friend Samuel Rust to be executors of this my last will and testament. In witness whereof I have hereunto set my hand and seal this 2nd day of November 1757.
Signed sealed and delivered in the presence of Peter Lamkin
Thaddeus Jackson
Christopher M. Jackson
Magdalene Jackson
Elizabeth Rust
At a court held for Westmoreland County the 29th day of June 1762 this will was proved according to law by the oath of Thaddeus Jackson and Magdalene Jackson witnesses thereto and ordered to be recorded and on the motion of Matthew Lamkin one of the executors in the said will named who made oath according to law together with George Simpson and Benedict Middleton his securities entered into and acknowledged bond with condition as the law directs, certificate is granted him for obtaining a probate thereof in due form; previous to which Ann Lamkin, the widow and relict of the said testator in the said will named personally appeared in court and refused to take upon herself the burthen of the execution thereof and absolutely renounced all benefit and advantage which she might have a claim under the said will.
Test: James Davenport CCW

Page 137.
Weaver to Weaver Deed of Gift
Know all men by these presents that I Adam Weaver the County of Westmoreland in Virginia. Now know ye that I Adam Weaver for the entire love and affection I bear to my son Benjamin Weaver to freely and truly give and grant and confirmed to him and to the heirs of his body my Negro boy Bristoe[?], but if he should die without heirs then I give the said Negro Bristoe to my son Zachariah Weaver and his heirs and if he should die then to the next heir at law only reserving I and my wife Anna Minor Weaver's natural lives in the said Negro and after her decease then the said Negro is to descend as above mentioned. In confirmation whereof I have hereunto set my hand and affixed my seal this 15th day of May 1762.
Signed sealed and delivered in the presence of us Adam Weaver (his mark)
Augustine Sanford
James Sanford
At a court held for Westmoreland County the 29th day of June 1762 this deed of gift was acknowledged by Adam Weaver party thereto and ordered to be recorded.
Test: James Davenport CCW

Page 138.
Monroe to Washington Articles of Marriage
This indenture made the 17th day of December 1761 between Andrew Monroe of the County of

Westmoreland of the one part and Margaret Washington in the County of Stafford of the other part. Witnesseth that whereas a marriage is intended between Andrew Monroe and Margaret Washington, now the said Andrew Monroe for himself his heirs &c, doth covenant promise in agreed to and with the said Margaret Washington her heirs &c to quit all claim or claims that he the said Andrew Monroe may or shall have to all or any part of her estate by virtue of the aforesaid marriage and that she the said Margaret Washington from all time in times hereafter may peaceably occupy and enjoy the before mentioned estate as if marriage had never been, the proper use and behoof of her or to her assigns without any disturbance or hindrance whatsoever by Andrew Monroe his heirs &c. in witness whereof the said party to these presents have hereunto set his hand and seal the day and year above written.

Sealed and delivered in presence of Andrew Monroe
Edward Pomfret
William Kendall
Margaret French (her mark)
Alexander McHarg

At a court held for Westmoreland County the 27th day of July 1762 these articles of marriage indented were acknowledged by Andrew Monroe party thereto and ordered to be recorded.
Test: James Davenport CCW
[Margaret Storke, widow of John Washington]

Page 139.
William Quisenbury's [Quisenberry] Will

In the name of God Amen, I William Quisenbury, Sr., of the Parish of Washington and County of Westmoreland being weak of body but perfect senses and memory do make and ordain this my last will and testament in manner and form following.

Item I give unto my daughter Eleanor Bayne one shilling sterling.

Item I give to my grandsons, Nicholas Quisenbury, John Mothershead and William Dodd each one shilling sterling.

Item I give to my son William Quisenbury the land he now lives on, beginning at a marked tree which is a white oak standing in the mouth of a branch, which divides the land I now live on from the said land running up the said branch to a marked tree on the head of the said branch, then along a line of marked trees to the head of a branch called Bolton's Spring, then down the said branch to the line of Butler's then along the said line to the main road, and running along the said road to the line of Naughty's, then along the said line to the first beginning.

Item I give to my two daughters Ann Quisenbury and Elizabeth Quisenbury all the remainder part of my land to them and their heirs of their body forever.

Item I give to my two daughters Ann Quisenbury and Elizabeth Quisenbury all the remainder part of estate both within doors and without.

Lastly, I appoint my two daughters Ann Quisenbury and Elizabeth Quisenbury executors of this my last will and testament. In witness whereof I have hereunto set my hand and seal this 27th day of May 1762.

Signed sealed and delivered in presence of us William Quisenbury, Sr.
James Clark
William Dodd
William Weaver (his mark)

At a court held for Westmoreland County the 27th day of July 1762 this will was proved according to law by the oath of James Clark, William Dodd and William Weaver the witnesses thereto and ordered to be recorded and on motion of Ann Quisenbury and Elizabeth Quisenbury executors named in the said will who made oath according to law and together with John Pope and William Dodd their securities entered into and acknowledged bond with condition as the law directs, certificate is granted them for obtaining a proof thereof in due form.
Test: James Davenport CCW

Page 140.
Pickerell & Baley to Baley Deed of Gift

This indenture made the 22nd day of January 1762 between Henry Pickrell, carpenter living in Loudoun County and James Baley, Sr., of Cople Parish in the County of Westmoreland and Ann Baley his wife of the one part and Stephen Baley of the same parish and county of Westmoreland aforesaid of the other part. Witnesseth that as well for natural love and affection and in consideration of five shillings current money the said Henry Pickrell, James Baley and Ann Baley his wife doth sell unto the said Stephen Baley a tract of land lying in the Parish of Cople and County of Westmoreland lying on Nominy River by estimation 350 acres being the land which Youell Watts or Watkins, deceased formerly devise to Patrick Spence, Gent., deceased by his last will and testament binding on the land of Youell Holland, deceased, and upon the land John Turberville, Gent., and upon the land of John Baker; the said land was devised to the said Watts or Watkins by the last will of his grandfather Thomas Youell, Gent. In witness whereof the said parties to these presents have interchangeably set their hands and seals the day and year first above written.

Signed sealed and delivered in presence of — Henry Pickrell
James Baley, Jr., — James Baley
William Rust — Ann Baley
William Gilbert
William Baley

At a court held for Westmoreland County the 27th day of July 1762 this indenture of bargain and sale and receipt thereon was proved by the oath of James Baley, Jr., William Gilbert and William Baley and Ann Baley wife of the said James Baley personally appeared and being first privy examined as the law directs voluntarily relinquished her right of dower in the lands conveyed by the said indenture.
Test: James Davenport CCW

Page 143.
Pope to Orr Indenture
This indenture made the 8th day of January 1762 between John Pope of the Parish of Washington and County of Westmoreland, planter of the one part and John Orr of the parish of Hanover and county of King George, Gent., of the other part. Whereas William Flood by indenture bearing date [blank] 1748 sold unto John Pope and his heirs a tract of land containing 109 acres being in the Parish of Washington and county aforesaid, and whereas by a decree of the general court bearing date at the capitol the 10th day of October 1759 it was decreed in a suit brought by John Pope against William Flood and Nicholas Flood that the aforesaid William Flood pay back to John Pope 43 pounds 7 shillings and 10 pence and that the said John Pope reconvey the lands purchased by him of the said William Flood to William Flood; and whereas William Flood has repaid to John Pope the aforesaid sum and hath fully performed the said decree on his part to be performed. Now this indenture witnesseth that John Pope for the consideration aforesaid and the for the performance of the decree has sold the said land to John Orr. In witness whereof the parties to these presents have hereunto set their hands and seals the day and year first within written.

Sealed and delivered in presence of us — John Pope
Isaac Robinson
William Flood
Lawrence Butler (his mark)
Christopher Butler

Received of John Orr the sum of 53 pounds 5 shillings and 2 pence in full of the within decree obtained against him. Witnesses my hand this 8th day of January 1762. John Pope
At a court held for Westmoreland County the 31st day of August 1762 this indenture together with a memorandum of livery of seizen and receipt thereon endorsed and acknowledged by John Pope, party thereto and ordered to be recorded.
Test: James Davenport CCW

Page 146.
Bennett & Wife to Bennett Deed of Gift
To all people &c, we Thomas Bennett and Elizabeth Bennett his wife of the County of

Westmoreland in consideration of the natural love and affection we have and bear our son Charles Bennett and also for other good causes and considerations me thereunto moving have given by these presents after our deaths young Negro woman Abigal and her increase. In witness whereof me have hereunto set our hands and seals this 28th day of August 1762.

Signed sealed and delivered in presence of Thomas Bennett, Sr.
Joseph Jeffries Elizabeth Bennett (her mark)
Daniel Bennett

At a court held for Westmoreland County the 31st day of August 1762, this deed of gift was proved by the oaths of both the witnesses thereto and ordered to be recorded.
Test: James Davenport CCW

Page 147.
Newton to Grace Lease

This indenture made the 16th day of September 1762 between Willoughby Newton, Gent., Of the County of Westmoreland of the one part and William Grace and Ann Grace his wife of the aforesaid County, planter of the other part. Witnesseth that Willoughby Newton in consideration of the yearly rents and covenants customized and to farm let unto William Grace and Ann Grace his wife all that plantation whereon John Allison now lives supposed to contain 100 acres lying in the Parish of Cople and County of Westmoreland and is bounded as followeth; beginning at a red oak corner tree Allison and Grace, near the road leading to Capt. Newton's house, thence down the said road to a hickory tree standing on the bent of a ditch near a small branch, thence to a medlar tree in an old field, thence to a holly by a small path leading from the said Newton's the said Grace's , then straight to the northwest corner of the corn field the said Grace now tendeth, thence along the said Grace's land to the beginning. To have and to hold the said land and other the premises hereby demised for and during the natural life of William Grace and Ann Grace his wife or the longest liver yielding and paying yearly and every year 800 pounds of crop tobacco unto Willoughby Newton on the 25th day of December yearly. In witness whereof the said parties to these presents have hereunto set their hands and seals the day and year first above written.

Sealed and delivered in the presence of Willoughby Newton
Robert Middleton William Grace
Samuel Payne

At a court held for Westmoreland County the 28th day of September 1762 of this indenture of lease was acknowledged by him Willoughby Newton, Gent., party thereto and ordered to be recorded.
Test: James Davenport CCW

Page 149.
Fleming to Wright Indenture

This indenture made the 30th day of August 1762 between John Fleming of Cople Parish in Westmoreland County the one part and Francis Wright of the same parish and county of the other part. Witnesseth that John Fleming in consideration of 100 pounds current money has sold to Francis Wright the tract of land containing 48 acres (a graveyard 30 ft.^{2} excepted) being the land whereon the said Fleming now liveth in the land which John Fleming bought of Alexander Fleming and is the same land which Peter Smith the elder, devised to Mary Fleming, mother of Alexander Fleming and John Fleming and after her death descended to the said Alexander Fleming. In witness whereof the parties to these presents have interchangeably set their hands and seals the day and year first above written.

Signed sealed and delivered in presence of John Fleming (his mark)
William Taylor
Peter Fleming
John Fleming
William Cox

At a Court held for Westmoreland County the 28th day of September 1762 this indenture of feoffment together with the memorandum of livery of seizen and receipt thereon endorsed and acknowledged by John Fleming party to thereto and ordain to be recorded.
Test: James Davenport CCW

Page 152.
Lamkin to Rust Indenture
This indenture made this 23rd day of July 1760 20 George Lamkin the County of Westmoreland of the one part and Vincent Rust of the County aforesaid of the other part. Witnesseth that George Lamkin in consideration of 160 pounds current money of Virginia has sold to Vincent Rust the parcel of land containing by estimation 127 acres; binding on the land of the said Vincent Rust: the land of Mr. Fleet Cox, the land of Thomas Bennett, Jr., and the land of Mr. Thomas Bennett, Sr., which said land was given to George Lamkin by his father Peter Lamkin by will bearing date the second day of November 1757. In witness whereof the said George Lamkin have hereunto set his hand and affixed his seal the day and year first above written.
Signed sealed and delivered in the presence of us George Lamkin
Matthew Lamkin
Michael Gilbert
John Thrailkill [Threlkeld]
At a Court held for Westmoreland County 28th day of September 1760, this indenture of feoffment together with the memorandum of livery of seizen thereon endorsed was proved by the oaths of Matthew Lamkin, Michael Gilbert and John Thrailkill the witnesses thereto, and a receipt thereon also endorsed was proved by the oath of Michael Gilbert and together with the said indenture and memorandum ordered to be recorded.
Test: James Davenport CCW

Page 155.
Smith to Dameron Indenture
This indenture made 31st day of August 1762 between James Smith and Sarah Smith his wife of the Parish of Cople and County of Westmoreland the one part and John Dameron the parish of Wicomico in County of Northumberland of the other part. Witnesseth that James Smith and Sarah Smith his wife in consideration of 170 pounds 7 shillings and 9 pence current money of Virginia and for diverse other causes them thereunto moving have sold to John Dameron a tract of land containing 158 ½ acres and lying in the Parish of Cople and County of Westmoreland and partly in the parish of St. Stephen's in the aforesaid County of Northumberland it being part of a patent granted by the proprietor's of the Northern Neck of Virginia unto John Hartley, deceased, father to the said Sarah Smith and by him bequeath by his will to the said Sarah Smith and bounded as follows; beginning at a marked red oak corner to Benedict Middleton's, running thence along the line of John Cralle South 47.30° East 42 poles to another red oak, thence South 49.30° East 60 poles to another red oak, thence South 48° East 14 poles along Cralle's line to the marshy Swamp, thence down the said swamp it several courses to the mouth of a branch which divides this land from the land of Benedict Middleton and thence up the said branch and along Middleton's line to the first mentioned red oak. In witness whereof the parties to these presents have set their hands and fixed their seals the day and year above written.
Signed sealed and delivered in presence of us James Smith
Mathias Self Sarah Smith (her mark)
John Hornsby
Hannah Rence
James Crawley
At a court held for Westmoreland County 28th day of September 1762 this indenture of feoffment in a memo of livery of seizen thereon endorsed proved by the oaths of Mathias Self: John Hornsby and Hannah Rence witnesses thereto and Sarah Smith wife of James Smith personally appeared and the first privy examined as the law directs voluntarily relinquished her right of dower estate conveyed by the said indenture.
Test: James Davenport CCW

Page 158.
Pritchett's wife to Cox Privy Examination
To Richard Henry Lee and John Newton Westmoreland County, Gent. Whereas Rodham Pritchett

the County of Westmoreland by his indenture of feoffment bearing date the 24th day of October 1762 has conveyed unto Fleet Cox the said County of Westmoreland in fee simple estate 40 acres of land lying in the parish Cople in County of Westmoreland and whereas Ann Pritchett and cannot conveniently travel to our court to make acknowledgment. Therefore, we do give you or two of you power to receive the acknowledgment which she shall be willing to make. Witness James Davenport, clerk of our court the 20th day of April 1762.
Test: Joseph Lane DCCW
Westmoreland to Wit:
We Richard Henry Lee and John Newton to His Majesties Justices of the peace for the County aforesaid and mentioned in the within writ of dedimus have examined Ann wife of Rodham Pritchett privately and apart from her husband and find that she doth willingly consent to the conveyance within mentioned and she is willing same shall be recorded. Given under our hands and seals this fourth day of June 1762.
Richard Henry Lee
John Newton
At a Court held for Westmoreland County the 28th day of September 1762 this commission for the privy examination of Ann Pritchett's wife of Rodham Pritchett and a certificate of the execution thereof being returned was ordered to be recorded.
Test: James Davenport CCW

Page 160.
Sanford to Wife and her Belfield Children Agreement
Know all men by these presents that I John Sanford of the County of Westmoreland am held and stand firmly bound to Mary Sanford my wife and her two daughters Frances Belfield and Nancy Belfield of the said county in the full sum of 120 pounds current money. Sealed with my sealed and dated this 25th day of March 1761. The condition of the above obligation is such that whereas the above bound John Sanford has with the said Mary Sanford: his wife when he intermarried with her sundry sorts of household furniture which furniture is accounted to be worth 60 pounds current money and he doth by this obligation oblige himself to pay the said sum of 60 pounds to Frances Belfield and Nancy Belfield on demand after decease of the said Mary Sanford their mother or to return them all and every article of the said household furniture that then the above obligation to be void and of non-effect otherwise to remain in full force and virtue.
Signed sealed and delivered in presence of us John Sanford
Alexander Spark
Edward Sanford
Katherine Sanford
At a Court held for Westmoreland County the 28th day of September 1762 this bond for performance of covenants was proved by the oath of Alexander Spark, Edward Sanford and Katherine Sanford the witnesses thereto and ordered to be recorded.
Test: James Davenport CCW

Page 161.
William Wheeler's Will
In the name of God Amen, I William Wheeler of Westmoreland County in Washington Parish being sick and weak in body but of perfect soundness of memory do make and ordain this my last will and testament
First, I give unto my wife Elizabeth Wheeler all my land that I now live on as far as the branch between the and where Elliott Sebastian now lives and up the said branch to Balthrop's line during her natural life and after her death to my son Thomas Wheeler and his heirs forever.
Item I give unto my daughter Sarah Horton that parcel of land that Elliott Sebastian now lives on bounded by the aforesaid branch to Balthrop's line to her and her heirs forever.
Item I give unto my wife Elizabeth Wheeler Negro wench Sarah and Negro boy Tom during her natural life and after her death to her daughter Elizabeth Strother and her heirs forever.
Item I give unto my wife Elizabeth Wheeler one still during her natural life and at her death to my daughter Sarah Horton and her heirs forever.

Item I give unto my daughter Sarah Horton 10 pounds cash to her and her heirs forever.
Item I gave it to my son Thomas Wheeler 10 pounds cash to him his heirs forever and all my wearing clothes and my gun.
Item I give unto my son Richard Wheeler five shillings.
Item I give unto my son John Wheeler five shillings.
Item I desire all the rest of my estate to be equally divided between my wife Elizabeth Wheeler and my son Thomas Wheeler and my daughter Sarah Horton to them and their heirs forever.
And I the said William Wheeler to make order and constitute my wife Elizabeth Wheeler executrix of this my last will and testament. In witness whereof I have hereunto set my hand and seal this 18th day of November 1761.
Signed sealed and published in the presence of William Wheeler
Robert Strother
Enoch Strother
Mary Rogers
At a Court held for Westmoreland County the 28th day of September 1762 this will was proved according to law by the oath of Robert Strother and Enoch Strother witnesses thereto and ordered to be recorded and on the motion of Elizabeth Wheeler, widow and executrix named in the said will who made oath according to law and together with the said Robert Strother and executor and Thomas Robins her securities entered into and acknowledged bond with condition as the law directs, certificate is granted her for obtaining a probate thereof in due form.
Test: James Davenport CCW

Page 162.
Alexander Moxley Will
In the name of God Amen, I Alexander Moxley of Westmoreland County, planter being sick and weak but in perfect sense and memory do make this my last will and testament in manner and form following.
I give and bequeath to my wife Frances Moxley and her heirs Negro girl Hannah.
I give and bequeath to my brother John Moxley's son Rodham Moxley and his heirs forever Negro boy Nick.
I give and bequeath to my cousin Joseph Moxley my cambset coat and britches.
I give and bequeath to my father John Moxley all my clothes not before given.
I give and bequeath to my wife Frances Moxley and her heirs forever all the rest of my personal estate not before given, but of which my debts are to be paid and in case there is not sufficient then each of the two first given legacies to be [used] in proportion to the debts.
Item case my wife should be with child that I give all my estate to the child she is with.
Lastly, I constitute and appoint my wife Frances Moxley whole and sole executrix this my last will and testament. In witness whereof I have set my hand and seal this 25th day of August 1762
Signed sealed published in the presence of us Alexander Moxley
Richard Lee
William Pierce
George Carter
At a court held for Westmoreland County the 28th day of September 1762 this will was proved according to law by the oath of Richard Lee and William Pierce, witnesses thereto and ordered to be recorded and on the motion of Frances Moxley: widow and executrix named on the same will made oath according to law he together with Henry Dunkin or security entered into and acknowledged bond with condition as the law directs, certificate is granted to her for obtaining a probate thereof in due form.
Test: James Davenport CCW

Page 163.
Elizabeth Davis Will
In the name of God Amen, I Elizabeth Davis of Westmoreland County in Washington Parish being sick and weak of body but in perfect sense and memory do make and ordain this to be my last will and testament and form as followeth.

I give and bequeath to my sister Frances Davis Negro man Tony left to me in my father's will, and all the rest of my estate be it any kind whatsoever and further I appoint Frances Davis and Mary Davis my executors to this my last will and testament. In witness whereof I have set my hand and seal this 30th day of May 1759.

In the presence of — Elizabeth Davis
John Weedon
Augustine Weedon
Elizabeth Weedon (her mark)
Jane Weedon (her mark)
Rebecca Weedon (her mark)

At a court held for Westmoreland County the 28th day of September 1762 this will was proved according to law by the oath of Augustine Weedon and Elizabeth Weedon witnesses thereto and ordered to be recorded and on motion of Mary Davis one of the executrix's named in the said will who made oath according to law and together with the said Augustine Weedon her security entered into and acknowledged bond with condition as the law directs, certificate is granted her for obtaining a probate thereof in due form.
Test: James Davenport CCW

Page 164.
<u>Linton's Wife to Simpson Privy Examination</u>
To Willoughby Newton, Richard Lee, and John Newton. Whereas John Linton the County of Westmoreland and Mary Ann Linton his wife by their indenture of feoffment bearing date the 28th day of February 1761 have conveyed unto Joseph Simpson, clerk of the County of Richmond the fee simple estate of 166 acres of land lying in the Parish of Cople and County aforesaid and whereas Mary Ann Linton cannot conveniently travel to record to make acknowledgment of the said conveyance, therefore we do give unto you or any two of you power to receive the acknowledgment which she would be willing to make. Witness George Lee, clerk of our court the second day of March 1761.
Westmoreland Sct.
By virtue of a commission for the examining Mary Ann Linton wife of John Linton with the commission directed to us did go to her and did take her apart from her said husband and examined or concerning her acknowledgment of the said deed for 166 acres of land as directed by the commission and she saith that she doth freely and voluntarily of her own accord acknowledge the said deed. Certified under our hands and seals the 16th day of November 1762.
Willoughby Newton
John Newton
at Court held for Westmoreland County the 30th day of November 1762 this commission in the certificate of execution thereof being returned or ordered to be recorded
Test: James Davenport CCW

Page 165.
<u>Thomas Pritchett Nuncupative Will</u>
Westmoreland Sct., This day Thomas Robinson and Elizabeth Lee made oath that on the 24th of this instant May, Thomas Pritchett who then lay sick at the said Robinson's house told him and the said Elizabeth Lee that it was his desire that his estate should be equally divided among all his children and also that his brother James Pritchett should administer upon his said estate and further saith that the said Pritchett was of sound mind and memory as they believed at the time of his pronouncing the above words and that the said Pritchett departed this life on Thursday, the 27th of May following.

Witness our hands and seals — Thomas Robinson (his mark)
Sworn to this 29th day of May 1762 — Elizabeth Lee
Thomas Chilton, Jr.

At a court Westmoreland County the 30th day of November 1762 this writing purporting the nuncupative will of Thomas Pritchett: deceased was proved according to law by the oath of Thomas Robinson and Elizabeth Lee, the witnesses thereto and ordered to be recorded and on the

motion of William Flood who made oath according to law together with Richard Parker his security entered into and acknowledged bond with condition as the law directs, certificate is granted him for obtaining letters of administration of the said Thomas Pritchett with the said will annexed in due form; James Pritchett the executor named in the said will who was appointed guardian to the orphans of the said testator having been duly summoned to contest the probate of the said writing in behalf of the said orphans was solemnly called but did not appear.
Test: James Davenport CCW

Page 166.
Lee: Booth & Washington to Ransdell Indenture
This indenture made the 25th day of May 1762 between Richard Lee of the County of Charles and province of Maryland, Esq. and Grace Lee his wife, William Booth of the Parish of Cople in the County of Westmoreland and colony of Virginia, Gent., and Elizabeth Booth his wife, and Augustine Washington of the Parish of Washington in the County and colony last mentioned, Gent., Ann Washington his wife of the one part and Edward Ransdell of the Parish of Cople and County of Westmoreland, Gent., of the other part. Whereas Henry Ashton late of the parish and county last mentioned, Gent., deceased left issue at the time of his death by Elizabeth his wife only three daughters; (1) Frances Ashton who intermarried with George Turberville, late of the County of Westmoreland, Gent., deceased having left issue only one daughter Elizabeth Turberville. (2) Anne Ashton the second daughter who intermarried with William Aylett, late of the said County of Westmoreland, Gent., deceased having left issue two daughters, the said Elizabeth Booth and Ann Washington parties to these presents and (3) and the third daughter Grace Lee also party to this presents. And whereas the said Elizabeth Turberville the granddaughter of Henry Ashton is seized and possessed in fee tail as heir to her mother Frances Turberville of and in one certain tract of land containing by estimation 68 acres situated and lying in the said Parish of Cople in the County of Westmoreland and not far from Westmoreland Courthouse which said tract of land is bounded as followeth; beginning at a white oak in the line of Minor extending thence North 66 ½° East 34 poles to a hickory, thence North 30° East 110 poles to a walnut in Sturman's old field in McCarthy's line, thence South 47 ½° East 96 poles to a corner stone: thence South 30° west 62 poles to a red oak corner to Browne's, thence to the beginning; and whereas Elizabeth Turberville has from her birth afflicted with fits which has deprived her in a great manner of her reason so that it is impossible she can make any disposition of her estate and there is no probability of her having any issue in which case one half of the said tract or parcel the land reverts to the said Grace Lee party to these presents and the other half be equally divided between Elizabeth Booth and Ann Washington parties to these presents; and whereas Richard Lee and Grace Lee his wife, William Booth and Elizabeth Booth his wife and Augustine Washington and Ann Washington his wife have respectively agreed to and with the said Edward Ransdell to sell and dispose of the said tract of land to him. Now this indenture witnesseth that Richard Lee and Grace Lee his wife, William Booth and Elizabeth Booth his wife and Augustine Washington and Ann Washington his wife in consideration of 36 pounds 11 shillings current money of Virginia to Richard Lee, 18 pounds five shillings and six pence of like money to William Booth and 18 pounds five shillings and six pence like current money of Virginia to Augustine Washington have sold to Edward Ransdell the before mentioned tract of land containing 68 acres. In witness whereof the parties to these presents have hereunto set their hands and seals the day and year first above written.
Richard Lee
Grace Lee
William Booth
Elizabeth Booth
Augustine Washington
Ann Washington
At a Court held for Westmoreland County the 30th day of November 1762 this indenture and the receipt endorsed were proved as to Richard Lee and Grace Lee his wife parties thereto by the oath of Leroy Hipkins, Thomas Edwards and Edward Ransdell, Jr., the witnesses thereto, and At a court held for the county the 26th day of May last past the said indenture was acknowledged by William Booth and Elizabeth Booth his wife she being first privy examined as the law directs, and Ann

Washington now the widow of Augustine Washington, deceased and the receipt endorsed were also acknowledged by William Booth and Ann Washington together with the said indenture in ordered to be recorded.
Test: James Davenport CCW

Page 171.
Blair to Ashton Indenture
Indenture made the 27th day of August 1762 between James Blair and Sarah Blair his wife of the Parish of Washington and County of Westmoreland of the one part and John Ashton, the younger of the aforesaid Parish in County, Gent., Of the other part. Witnesseth that James Blair in consideration of 350 pounds current money of Virginia has sold unto John Ashton a tract of land known by the name of the "Glebe" lying in the aforesaid parish and county and containing 100 acres and bounded as followeth; beginning at a marked poplar tree standing upon the main road which poplar is a line tree between the premises and the land of Mrs. William Bernard, thence along the said Bernard's line to Machodoc Creek, thence up the creek to the line of a tract of land belonging to the said John Ashton party to these presents, thence along the said line to a marked post standing on the road side, thence along the said road to the beginning. In witness whereof the said James Blair and Sarah Blair his wife have hereunto set their hands and seals the day and year above written.
Signed sealed and delivered in presence of James Blair
Thomas Taylor Sarah Blair
James Berryman
William Berryman
The commission for the privy examination of Sarah Blair was completed by James Berryman and William Berryman 27 August 1762.
At a Court held for Westmoreland County the 30th day of November 1762 this indenture and the receipt endorsed were acknowledged by James Blair, party thereto and together with a commission annexed for taking the acknowledgment and privy examination of Sarah Blair the wife of James Blair and a certificate of the execution thereof ordered to be recorded.
Test: James Davenport CCW

Page 174.
John Balthrop's Will
I John Balthrop of Washington Parish and the County of Westmoreland being very sick and weak of body but of perfect sense and memory do make and ordain this to be my last will and testament in manner and form following.
Item I give and bequeath my lands to be equally divided between my two sons William Balthrop and John Balthrop and my desire is that after the division is made that my son William Balthrop may have his choice.
Item I give to my daughter Sarah Balthrop, Negro girl Winney.
Item I give to my daughter Elizabeth Balthrop, Negro girl Judith.
Item I give and bequeath to my daughter Margaret Balthrop, Negro boy Will.
All the rest of my Negroes and personal estate of what kind soever I give to my beloved wife as long as she remain a widow and after her marriage or death to be equally divided between my daughter Frances Kirk, son William Balthrop, son John Balthrop, son Sharp Balthrop, daughter Nancy Balthrop, son James Balthrop and son Augustine Balthrop.
I constitute and appoint my beloved wife Jemima Balthrop to be the executor of this my last will and testament. In witness hereof I have hereunto set my hand and seal this 28th day of August 1762.
Sign and sealed in presence of John Balthrop
James Dishman
James White
John Wilkerson
At a court held for Westmoreland County the 30th day of November 1762, this will was proved according to law by the oaths of James White and John Wilkerson, witnesses thereto and ordered to be recorded, and on the motion of Jemima Balthrop: widow and executrix in the said will named,

who made oath thereto according to law and together with John Wilkerson and John Baley her securities entered into and acknowledged bond as the law directed, certificate is granted her obtaining a probate thereof in due form.
Test: James Davenport CCW

Page 175.
Eskridge to Lowe Indenture
This Indenture made 27th November 1762 between Robert Eskridge of the county of Richmond, planter of the one part, and Richard Lowe of the County of Westmoreland, planter of the other part. Witnesseth that Robert Eskridge in consideration of 60 pounds current money of Virginia and the further sum of 26 pounds 5 shillings to be paid at or before the last day of July next, hath sold to Richard Lowe has sold a tract lying in Yeocomico Neck being the land granted to Robert Eskridge by patent bearing date the 1st day of May 1762 and bounded as follows: beginning at a peach tree where formerly stood a red oak a corner between William Butler and Robert Ball and late in possession of Abigal Dunbar extending thence East by North 82 ¼ poles to two small pines and a sweet gum in a line of George Jeffries, thence along the said line South 142 poles to a large white oak, thence North West along Thomas Butler's line 165 poles to a dogwood near the head of a small cove of Yeocomico River from thence to the beginning; containing 51 acres or thereabouts. In witness whereof the day and year first above written.
Sealed and delivered in the presence of — Robert Eskridge
George Simpson — Richard Lowe
John Eidson
John Thornton
At a Court held for Westmoreland County the 30th day of November 1762 this indenture and memorandum of livery of seizen endorsed were acknowledged by Robert Eskridge in ordered to be recorded, previous to which the wife of Robert Eskridge personally appeared in being first privy examined as the law directs voluntarily relinquished her right of dower in the lands conveyed by the said indenture.
Test: James Davenport CCW

Page 177.
Eskridge to Lowe Bond
Know all men by these presents that Robert Eskridge and Samuel Eskridge the County of Richmond are held and firmly bound unto Richard Lowe of the County of Westmoreland, planter in the sum of 200 pounds current money of Virginia to which payment well and truly to be made. Sealed with our seals dated this 29th day of November 1762. The condition of this obligation is such that if the above bound Robert Eskridge in stem Eskridge shall keep all and every the covenants on their part in one indenture of feoffment bearing date with these presents and between the above bound Robert Eskridge of the one part and Richard Lowe of the other part in all things according to the intent and meaning of the said indenture then the above written obligation to be void and of non-effect, or otherwise to be remain in full force and virtue.
Sealed and delivered in presence of — Robert Eskridge
George Simpson — Samuel Eskridge
John Eidson
John Thornton
At a court held for Westmoreland County the 30th day of November 1762 this bond was acknowledged by Robert Eskridge party thereto and ordered to be recorded.
Test: James Davenport CCW

Page 178.
Horrell to Rust Bond
Know all men by these presents that I John Horrell of Westmoreland county and Parish of Cople am held and firmly bound to Jeremiah Rust of the aforesaid county and parish in the just and full sum of 1,000 pounds current money of Virginia to which payment well and truly to be made. Sealed with our seals dated this 29th day of April 1762. The condition of this obligation is such that

whereas the above bounden John Horrell has sold unto Jeremiah Rust all the whole right of the estate left him by his father consisting of Negroes and household furniture &c. now if the said John Horrell shall well and truly observe all and singular the covenants in the agreement as follows: the above mentioned Rust was to give the above bound Horrell 50 pounds for the right of the estate left him by his father and in case the said Rust did recover the said estate, he is to give 5 pounds more. Now if the above bound John Horrell as well and truly fulfilled all covenants in the above obligation to be void and of no effect or else to stand in full force power and virtue.

Signed in presence of us John Horrell
Christopher Mothershead
William Sturman (his mark)
John Riley (his mark)

At a court held 30 November 1762 this bond was proved by the oath of William Sturman and John Riley, witnesses thereto and ordered to be recorded
Test: James Davenport CCW

Page 179.

Elizabeth Berryman's Will

In the name of God Amen, I Elizabeth Berryman of the County of Westmoreland being weak in body but of sound and disposing mind and memory do constitute and appoint this my last will and testament in manner following.

Whereas my husband Benjamin Berryman by his last will, authorize me to make distribution all his slaves to his six sons for the survivors of them and whereas three of the said sons; Newton Berryman, John Berryman and Henry Berryman, died before they came of age and were not possessed of any of their fathers estate. And whereas William Berryman, James Berryman and Maximilian Berryman are the surviving to sons, I give all the slaves to be divided with their increase as follows; Imprimis, I give to my son William Berryman old Negro Jack and Grace and their children and Bob which is in his possession and Sall which I delivered to him as part of his father's estate some years passed but being a little Negro girl, that attended me I desired my son William to let her stay and wait on me which is now with me, as also I give him Rachael and Nell and Beck their mother, to him and his heirs and assigns forever and also my father's old silver tankard without a lid and my father's coat of arms. As also I give to my said son William Berryman all the lands I upon Cossum Bennett in the County of Westmoreland which I have given him by a deed in due confirmed to him his heirs forever.

Item I give to my son James Berryman Negroes; George, Jack, Anthony, Ben, Aaron, Suke, Nace, Mary, Tim, Ned, Jude, Peggy and her youngest child Gerrat, Winney and Betty.

Item I give to my son Maximilian Berryman 14 Negros which he has in his possession as also; Sally, Lilla and Frank Richard yet in my possession.

Item my will and desire is that my stock and household stuff of what kind soever tobacco, corn, money &c, shall be equally divided between my three children that is to say William Berryman, James Berryman and Katherine Vowles.

Item my son Benjamin Berryman at his part of his father's estate before his death.

Item my daughter Rose Taliaferro at her part of her father's estate before his death.

Item my daughter Frances Foote had her part since her father's death according to his will and gave a receipt for it.

Item my daughter Sarah Douglass, has had her part of the Negroes.

Item my daughter Katherine Vowles has had her part of the Negroes.

The reason of my giving my son William Berryman 17 Negroes and my son James but 16 Negroes is because some Negroes that my son William is possesed of are very deficient for Old Jack and Grace are almost past labour, and one Negro fellow with one eye and one hand, and another crippled lad of very little use. Therefore, I think the division I have made will make them equal according to quantity and quality.

Item I appoint my sons William Berryman and James Berryman executors of this my last will and testament. In witness whereof I have hereunto set my hand and seal this 14th day of June 1762.

Signed sealed and delivered in presence of. Elizabeth Berryman (her mark)
Gerard Blackistone Causine

Josias Causine
Thomas Clark
William Staples
At a court held for Westmoreland County the 22nd day of February 1763, this last will and testament of Elizabeth Berryman: deceased was proved according to law by the oath of Josias Causine and William Staples witnesses thereto and ordered to be recorded and on the motion of William Berryman, one of the executors named in the said will who made oath according to the law and together with Willoughby Newton his security entered into and acknowledged bond with condition as the law directs, certificate is granted him for obtaining a probate thereof in due form, liberty being reserved to James Berryman the other executor named in the said will to join in probate when he shall think fit.
Test: James Davenport CCW

Page 181.
King to Rust Indenture
This indenture made the 14th day of December 1762, between John King of Loudoun County, planter and Mary King his wife of the one part and Vincent Rust of the County of Westmoreland, planter of the other part. Witnesseth that John King and Mary King his wife in consideration of 15 pounds current money of Virginia has sold to Vincent Rust a parcel of land whereon Edward Pack lived being by estimation 60 acres which said land was also given to Jane Ashton God daughter to William Smith [d. 1707] for her natural life as will appear by his last will and testament, which land after the Jane Ashton's death vested in the said John King as heir at law to the said William Smith. In witness whereof the said John King and Mary King his wife hath hereunto set their hands and seals the day and year first above written.
Signed sealed and delivered in presence of us John King
John Short
William Baley
Stephen Baley (his mark)
William Walker
At a court held for Westmoreland County the 22nd day of February 1763 this indenture and the memorandum of livery of seizen and receipt endorsed were proved by the oaths of William Bailey: Stephen Bailey: and William Walker witnesses thereto and ordered to be recorded.
Test: James Davenport CCW

Page 184.
Daniel Tebbs Will
In the name of God Amen, I Daniel Tebbs of the Parish of Cople and County of Westmoreland being in good health of body and perfect mind and memory do make and ordain this to be my last will and testament.
Imprimis, I give and bequeath to my son William Tebbs the land I purchased of Samuel Earle, Presley Cox and part of Thomas', the line to be from the head of the branch below my orchard, a straight line to a white oak standing in the edge of Samuel Rust's old field that was formerly a corner to Thomas' and Earle's, and all the land I bought of Charles Eskridge: also a mill called Courtney's Mill, and a Negro boy named Young Topsom.
Item I give to my dear beloved wife Elizabeth Tebbs the use of my dwelling plantation with 300 acres of land adjoining thereto to be taken out of my son Daniel Tebbs part of land with her choice of three of my Negroes during her natural life.
Item I give unto my son Daniel Tebbs Negro Till, and all the other part of my land with the mill called the Church Mill.
Item I give to my daughter Mary Tebbs, three Negroes; Nan, Janney and Nelly.
Item I give to my daughter Elizabeth Tebbs two Negroes; Frank and Johney.
Item I give all the rest of my Negroes to be equally divided between my children, Daniel Tebbs, Mary Tebbs: Elizabeth Tebbs: and William Tebbs.
I therefore give my executors full power and authority to make over lawful deeds for that land I sold to John Garner, lying in Prince William County according to the said Garner's will, as the deed I

gave him passed before it was proved on the south side of Broad Run.
I do hereby constitute and appoint my beloved wife Elizabeth Tebbs (if she should be the longest liver) my friends the Hon. Philip Ludwell Lee, Esq., and Samuel Rust my executors and guardians to my children till they come of age.
In witness whereof I have hereunto set my hand and seal this 25th day of May 1760
Sealed and delivered in presence of Daniel Tebbs
At a court held for Westmoreland County the 22nd day of February 1762 this last Will and Testament of Daniel Tebbs, deceased was presented into Court by Samuel Rust, one of the executors therein named and no witnesses being subscribed thereto Thomas Bennett, Jr. and Richard Atwell severally made oath that they are well acquainted the testators handwriting and verily believe the said will and the name thereto subscribed to be the proper hand writing of the said testator and therefore it is ordered that the same be recorded. And on the motion of the said Samuel Rust who made oath according to law and together with Willoughby Newton and Joseph Lane his securities entered into and acknowledged bond with condition, as the law directs, certificate is granted him for obtaining a probate thereof in due form.
Test: James Davenport CCW

Page 185.
Peirce to Peirce [Pierce] Indenture
This indenture made the first day December 1762 between William Peirce and Foxall Sturman of the Parish of Cople in the County of Westmoreland the one part and Joseph Peirce of the said parish and county of the other part. Whereas in a suit in Chancery brought by William Peirce and Margaret Peirce his wife against Dozier Templeman acting executor of Thomas Templeman, deceased, William Templeman and Richard Hodgson Templeman and Mary Templeman, and thence by the said Dozier Templeman, their next friend. It was ordered and decreed among other things at the said William Peirce, Joseph Peirce and Foxall Sturman or any two of them should advertise the two Negroes and tract of land in the bill mentioned to be sold at six months credit to the highest bidder as by the said order bearing date At a court held for Westmoreland County the 30th day of July 1760, and whereas William Peirce and Foxall Sturman in pursuance of the said order in decree did advertise the land and Negroes to be sold for six months credit to the highest bidder and at the day of sale thereof the said Joseph Peirce did bid the sum of 37 pounds 3 shillings for the said land which was the highest sum bid for the same. Now this indenture witnesseth that William Peirce and Foxhall Sturman by virtue of the said order in decree in consideration of the said sum of 37 pounds 3 shillings have sold unto Joseph Peirce a tract of land containing by estimation 102 acres lying in the Parish of Cople and County of Westmoreland contiguous to a tract of land belonging to and in possession of the said Joseph Peirce bounded as by a plot hereunto annexed may appear. In witness whereof the parties to these presents have hereunto set their hands and seals the day and year first above written.
Sealed and delivered in the presence of us William Peirce
James Davenport Foxhall Sturman
Richard Parker
John Augustine Washington
Edward Ransdell
Leroy Hipkins
At a court held for Westmoreland County the 22nd day of February 1763 this indenture of bargain and sale and receipt thereon endorsed was proved by the oath of James Davenport, Edward Ransdell and Leroy Hipkins witnesses thereto and ordered to be recorded.
Test: James Davenport CCW

Page 187.
Lee to Lee Lease
This indenture made this sixth day of January 1763 between the Hon. Philip Ludwell Lee of the County of Westmoreland, Esq. of the one part and Richard Henry Lee of the same County, Esq. of the other part. Witnesseth that Philip Ludwell Lee in consideration of five shillings current money and the said rents and covenants herein after mentioned to be paid or performed has demised and

to farm let by these presents unto Richard Henry Lee a tenement lying in Cople Parish, Westmoreland County between the land of Maj. Thomas Chilton and the Hollows's Marsh plantation belonging to Philip Ludwell Lee and bounded as followeth; beginning at a hickory on the head of the northwest side of a marsh which marsh is on the north west side of the road built by Richard Henry Lee, extending thence South 68° West 6 poles South 78° West 18 poles, South 66 ½° West 14 poles, South 78° West 10 poles, North 84 ½° West 18 pole, North 83° West 31 poles, North 77° West 13 ½ poles, South 61° West 7 poles, North 89° West 32 poles, South 73° West 14 pole, South 83° West 14 ½ poles, to a willow in the fork of two marshes, thence up the ridge South 80° West 20 poles to a chestnut tree South 50° West 18 poles, to another chestnut South 62° West 26 poles to a chestnut oak, South 64 ½° West six poles, to another chestnut oak, South 52° West 11 poles to a red oak, South 53° West 32 poles, to a small chestnut, South 75 ½° West 59 poles to a small red oak, South 55° West 26 poles, a small red oak, North 75° West 20 poles, to a black gum, Northwest 68 poles to the Hollows's Marsh Road where three saplings are marked, thence up the said Road., South 88 ¼ West 39 poles, to a double bodied maple on the north side of the said road, thence North 32° East 28 poles to a chestnut oak, North 21° East 15 poles, to a small red oak, thence South 84° East 34 poles, to one red and two white oaks marked, North 49° East 22 poles, to a small white oak by the side of a branch, thence down the branch, North 2° West 38 poles to a large red oak, North 76 ½° West 18 pole, to a red oak in the brow of a hill, thence [?] 36 ½°West 42 poles, to a chestnut, South 21° West 13 poles to another chestnut South 11 ½° West 10 poles, to a chestnut South 10° West 18 poles to a stake South 22° West 20, to another stake in South 50° West 36 poles, to a red oak by the before mentioned Road, thence up the Said Rd., North 60° West 20 poles to two small white oaks on the south side of the road, South 22° West 36 poles, to one white and two red Oaks South 9° West 20 poles to a white oak at the head of a branch and South 61 ¼ East 120 poles to a small black oak and a hickory near an old Field, North 70° East 58 poles, to a stake in the old field South 42° East 17 poles to a white oak on the land east side of the said old field, South 28° East 32 poles to a small red oak South 57° East 12 poles, to another small red oak South 77° East 32 poles, to a red oak South 7 ½° East 17 ½ poles to a small black oak on the brow of a hill thence East 10 poles to a small red oak North 75° East 22 poles to a red oak South 77 ¼ East 75 ¼ poles to a stake on the south east side of a branch, thence down the said branch and ditch on the south and east side thereof including all the middle ground, 307 ½ poles, to a dam or ditch at the head of a marsh, thence crossing the marsh North 9 ½° West 15 poles to the north and thereof thence down the side of the marsh in a straight line 106 poles to the landing at the head of a creek, thence up the creek and gut including all dry land to a white oak on south side of the branch, thence crossing the marsh South 18° West 15 poles to the beginning hickory; including 500 acres of land together with all houses, buildings, yards, gardens, orchards, etc. To have and to hold the above-mentioned land for the natural lives of Richard Henry Lee, Anne Lee his wife and Samuel Lee, son of Richard Henry Lee for and during the lives of the longest liver, yielding and paying during the said term the yearly rent of 2,650 pounds tobacco upon the first day of December in every year to Philip Ludwell Lee. In witness whereof the parties of these presents have hereunto interchangeably set their hands and affixed their sales the day and year above written.

Sealed and delivered in the presence of
John Augustine Washington
James Davenport
Anthony Stewart

Philip Ludwell Lee
Richard Henry Lee

At a Court held for Westmoreland County the 22nd day of February 1763 this indenture of lease was proved by the oath of John Augustine Washington, James Davenport and Anthony Stewart the witnesses thereto and ordered to be recorded.
Test: James Davenport CCW

Page 191.
<u>Ariss & Wife to Sanford Lease</u>
This indenture made the 4th day of September 1762 between John Ariss, builder and Elizabeth Ariss his wife of the county of Richmond of the one part and Edward Sanford of the County of Westmoreland, inspector of the other part. Witnesseth that John Ariss and Elizabeth Ariss his wife

in consideration of 5 shillings hath demised and to farm let unto Edward Sanford all that tract of land lying in the Parish of Washington and County of Westmoreland formerly sold by Humphrey Pope to Samuel Demovel [Damourvell], the father of Sampson Demovel and by the said Sampson Demovel sold the land to John Ariss, which said land was surveyed by William Garland, surveyor the 8th day of August 1755 for 311 acres. To have and to hold the tract of land during the term of one whole year the day next before the date of these presents under the intent that by virtue hereof and of the statute for transferring uses into possession said Edward Sanford may be in actual possession of the tract or parcel of land. In witness whereof the parties to these presents have hereunto set their hands and seals the day and year first above written.

Sealed and delivered in the presence of us — John Ariss
William Booth — Elizabeth Ariss
William Rountree
Edward Ransdell

At a court continued and held for Westmoreland County the 30th day of March 1763 this indenture was proved by the oath of William Booth, William Rountree and Edward Ransdell witnesses thereto and ordered to be recorded.
Test: James Davenport CCW

Page 192.
Ariss & Wife to Sanford Release

This indenture made the 6th day of September 1762 between John Ariss, builder and Elizabeth Ariss his wife of the county of Richmond of the one part and Edward Sanford of the County of Westmoreland, inspector of the other part. Witnesseth that John Ariss and Elizabeth Ariss his wife in consideration of 150 pounds current money of Virginia has sold and released unto Edward Sanford in his actual possession now by virtue of an indenture of lease made for one whole year all that tract of land lying in the Parish of Washington and County of Westmoreland formerly sold by Humphrey Pope to Samuel Demovel [Damourvell], the father of Sampson Demovel and by the said Sampson Demovel sold the land to John Ariss, which said land was surveyed by William Garland, surveyor the 8th day of August 1755 for 311 acres and bounded as followeth: beginning at the letter "A" and where stands a spanish oak near a cross path and on the south side of the said path extending thence South by West 141 ½ poles to the small corner Hickory letter "B" , thence South 73° East 12 pole to the head of a branch at the letter "C" , and continued the same course along a line of marked trees to the main swamp 22 poles, thence down the said swamp several courses and distances to the letter "D", formerly stood a poplar part is a corner now a red oak, thence North West 178 pole to a ditch of Col. Philip Ludwell Lee's near a corner white oak, thence along the said ditch 180 poles, thence leaving the said ditch North 33° East 47 poles to the letter "G" where formerly stood a locust post in a valley, thence West by South all poles to the post before mentioned which course to be continued 14 poles more, thence along the said ditch it several turnings 223 poles to the path that leads to Col. Lee's plantation where stands a white oak marked as a corner on the north side thereof, thence along the said path several turnings 148 poles to the beginning containing by estimation 311 acres. In witness whereof the parties to these presents have hereunto set their hands and seals the day and year first above written.

Sealed and delivered in the presence of us — John Ariss
William Booth — Elizabeth Ariss
William Rountree
Edward Ransdell

At a court continued and held for Westmoreland County the 30th day of March 1763 this indenture and the receipt endorsed, was proved by the oath of William Booth, William Rountree and Edward Ransdell witnesses thereto and ordered to be recorded.
Test: James Davenport CCW

Page 196.
Thomas Bennett's Will

In the name of God Amen, I Thomas Bennett, Sr., sick of body but of perfect sense and memory do ordain this my last will and testament.

Item my land to be divided between two sons Daniel Bennett and Charles Bennett and my son Charles to have that half next to the creek.
Item my desire is that neither of my sons shall cut the entail to sell their parts to any other person than from one brother to another. And if both brothers die without heir, their parts shall go to my son Joseph Bennett.
Item I give to my son Thomas Bennett 40 shillings sterling money of Great Britain to be paid by my executor.
Item give my son Daniel Bennett young Negro man Sam but if my son Daniel Bennett dies without heir and Negro should go to my son Charles Bennett.
Item I give and bequeath to my son Charles Bennett three Negro women and one Negro child; Judah, Maria, Abigail and John and there their increase, but my son Charles Bennett dies without heir the Negroes to go to son Daniel Bennett.
Item give to my son Solomon Bennett one cow and calf.
Item my will and desire is that my loving wife have the use of estate for and during her natural life and after her death Negroes to go to them, bequeath [this is literally how it reads. He, probably meant that the negroes would go to her kids] and the rest of my estate to be divided my children; Joseph Bennett: Solomon Bennett, Daniel Bennett: Charles Bennett: Mary Bennett.
Item I do hereby make constitute and appoint my two sons Daniel Bennett and Charles Bennett. executors of this my last will and testament. In witness whereof I have set my hand and seal this 8th day of December 1762.
Test, Jeremiah Jeffries Thomas Bennett
Presley Hall
John Short
At a court held for Westmoreland County the 31st day of May 1763 this last will and testament of Thomas Bennett, Sr., deceased was proved according to law by the oath Jeremiah Jeffries and Presley Hall, witnesses thereto and ordered to be recorded and on the motion Daniel Bennett and Charles Bennett the executors named in said will who made oath according to law and together with George Rust and Jeremiah Jeffries their securities entered into and acknowledged bond with condition as the law directs, certificate is granted him for obtaining a probate thereof in due form.
Test: James Davenport CCW

Page 198.
Bowcock & Wife to Campbell Indenture
This indenture made the 19th day of May 1763 between Thomas Bowcock and Amy Bowcock his wife of the Parish of Washington and County of Westmoreland of the one part and Archibald Campbell of the parish and county aforesaid, clerk of the other part. Witnesseth that Thomas Bowcock and Amy Bowcock his wife in consideration of 255 pounds 6 shillings and 6 pence current money of Virginia has sold to Archibald Campbell all that tract of land lying in the parish and county aforesaid containing 200 acres and bounded as follows; beginning at a white oak by the side of a road formerly leading to Mattox Ferry and running thence East 166 poles, thence North 40° West 85 poles to a white oak standing between this land and the land that formerly belonged to Bunch Roe, thence North 5° West 60 poles to a red oak between this land and the said Roe's land, thence North 17° East 100 poles to a live oak corner to this land and the said Roe's land, thence West 160 poles, thence South 1° East 206 poles to the road, thence down the road South 50° East to the beginning including all the land devised to the said Thomas Bowcock in the last will and testament of James Bowcock, deceased. In witness whereof the said Thomas Bowcock and Amy Bowcock his wife have hereunto set their hands and seals the day and year above written.
Signed sealed and delivered in the presence of Thomas Bowcock
Daniel Fitzhugh Amy Bowcock (her mark)
John Martin
Anthony McKittrick
Alexander McHarg
At a court held for Westmoreland County the 31st day of May 1763 this indenture and receipt were acknowledged by Thomas Bowcock and Amy Bowcock his wife parties thereto (she being first privy examined) and ordered to be recorded.

Test: James Davenport CCW

Page 199.

Gardner [Garner] to Morse [Moss] Indenture

This indenture made the fifth day of March 1763 between Thomas Garner of the Parish of Cople and County of Westmoreland of the one part and Obediah Morse [Moss] of the same parish and county of the other part. Witnesseth that Thomas Garner in consideration of 30 pounds current money has sold to Obediah Morse a tract of land containing by estimation 70 acres that fell to him being heir of his brother John Garner, deceased, being part of a tract of land granted by patent to William Walker 1662, lying in the Parish of Cople and County aforesaid and bounded by the lands of Samuel Rust and Thomas Beale and the branch and mill pond. In witness whereof the parties first to these presents have hereunto set his hand and seal this day and year first above written.
Sealed and delivered in the presence of us Thomas Garner
Samuel Rust
Jeremiah Jeffries
At a Court held for Westmoreland County the 31st day of May 1763 this indenture and the memorandum of livery of seizen and receipt endorsed were proved by the oath of Jeremiah Jeffries a witness thereto and at a court continued and held for the said County the 30th day of March last past the said indenture memorandum and receipt being proved by the oath of Samuel Rust and Robert Jeffries the two other witnesses, thereto are ordered to be recorded.
Test: James Davenport CCW

Page 201.

James Hore's Will

In the name of God Amen, this 12th day of April 1763 I James Hore of the Parish of Washington and County of Westmoreland though weak in body yet of sound and perfect memory and understanding do constitute make and ordain this my last will and testament as manner and form following.
Imprimis, I give and bequeath unto my godson Beckwith Butler mulatto girl Carey.
Item I give and bequeath to my cousin Sarah Hore the use of Negro man Sam during her natural life and after her decease to go to Elias Hore.
Item I give and bequeath William Berkley and his wife Peggy Berkley the use of Negro girl Kisey during their natural life and after their decease the Negro girl Kisey and her increase return to my godson John Berkley.
Item I give and bequeath unto Mary Nelson, Sr., the use of Negro Woman Betty [in her possession] during her natural life and after her decease to return to my godson William Nelson.
Item I give and bequeath unto Mary Nelson, Jr., Negro girl Lucy and Negro boy Benn.
Item I give and bequeath to James Hore son of my cousin Elias Hore: the plantation, and the lands I now live on.
Item I give and bequeath unto Mary Nelson, Sr., my riding horse "Buck".
Item I give and bequeath all the rest of my estate to be equally divided between John Triplett and my cousin Elias Hore.
Item my will and desire is that my estate may not be appraised.
Item I constitute, make and appoint my friend Lawrence Butler, John Triplett, Elias Hore and William Berkley to be my executors of this my last will and testament.
In witness whereof I have hereunto set my hand and seal the day and year first above mentioned.
Signed sealed and acknowledged in presence James Hore
William Craighill
George Hales
James Cannaday
John Nelson, Sr.
John Nelson, Jr.
At a court held for Westmoreland County the 31st day of Mary 1763 this last will of James Hore, deceased was proved according to law by the oaths to George Hales, James Cannaday and John Nelson, Jr., witnesses thereto and ordered to be recorded, and on the motion of John Triplett, Elias

Hore and William Berkley, three of the executors named in the said will who made oath according to law, and together with Benjamin Weeks, George Hales and Samuel Walker their securities entered into and acknowledged bond with condition as the law directs, certificate is granted him for obtaining a probate thereof in due form.
Test: James Davenport CCW

Page 203.
Ashton to Massey Lease
This indenture made the 27th day of November 1762 between John Ashton of the County of Westmoreland of the one part and Robert Massey of the county of King George of the other part.
Witnesseth that John Ashton in consideration of 5 shillings has sold unto Robert Massey all that tract of land lying in the Parish of Washington and County of Westmoreland containing 100 acres from the day of the date hereof for and during the term of one whole year from thence next ensuing yielding and paying yearly the rent of one ear of Indian corn to the intent and purpose that by virtue of these presents and of the statute for transferring uses into possession the said Robert Massey may be in the actual possession of the tract. In witness whereof the said John Ashton hath to this indenture set his hand and seal the day month and year first above written.
Sealed and delivered in the presence of John Ashton
William Bernard
John Weedon, Jr.
Samuel Dishman
Thomas Taylor
At a court held for Westmoreland County the 31st day of Mary 1763 this indenture was proved by the oath of Thomas Taylor, a witness thereto and at a court held for Westmoreland County the 29th day of March last past the said indenture having proved by the oaths of William Bernard & Samuel Dishman two others of the witnesses thereto is ordered to be recorded.
Test: James Davenport CCW

Page 204.
Ashton's wife to Massey Lease & Release
This indenture made the 28th day of November 1762 between John Ashton and Mary his wife of the Parish of Washington and County of Westmoreland of the one part and Robert Massey of the parish of Hanover and county of King George of the other part.
Witnesseth that John Ashton and Mary Ashton his wife in consideration of 100 pounds current money of Virginia has sold unto Robert Massey all that tract of land lying in the Parish of Washington and County of Westmoreland containing 100 acres already in his possession by virtue of a bargain and sale and by the statute for transferring uses into possession. In witness whereof the said John Ashton and Mary Ashton his wife hath to this indenture interchangeably set their hands and seals the day month and year first above written.
Sealed and delivered in the presence of John Ashton
William Bernard Mary Ashton
John Weedon, Jr.
Samuel Dishman
Thomas Taylor
At a court held for Westmoreland County the 31st day of Mary 1763 this indenture was proved by the oath of Thomas Taylor, a witness thereto and At a court held for Westmoreland County the 29th day of March last past the said indenture and receipt being proved by the oaths of William Bernard & Samuel Dishman two others of the witnesses thereto is ordered to be recorded.
Test: James Davenport CCW

Page 207.
Lane to Lane Indenture
This Indenture made the 23rd day of May 1763 between Martha Lane: widow of the Parish of Cople and County of Westmoreland of one part and Joseph Lane of the aforesaid parish and county, Gent., of the other part. Witnesseth that Martha Lane in consideration of the natural love and

affection which she beareth unto Joseph Lane, her son as for the consideration that Joseph Lane having conveyed to James Lane, her son of the county of Loudoun 155 acres of land; doth by these presents confirm unto Joseph Lane (after her death) all that tract of land lying in the Parish of Cople and County of Westmoreland whereon the said Martha Lane now liveth containing 100 acres during her natural life which land was given to her by her father William Carr by will dated the 13th day of January 1702/3. In witness whereof the said Martha Lane hath hereunto set her hand and seal the day and year first above written.

Signed sealed and delivered in the presence of Martha Lane
Daniel McKenny
William Carr Tidwell
Thomas Davis

At a court held for Westmoreland County the 31st day of May1763, this deed of gift was proved by the oaths of Daniel McKenny, William Carr Tidwell and Thomas Davis the witnesses thereto and ordered to be recorded.
Test: James Davenport CCW

Page 209.
Ashton's Wife to Massey Privy Examination

To James Berryman, William Berryman and Archibald Campbell: Gent. Whereas John Ashton of the County of Westmoreland, Gent., and Mary Ashton his wife by their indentures of lease and release bearing date the 27th and 28th days of November 1762 have conveyed unto Robert Massey of the county of King George the fee simple estate of 100 acres being in the Parish of Washington and County of Westmoreland and whereas Mary Ashton cannot conveniently travel to our court to make acknowledgement of the conveyance. Therefore, we do give unto you or any two of you power to receive the acknowledgement the said Mary Ashton shall be willing to make. Witness James Davenport, clerk of our said Court the 30th day of March 1763

We have examined the within named Mary Ashton apart from her within named husband and she declared that she subscribed her name to the within mentioned deed voluntarily and without the threats of her husband. Given under our hands & seals this 23rd day of July 1763.
James Berryman
William Berryman

At a court continued and held for Westmoreland county the 27th day of July 1763. This commission and the certificate of the execution thereof being returned and ordered to be recorded
Test: James Davenport CCW

Page 210.
Garner & Wife to Rust Indenture

This Indenture made the 29th day of August 1763 between Bradley Garner and Katharine Garner his wife of the Parish of Cople and County of Westmoreland, planter of the one part and Samuel Rust of the parish and county aforesaid, inspector of the other part. Witnesseth that Bradley Garner and Katharine Garner his wife in consideration of 70 pounds current money of Virginia has sold to Samuel Rust all that tract of land that the said Bradley Garner purchased of Thomas Allison, Jr., by deed bearing date the 22nd day of July 1754 containing 100 acres being part of a tract granted by patent to William Hopkins in 1661, situate and lying in Yeocomico Forrest in the Parish of Cople and county aforesaid and bounded by the lands of the said Samuel Rust and Jeremiah Jeffries. In witness whereof the parties first to these presents have hereunto set their hands and seals the day and year first mentioned.

Sealed and delivered in the presence of us Bradley Garner
Presley Cox Katharine Garner
Marshall Daffan
Witmoth Garner (her mark)
Elizabeth Rust
Mary Daffan (her mark)

At a court held for Westmoreland County the 30th day of August 1763 this indenture of feoffment and a memorandum of livery of seizen and receipt thereon endorsed were acknowledged by

Bradley Garner and ordered to be recorded, and Catharine Garner wife of Bradley Garner personally appeared and first privy examined as the law directs, voluntarily relinquished her right of dower in the estate conveyed by the indenture.
Test: James Davenport CCW

Page 212.
Gray to Weedon Indenture
This indenture made the 19th day of August 1763 between Francis Gray of the Parish of Washington and County of Westmoreland of the one part and George Weedon the same parish and county, Esq., of the other part. Witnesseth that Francis Gray in consideration of 80 pound current money of Virginia has sold to George Weedon a tract of land lying in the Parish of Washington and the County of Westmoreland containing 5 acres and bounded as follows; beginning at a spanish oak, a corner tree dividing this land and a tract formerly purchased by George Weedon of John Washington of Gloucester County, Gent., deceased, extending thence along Weedon's line to a locus post, another corner to the said Weedon and the said Francis Gray, thence Southwesterly to a marked locust post, a corner set up by the said Francis Gray and dividing this land from Gray's land, thence Southeasterly by a marked poplar standing in a branch of Rozier's Creek, thence along the branch to the first beginning. Which said tract was formerly by me conveyed to William Strother, now deceased, and was recovered together with another tract in my possession of the said William Strother of me the said Francis Gray by John Washington who conveyed the said 5 acres together with the land recovered of me to James Blair who conveyed the whole to me the said Francis Gray. In witness whereof the said Francis Gray hath set his hand and seal the day and year first before written.
James Blair Francis Gray
Andrew Monroe
William Muir
Thomas Taylor
At a court held for Westmoreland county the 30th day of August 1763, this indenture of feoffment and a memorandum of livery and seizen and receipt thereon endorsed were proved by the oaths of James Blair, Andrew Monroe and William Muir, witnesses thereto and ordered to be recorded.
Test: James Davenport CCW

Page 216.
Butler to Butler Indenture
Know all men by these presents that we Mary Butler, relict of Caleb Butler, deceased and William Smith of the Parish of Washington in the County of Westmoreland, as well for the natural affection and filial love which I the said Mary Butler have and do bear unto my well beloved son Joseph Butler, as also for divers other good causes and considerations to me at this present time especially moving, as also for a valuable consideration to me, the said William Smith in hand paid the receipt whereof I do hereby acknowledge in William Smith to give grant and make over and confirm unto Joseph Butler and his heirs, two Negroes; Alec and Let and their increase. In witness whereof we have set our hands and seals this 4th day of March 1763.
Signed sealed and delivered in presence of Mary Butler
Alexander Thom William Smith
William Finch
George Butler
At a Court held for Westmoreland County the 30th day of August 1763 this deed of gift was proved by the oaths of Alexander Thom, William Finch and George Butler the witnesses thereto and ordered to be recorded.
Test: James Davenport CCW

Page 217.
Butler to Smith Indenture
This indenture made the 30th day of August 1763 between Mary Butler: widow of the Parish of Washington and the County of Westmoreland of the one part and William Smith of the same parish

and county of the other part. Witnesseth that the said Mary Butler in consideration of two Negroes; Alec and Let and their future increase mentioned in a certain deed bearing date the fourth day of March 1763 has granted and sold the tract of land lying in the parish and county aforesaid whereon I now live containing by estimation 250 acres only reserving to myself my natural life and the lands and premises aforementioned. In witness whereof the parties to these presents have interchangeably set their hands and seals the day and year above written.

Sealed and delivered in presence of Mary Butler
Alexander Thom's
William Finch
George Butler

At a Court held for Westmoreland County the 30th day of August 1763 this indenture of bargain and sale was proved by the oaths of Alexander Thom, William Finch and George Butler the witnesses thereto and ordered to be recorded.
Test: James Davenport CCW

Page 219.

Jarvis to Tidwell Indenture

this indenture made the 27th day of June 1763 between John Jarvis the Parish of Washington in the County of Westmoreland, planter (son and heir John Jarvis and Elizabeth Jarvis who was one of the daughters and copartners Abraham Field, deceased) and Sarah Jarvis his wife of the one part, and William Carr Tidwell of Parish of Cople in the said County of Westmoreland. Witnesseth that John Jarvis and Sarah Jarvis his wife in consideration of 4 pounds 11 shillings current money of Virginia and 1164 pounds of crop tobacco have sold to William Carr Tidwell all their right title and claim to a parcel of land lying in the said Parish of Cople and County of Westmoreland commonly called and known by the name of "Narrow's Point" on the upper side of Lower Machodoc River where the ship Catherine lies sunk containing 140 acres and bounded as followeth; beginning at the head of a Creek which divideth this land in the land formerly belonging to Capt. Thomas Youell, extending along the same creek East South East 160 poles to Lower Machodoc River, thence southerly 200 poles along the said river to a small that divideth this formerly belonging to Isaac Allerton, Esq., deceased and West northerly along the lands of the said Isaac Allerton first beginning. The said land was first granted to George Watts patent bearing date the 20th day of July 1661, and after the decease of George Watts the land descended by inheritance to William Watts his son and sole heir who by John Sturman his attorney duly and legally authorized thereto sold and conveyed the same to Abraham Smith, by deeds of lease and release bearing date the 23rd day of June 1691, and the said Abraham Smith sold and conveyed the said lands to James Lawhon/ Laughan, by deed of feoffment bearing date the ninth day June 1696, and the said James Lawhon/ Laughan sold and conveyed the land to Abraham Field who died possessed thereof without conveying or disposing of the same, whereupon it became the proper inheritance of his several daughters as coheirs one of whom intermarried with John Jarvis, and two of them died without heirs or conveying their right to the said land under whom the said John Jarvis party to these presents claims his right and title as son and heir at law. In witness whereof the parties first named have interchangeably set their hands and affixed their seals the day and year first written.

Signed sealed and delivered in presence of us John Jarvis
William Smith Sarah Jarvis
Joseph Butler
John Justiss
George Butler

At a Court held for Westmoreland County the 30th day of August 1763 this indenture of bargain and sale and the receipt thereon endorsed were proved by the oath of William Smith in George Butler witnesses thereto and had Court held for the said County the 26th day of July last past the said indenture and receipt being proved by the oath of John Justiss one other witnesses thereto were ordered to be recorded.
Test: James Davenport CCW

Page 223.

Mary Middleton's Will

In the name of God Amen, I Mary Middleton of the Parish of Cople and County of Westmoreland being in disposing sense and memory do make this my last will and testament in manner and form. Imprimis, I give and bequeath my right and title of the land I now live on and my part of Negro man Sam, as also all my movable estate except one feather bed and furniture to be equally divided between William Middleton and Thomas Middleton the two sons of Thomas Middleton: deceased.

Item I give and bequeath the bed above excepted with all the furniture belonging to Mary Brown the daughter of my brother Benjamin Middleton, provided she is alive at the time of my death. If not, then to the above William Middleton and Thomas Middleton.

Further my will is that Leazure Middleton, the widow of Thomas Middleton: deceased, shall have the use of all my estate (except the bed given to Mary Brown) during her widowhood to raise and maintain the above William Middleton and Thomas Middleton upon that they may have no necessity of being bound out for want of sustenance and I do ordain the said Leazure Middleton my whole and sole executrix of this my last will and testament.

I also appoint Thomas Brown as a trustee impowering him in case the said Leazure Middleton should marry or make willful waste of the above said estate, more than is necessary for the raising and supporting the said William Middleton and Thomas Middleton: to take it out of her hand into his own. Signed Sealed and published

The 6th day of March 1755 Mary Middleton

Witness: Samuel Harrison

George Knott (his mark)

Elizabeth Walker

Thomas Brown

At a court held for Westmoreland county the 27th day of September 1763, this last will and testament of Mary Middleton: deceased was proved according to law by the oaths of George Knott and Elizabeth Walker, witnesses thereto and ordered to be recorded, and on the motion of Leazure Middleton the executrix named in the will who made oath according to law and together with William Taylor her security entered into and acknowledged bond with condition as the law directs, certificate is granted her for obtaining a probate thereof in due form.

Test: James Davenport CCW

Page 224.

George Jeffries Will

In the name of God Amen, I George Jeffries of the Parish of Cople and County of Westmoreland being low and weak of body but of perfect sense and memory to make and ordain this to be my last will and testament.

Item I give my land to my sons William Jeffries and John Jeffries to be divided equally and in the suitablest manner to each of their plantations by any two persons that they shall choose and William Jeffries to have the plantation that I now live on and John Jeffries to have the plantation that Thomas Gallohoo/Gallahue now lives on and they shall neither lease, mortgage nor sell either of their lands to any person only to each other and my wife shall not be interrupted on the plantation she now lives on during her widowhood and shall keep all my movable estate quietly in her possession not to be interrupted by any person during her widowhood and after to her marriage to have what the law allows. After her death or marriage, the movable estate to be divided into four parts between George Jeffries, William Jeffries, John Jeffries and Marah Jeffries, and William to possess George Jeffries part and take care of him. In case George Jeffries should live till William Jeffries comes to age, and if not, for the movable estate to be equally divided amongst the other three children, above mentioned and what Elizabeth Jeffries, and Ann Jeffries hath received already to be their parts of my estate.

Jeremiah Jeffries and Elizabeth Jeffries, my wife, I leave full and sole executors of this my last will and testament. In witness whereof I the said George Jeffries do set my hand and seal this 30th day of August 1763.

In the presence of us George Jeffries

Daniel Walker

Corbin Myars

Thomas Jones (his mark)
At a court held for Westmoreland County the 25th day of October 1763 this last will and testament of George Jeffries, deceased was proved according to law by the oaths of Corbin Myars, and Thomas Jones witnesses thereto and ordered to be recorded, and on the motion of Elizabeth Jeffries the executrix named in the said will who made oath according to law and together with Corbin Myars and Thomas Jones her securities entered into and acknowledged bond with condition as the law directs, certificate is granted her for obtaining a probate thereof in due form.
Test: James Davenport CCW

Page 226.
James White's Will
In the name of God Amen, this 21st day of October 1762, I James White of Washington Parish and county of Westmoreland being very weak do make and ordain this to be my last will and testament in manner and form as followeth.
First, I bequeath to Alice Kersey one high bedstead bed and all the furniture belonging to it, 6 pounds cash, 1 large hog, and 14 bushels of corn.
Item, I give and bequeath to my son Benjamin White's three daughters, Janey White, Mildred White and Amey White 20 shillings apiece.
Item I give and bequeath to my son John White's two sons, Samuel White and John White, 1 shilling sterling apiece.
Item, I give to my son Daniel White my Negro man Dick, four days in every week, viz; Mondays, Tuesdays, Wednesdays, and Thursdays and no more.
Item, I give an bequeath the use of my Negro man Dick, the other three days in every week, viz; Fridays, Saturdays, and Sundays to my trusty neighbor John Wilkerson, Sr.
I give one coat, jacket and breeches, to my Negro man Dick.
Item I give and bequeath to my daughter Jemima Balthrop: one shilling sterling and no more of my estate.
Item I give and bequeath to my daughter Virlinda Gribsby, one shilling sterling and no more of my estate.
Item I give and bequeath to my son James White, one shilling sterling and no more of my estate.
Item I give to all the rest of my son Benjamin White's children one shilling sterling apiece and no more of my estate.
Item I give and bequeath to my granddaughter Winifred Balthrop: one trunk.
Item I leave all the rest of my estate of what nature or kind soever to be equally divided between by two sons Daniel White and Thomas White.
Lastly, I appoint my trusty neighbor John Bailey my executor of this my last will and testament. In witness whereof I have hereunto set my hand and seal this 21st day of October 1762.
Signed sealed and delivered in the presence of us James White, Sr.
Thomas Peach
John Wilkerson
Mary Wilkerson (her mark)
At a court held for Westmoreland County the 25th day of "October 1763 this will was proved according to law by the oaths of Thomas Peach and John Wilkerson, witnesses thereto and ordered to be recorded and on the motion of Daniel White who made oath according to law and together with Thomas Peach his security entered into and acknowledged bond with condition as the law directs, certificate is granted him for obtaining letters of administration of the estate of the said James White with the will annexed in due form, John Bailey the executor named in the same will having first personally appeared and refuses to take upon himself the burthen of the execution thereof.
Test: James Davenport CCW

Page 227.
Beale to Beale Deed of Gift
To all Christian People to whom these presents shall come, I Joseph Beale of the Parish of Cople and County of Westmoreland in consideration of the love good will and affection which I have and

do bear towards my loving son Thomas Beale of the same parish and county and for diverse other causes and considerations me thereunto moving but more especially for the support and maintenance which I and my wife Hannah Beale is to have from the said Thomas Beale my son for and during the natural lives of both of us or the longest liver have given by these presents unto my son Thomas Beale all and singular my lands, houses, buildings, fencing with all appurtenances thereunto belonging lying in the parish and county aforesaid together with all my stock of cattle, hogs, horses, mares, household furniture, working tools, implements, etc. in witness whereof I have hereunto set my hand and seal this 7th day of October 1763.

Signed sealed and delivered in the presence of us Joseph Beale (his mark)
John Norwood
Thomas Colston (his mark)

At a Court held for Westmoreland County the 29th day of November 1763 this deed of gift was acknowledged by Joseph Beale party thereto and ordered to be recorded.
Test: James Davenport CCW

Page 228.

Augustine Weedon's Will

In the name of God Amen, I Augustine Weedon Westmoreland County in the Parish of Washington being very sick and weak in body but of perfect sense and memory do make and ordain this to be my last will and testament in the form as followeth.
Item I give and bequeath unto my daughter Elizabeth Weedon: Negro woman Moll.
Secondly, my Negro woman Jemimah to my daughter Jean Weedon
Thirdly, I give Negro girl Grace to my daughter Rebecca Weedon.
Fourthly, I given to my daughter Mary Hilton Negro boy Will.
Fifthly, I give and bequeath Negro man Dick to my son John Weedon.
Sixthly, I give and bequeath Negro girl Kate to my son George Weedon
Seventhly, I give Negro boy Ben to my son Augustine Weedon.
Item I give unto my Sarah Weedon as it is not in my power to give her a Negro, my will and desire is that my daughter Sarah have as much cash made up and paid out of the all the estate as will make up 50 pounds current money.
I will and desire that my five daughters, my five beds between them and furniture.
Item I give my gun to my son John Weedon,
Item my young sorrel mare and saddle to my son George Weedon.
My will is that my three sons, John Weedon, George Weedon: and Augustine Weedon be bound out to a trade at the discretion of my executors.
I appoint and ordain John Hilton and Elizabeth Hilton my whole and sole executors to this my last will and testament is whereof I set my hand and seal this 20th day of September 1763.

Signed sealed and delivered in published in the presence of Augustine Weedon
Thomas Taylor
John Edrington
Robert Massey
John Weedon

At a court held for Westmoreland County the 29th day of November 1763 this last will and testament of Augustine Weedon, deceased was proved according to law by the oath of Thomas Taylor, John Edrington, and John Weedon witnesses thereto and ordered to be recorded and on the motion of John Hilton the executor named in the said will who made oath according to law together with John Weedon and Thomas Taylor his securities entered into and of knowledge bond with condition as the law directs, certificate is granted him for obtaining a probate thereof in due form.
Test: James Davenport CCW

Page 230.

Frances Davis' Will

In the name of God Amen, I Frances Davis Westmoreland County in the Parish of Washington am sick in body but in perfect sound sense and memory do make, ordain, and constitute this my last

will and testament in the following manner.
Item I give and bequeath unto my sister Ann Davis my Negro man Dick to her and her heirs.
I give and bequeath unto my sister Mary Davis my Negro man Tony.
All the rest of my estate to my sister Katherine Davis.
I appoint my sister Ann Davis & Mary Davis my executors to this my last will and testament. In witness whereof I set my hand and seal this 16th day of November 1763.
Signed sealed and delivered in the presence of Frances Davis (her mark)
John Weedon, Jr.
Butler Baker
Mildred Weedon (her mark)
Winifred Baker (her mark)
At a court held for Westmoreland County the 29th day of November 1763, this last will and testament of Frances Davis: deceased was proved according to law by the oaths of John Weedon, Jr., and Butler Baker witnesses thereto and ordered to be recorded and on the motion of Mary Davis the executrix last named in the said will, who made oath according to law, and together with John Hilton & Butler Baker her securities entered into and acknowledged bond with condition as the law directs, certificate is granted her for obtaining a probate thereof in due form liberty being reserved to Anne Davis the other executrix to join in the probate when she shall think fit.
Test: James Davenport CCW

Page 231.
Anne Davis Will
In the name of God Amen, I Anne Davis Westmoreland County in Washington Parish being sick and weak in body but in perfect sense and memory do make, ordain and constitute this my last will and testament in the following manner.
Item I give and bequeath to my daughter Ann Davis Negro woman Nell.
Item my will is that all the rest of my estate shall be equally divided between my five daughters and appoint my daughters Ann Davis and Mary Davis my executors to this my last will and testament. In witness whereof I set my hand and seal this 12th day of October 1763
Signed sealed and delivered in the presence of Ann Davis (her mark)
John Weedon
Butler Baker
Frances Baker
Ann Davis (her mark)
At a court held for Westmoreland County the 29th day of November 1763, this last will and testament of Ann Davis, deceased was proved according to law by the oaths of John Weedon, and Butler Baker witnesses thereto and ordered to be recorded and on the motion of Mary Davis the executrix last named in the said will, who made oath according to law, and together with John Hilton & Butler Baker her securities entered into and acknowledged bond with condition as the law directs, certificate is granted her for obtaining a probate thereof in due form liberty being reserved to Anne Davis the other executrix to join in the probate when she shall think fit.
Test: James Davenport CCW

Page 232.
Rice to Haselrigg Indenture
This indenture made the 29th day of November 1763 between William Rice and Jemima Rice his wife of the parish Cople and the County of Westmoreland of the one part and William Hazelrigg the said parish and county of the other part. Witnesseth that William Rice and Jemima Rice his wife in consideration of 19 pounds five shillings current money has sold to William Hazelrigg a tract of land with the appurtenances lying in the Parish of Cople and County of Westmoreland containing by estimation 25 acres, 3 rods and 9 poles of land; beginning at a sapling marked for this corner to this land in standing on the north west side of a road and on the land dividing William Rice and William Hazelrigg, and running North 43° East 59 poles to a marked red oak corner to William Hazelrigg, then North 31 ½° East 58 poles to another marked red oak corner to William Rice and land lately held by Dozier Templeman, deceased, thence North 89° West 80 ½ poles to a red oak sapling and

standing on the South easternmost side of the aforesaid road part by the said Rice and Hazelrigg for the corner to this land, thence South 6° 15 E. 90 3/8 poles to the first beginning. In witness whereof the said parties to these presents have interchangeably set their hands and seals the day and year first above written.

Sealed and delivered in the presence of us — William Rice
William Pierce — Jemima Rice (her mark)
Richard Sutton
Alexander Spark

At a Court held for Westmoreland County the 29th day of November 1763 this indenture was acknowledged by William Rice and Jemima Rice his wife parties thereto the first being privy examined as the law directs and ordered to be recorded.
Test: James Davenport CCW

Page 234.

Marmaduke to Peirce [Pierce]

This indenture made the 20th day of October 1763 between Christopher Marmaduke of the Parish of Cople and the County of Westmoreland and Mary Marmaduke his wife of the other part and Joseph Pierce of the said parish and county of the other part. Witnesseth that Christopher Marmaduke and Mary Marmaduke his wife in consideration of 10 pounds 16 shillings and 7 pence and sold to Joseph Pierce a parcel of land containing by estimation 28 acres, 3 rods, and 21 poles lying in the said parish and county and bounded as followeth; beginning at a marked white oak standing near a road and corner to land held by William Porter in the aforesaid Christopher Marmaduke and running South 29 ½° East 61 poles to the line dividing this land from Mr. Edward Ransdell's in the said Joseph Pierce's, thence North 69 ½° West 52 poles to another marked red Oak corner to the said Joseph Pierce thence northeasterly to the first beginning. In witness whereof the parties to these presents have hereunto set their hands and seals the day and year first above written.

Sealed and delivered in the presence of us — Christopher Marmaduke
Richard Barnett — Mary Marmaduke (her mark)
Edward Ransdell, Jr. ,
Richard Neale
Daniel Marmaduke

At a Court held for Westmoreland County the 29th day of November 1763 this indenture of bargain and sale and the receipt endorsed were proved by the oaths of Richard Barnett, Edward Ransdell, Jr., and Daniel Marmaduke witnesses thereto and ordered to be recorded
Test: James Davenport CCW

Page 237.

John Wilkerson [Wilkinson] Will

In the name of God Amen, I John Wilkerson Westmoreland County being very sick and weak but in perfect sense and memory do make and appoint this my last will and testament in manner and form as followeth.

Item I give unto my son Benjamin Wilkerson my land whereon I now live to him and his heirs and for want of such heirs to return to my son John Wilkerson and his heirs.

Item my will is that my land and all the rest of my estate be and remain in the hands of my loving wife till her natural death or day of marriage; if my wife should marry then to have no more than the law will give her.

Item my will is that after my wife's decease that my estate will be equally divided amongst all my children. As witness my hand and seal this 21st day of February 1764.

Signed sealed in the presence of us — John Wilkerson (his mark)
John Wilkerson
James Wilkerson (his mark)
George Wilkerson

At a Court held for Westmoreland County the 27th day of March 1764 this last Will and Testament

of John Wilkerson, deceased was proved according to law by the oath of John Wilkerson and James Wilkerson witnesses thereto and ordered to be recorded and on the motion of Margaret Wilkerson, widow and relict of the said deceased who made oath according to law and together with Benjamin Wilkerson and John Wilkerson her securities entered into and acknowledged bond with conditioned as the law directs, certificate is granted her for obtaining letters of administration of the estate of the said John Wilkerson with the said will the next in due form.
Test: James Davenport CCW

Page 238.
Allerton to Lee Indenture
This indenture made the seventh day of February 1764, Ann Allerton the Parish of Cople and County of Westmoreland of the one part and Richard Lee of the said parish and county, Esq. of the other part. Whereas on the death of James Steptoe, late of the said County of Westmoreland, Gent., deceased, the tract of land whereon he lived known by the name of Hominy Hall descended to the said Ann Allerton and her sister Elizabeth Steptoe (who has since intermarried with the Hon. Philip Ludwell Lee, Esq.) the daughters of James Steptoe by Mary Steptoe his wife in fee simple as coheirs of the said Mary who died before the said James Steptoe and whereas the said Ann Allerton after the death of her father intermarried with Willoughby Allerton, late of the said county, Gent., deceased who in his lifetime with the said Ann Allerton brought a suit in Chancery in the County Court of Westmoreland against Elizabeth Steptoe in order to have a division of the said tract of land and it was ordered by the said court on the 27th day of June 1758 with the consent of parties that Richard Jackson, Daniel Tebbs and John Crabb should divide the said land between the parties having regard to quantity and quality; in obedience to which order they on the 22nd day of July 1758 did divide the same agreeable to a plot thereof to their report the next by which it appears they allotted to the said Ann Allerton 77 acres 2 rods and 32 perches of land next to the river including the dwelling house and bounded by a line run parallel with the river that divides the tract from Critcher's land to Marsh Gutt which course is North 45° West and runs 184 poles, and to the said Elizabeth Steptoe they allotted the remainder of the said tract or parcel of land containing 204 acres and 13 perches which said report together with the plot aforesaid was afterwards returned to the County Court of Westmoreland and At a court held for the said County the 25th day of July in the year last mentioned. Now this indenture witness that and Allerton in consideration of 155 pounds current money of Virginia as sole to Richard Lee all that said dividend of land containing 77 acres, 2 rods and 32 perches. In witness the parties to these presents have hereunto set their hands and seals the day and year first above written.
Sealed and delivered in presence of us Ann Allerton
Richard Henry Lee
Benjamin Weeks
Francis Lightfoot Lee
William Lee
Jesse Price
At a Court held for Westmoreland County the 27th day of March 1764 this indenture of bargain and sale and receipt thereon endorsed were proved by the oath of Richard Henry Lee, Francis Lightfoot Lee and William Lee witnesses thereto and ordered to be recorded
Original Test by James Davenport CCW

Page 241.
Lee to Garner Indenture
This indenture made the 7th day of January 1764 between Richard Lee of the Parish of Cople in the County of Westmoreland, Esq. of the one part and Bradley Garner of the said parish and county, planter of the other part. Witnesseth that the said Richard Lee in consideration of 259 pounds 5 shillings sterling money of Great Britain has sold a tract of land which the said Richard Lee purchased of Abraham Garner, deceased by indenture of bargain and sale bearing date the 21st day of February in the first year of the reign of our Sovereign Lord King George III containing by estimation 234 acres in witness whereof the parties to these presents have hereunto set their hands and seals the day and year first above written.

Sealed and delivered in presence of us Richard Lee
Joseph Lane
At a Court held for Westmoreland County the 27th day of March 1764 this indenture bargain and sale and receipt thereon endorsed were acknowledged by Richard Lee, Esq. party thereto and ordered to be recorded. Teste

Page 243.
John Baker's Will
In the name of God Amen, I John Baker the Parish of Washington and County of Westmoreland being sick and weak of body but of perfect sound mind and memory do make and publish this my last will and testament in manner and form following.
Item I give and bequeath between my two daughters Frances Baker and Winney Baker, Negro fellow Mingo.
Item I give and bequeath unto my beloved wife Katherine Baker all my whole estate both real and personal not already given during her natural life and after her decease I land and all the rest of my personal estate to be sold (the Negro boy Ben to be excepted which I give to my son James Baker after the decease of my wife and after the sale of my real and personal estate) my debts to be paid and the remainder to be equally divided amongst my four children; James Baker, Samuel Baker, Rebeccah Baker and Richard Baker.
I also do make, constitute, and appoint my beloved wife Katherine Baker and Robert Massey joint executors of this my last will and testament. Signed, sealed, witnessed and delivered in the presence of us this 11th day of February 1764. John Baker
William Hodgson
Robert Massey
William Settle
At a court held for Westmoreland County the 27th day of March 1764 this last will and testament of John Baker, deceased was proved according to law by the oaths of William Hodgson and William Settle witnesses thereto and ordered to be recorded and the motion of Katherine Baker and Robert Massey the executors named in the said will who made oath according to law and together with John Chancellor and John Bulger their securities entered into and acknowledged bond with condition as the law directs, certificate is granted him for obtaining a probate thereof in due form. Teste

Page 244.
Brown to Fisher lease
This indenture made in 1764 between John Brown of Washington Parish and county of Westmoreland, planter of one part and William Fisher of the same parish and county, planter of the other part. Witnesseth that John Brown in consideration of the annual rent of 500 pounds tobacco hath let to farm let 50 acres of land being the place whereon William Fisher now lives and binding on Price's line. To have and to hold the said land from the day of the date hereof for and during the said William Fisher and Margaret Fisher his wife life paying to the said John Brown the before said annual rent after the first day of January yearly commencing January 1st, 1766. In consideration whereof, the said Fisher is to aid and assist in building of the said John Brown a dwelling house. In witness whereof the parties aforesaid have either to other to these presents interchangeably set their hands and seals the day above written this 9th day of February 1764.
Signed, sealed and delivered in presence of us John Brown
Thomas Spilman William Fisher
Elizabeth Pritchett (her mark)
Pegge Spilman (her mark)
N.B. the said William Fisher is to have timber and firewood of any part of the said John Brown's land for the use of the plantation.
At a court continued and held for Westmoreland County the 28th day of March 1764, This indenture of lease was acknowledged by John Brown and William Fisher the parties thereto is ordered to be recorded. Teste

Page 245.

Bulger (Sheriff) to Muse Indenture

This indenture made the 29th day of March 1764, between John Bulger: deputed sheriff under Richard Jackson, sheriff of the Parish of Washington and County of Westmoreland of the one part and John Muse of Washington Parish and Westmoreland County of the other part. Witnesseth that whereas Humphrey Pope of Westmoreland died indebted to William Black, merchant in the sum of 58 pound, 19 shillings, and 8 pence together with lawful interest thereon from the 9th day of March 1760, til payment afterwards, to wit; on the 27th of October 1762, the said Black obtained a judgment in the Honble General Court against Sarah Pope, widow and devise and John Pope, heir at law of the said Humphrey Pope: deceased, and John Augustine Washington executor of John Bushrod, Gent., late sheriff of Westmoreland county for the aforesaid sum, then by virtue of the said judgment the said William Black obtained a writ of execution to him the said Richard Jackson, then sheriff, directed commanding him of the lands and tenements of Humphrey Pope: deceased in the hands of Sarah Pope: widow and devise and John Pope heir at law and of the goods and chattles of John Bushrod, Gent., late sheriff in the hands of John Augustine Washington, executor of the said John Bushrod should cause to be made the aforesaid sum then pursuant to the said writ for and in consideration of the sum of 40 pounds current money to him the said John Bulger in hand paid by the said John Muse: at or before the insealing and delivery of these presents the receipt whereof the said John Bulger deputed hereby acknowledged has sold unto John Muse that tract of land with appurtenances lying in the Parish of Washington and county of Washington containing 137 acres and 21 poles as appears by deed passed from Joseph Butler to Humphrey Pope dated the 28th of August 1748. In witness whereof the parties have set their hands and seals the day and year first mentioned.

Sealed and delivered in presence of us John Bulger
Benjamin Weeks
Gerrard Hutt
William O'Bryan Goff

At a court continued in health Westmoreland County the 28th day of March 1764 this indenture of bargain and sale and receipt thereon endorsed were acknowledged by John Bulger party thereto and ordered to be recorded. Teste

Page 248.

Lee's Wife to Ransdell Privy Examination

To the justices of the peace of Charles County in the province of Maryland, Gent. Whereas Richard Lee of the province of Maryland, Esq. and Grace Lee his wife, William Booth of the County of Westmoreland in the colony of Virginia and Elizabeth Booth his wife and Augustine Washington of the same County and colony and Ann Washington his wife by their certain indenture of bargain and sale bearing date the 25th day of May last past have sold and conveyed unto Edward Ransdell the fee simple estate of 68 acres of land lying in the County of Westmoreland in the said colony and whereas the said Grace Lee cannot conveniently travel to our court to make acknowledgment of the said conveyance. Therefore, we do give unto you or any two of you power to receive the acknowledgment which the said Grace Lee shall be willing to make. Witness James Davenport, clerk of our said court the first day December 1762.

Maryland, Charles County Sct.

By virtue of the commission to us directed we did personally go to Grace Lee wife of the within named Richard Lee and examined her privy and apart from her husband and she did acknowledge the indenture of bargain and sale to be her act and deed and that she did freely and voluntarily without the persuasions or threats of her husband and was willing the same should be recorded in Westmoreland County Court. Given under our hands and seals this 21st day of May 1764
Ellen Davis
John Winter

Maryland, Charles County Sct.

I hereby certify that the above-mentioned Ellen Davis and John Winter, gentlemen who signed the above was at the time of signing the same and still are two of his lordships the Right Hon. the Lord Proprietor's Justices of the Peace for the County aforesaid legally authorized and assigned to

whom full faith and credit is ought to be given as well in justice court has thereout.
In testimony whereof I have hereunto set my hand and affixed the public seal of the County aforesaid this 22nd day of May 1764.
Philip Richard Fendall, clerk
Charles County court
At a Court held for Westmoreland County the 29th day of May 1764 this commission and the certificates of the execution thereof being returned and ordered to be recorded. Teste

Page 250.
Bernard to Bernard Indenture
To all to whom these presents shall come be it known that I Richard Bernard of the County of Westmoreland for divers good causes and considerations but more especially for the parental love and affection which I have to my son William Bernard, and by these presents do give grant and make over unto my said son the following Negro slaves; Ben, Jane, and the 11 following children from Jane, viz; Ben, Mill, Sarah, Matt, Benn, Dal, Nan, George, Joshua, Phill and James, Nat son of Mill, and Gus the son of Sarah, and all 15 to hold to my said son William Bernard his heirs and assigns forever and I the said Richard Bernard in testimony thereof have hereunto set my hand and seal this 20th day of May 1764.
In the presence of Richard Bernard
John Monroe
At a Court held for Westmoreland County the 29th day of May 1764 this deed of gift was proved by the oath of John Monroe a witness thereto is ordered to be recorded
test

Page 250.
Triplett to Monroe Lease
This indenture made the 9th day of May 1764 between John Triplett, Sr., of the Parish of Hanover in County of King George, Gent., of the one part and George Monroe, Jr., of the Parish of Washington and County of Westmoreland of the other part. Witnesseth that John Triplett in consideration of five shillings current money has sold unto George Monroe, Jr. all that plantation containing 200 acres lying at the head of Weedon's Run in the parish and county aforesaid, bounded as follows;
beginning at a spanish oak near Whites corner running
North 20° West 98 pole to a red Oak,
thence South 76° West 120 pole,
thence South 77° West 94 pole,
thence South 32 ½° East 10 pole,
thence South 10° East 44 pole to a white oak corner of White's patent,
thence down Spilman's path South 12° 15' West 14 Pole along the said path South 3° East 26 pole,
thence along the aforesaid path South 7° East 52 pole to a white oak, Spanish oak and box oak, standing at Baley's Road,
thence down the said road, North 72° East 20 pole,
thence South 83° East 20 pole,
thence South 66 ¾° East 30 pole,
thence South 69 ¾° East 20 pole,
thence North 85 ½° East 24 pole,
thence South 88 ¾° East 22 pole,
thence South 57° East 24 pole,
thence South 81° East 16 pole,
thence South 71° East 22 pole,
thence North 71° East 12 pole,
thence North 62° East 14 pole,
thence South 62 ¾° East 29 pole, to three white oaks on Baley's Road,
thence North 126 pole to a red oak,
thence North 50° West 18 pole to the beginning.
To have and to hold the said plantation for the term of one whole year from thence next ensuing

yielding and paying the yearly rent of one ear of Indian corn to the intent that by virtue of these presents and by force of the statute for transferring uses into possession the said George Monroe, Jr., may be enabled to take grant and release of the reversions and inheritance thereof to him and his heirs forever. In witness whereof the said John Triplett has hereunto set his hand and seal the day and year first above written.

Sealed and delivered in the presence of John Triplett
William Piper
John Robinson
Roderick Perry

At a Court held for Westmoreland County the 29th day of May 1764 this indenture was acknowledged by John Triplett party thereto and ordered to be recorded test

Page 251.

Triplett to Monroe Release

This indenture made the 10th day of May 1764 between John Triplett, Sr., of the Parish of Hanover in County of King George, Gent., of the one part and George Monroe, Jr., of the Parish of Washington and County of Westmoreland of the other part. Witnesseth that John Triplett in consideration of 80 pounds lawful money of Virginia has sold and released unto George Monroe, Jr. all that plantation containing 200 acres lying at the head of Weedon's Run in the parish and county aforesaid, now in the possession of George Monroe, Jr., by virtue of a bargain and sale made by John Triplett for the term of one year and by indenture bearing date the day next before the day of the date hereof and by force of the statue for transferring uses into possession . [boundaries in above lease]. In witness whereof the said John Triplett hath hereunto set his hand and seal the day and year first above written.

Sealed and delivered in presence of us John Triplett
William Piper
John Robinson
Roderick Perry

At a Court held for Westmoreland County the 29th day of May 1764 this indenture and the receipt thereon endorsed or acknowledged by John Triplett party thereto and ordered to be recorded. Teste

Page 257.

Knott to Goff Indenture

This indenture made 29th day of May 1764 between Farnifold Knott and Sissy Knott his wife of the Parish of St. Stephen's in County of Northumberland of the one part and William O'Bryan Goff of the Parish of Cople and County of Westmoreland of the other part. Witnesseth that the said Farnifold Knott and Sissy Knott his wife in consideration of 25 pounds current money of Virginia have sold to William O'Bryan Goff a tract of land containing 100 acres or thereabouts lying in Yeocomico Neck in the County of Westmoreland and now in the tenure and occupation of John Harrison, Jr., and bounded as follows; beginning at a marked white oak standing on the line that divides this land from the lands of Jeremiah Garland, thence along a line of marked trees northwest to a marked white gum, thence West to another marked white oak, thence southerly along a line that divides this land from the land of William Butler and being part of a dividend of land that belonged to George Jeffries and also being the same tract of land that George Jeffries by deed of gift bearing the date the 25th day of June 1733 gave to his brother Edmund Jeffries and more particularly it being the land called "Fishers" whereon John Fisher formerly lived. In witness whereof the said Farnifold Knott and Sissey his wife to these presents hath set their hands and fixed their seals the day month and year first written.

Signed sealed and delivered in the presence of us Farnifold Knott
Jacob Johnstone (his mark) Sissey Knott
Joseph Milleken
John Norwood

At a court held for Westmoreland County the 29th day of May 1764 this indenture and the memorandum of livery of seizen endorsed or acknowledged by Farnifold Knott and Sissy Knott his wife parties thereto she being first privy examined and ordered to be recorded. Teste

Page 260.

Read to Crabb Indenture

This indenture made the 12th day of May 1764 between Richard Read of the Parish of Cople and County of Westmoreland of the one part and John Crabb of the same parish and county of the other part. Witnesseth that Richard Read in consideration of 250 pounds current money of Virginia has sold to John Crabb a tract containing 333 acres or thereabouts be the same that was left by Coleman Read to the aforesaid Richard Read after the death of his mother Ruth Read who is now living on the said land which is bounded as followeth; beginning at a marked white oak standing by a branch called Smith's Spring Branch and running from thence to Gerrard Hutt's line, thence has a swamp called the Old Field Swamp joining on John Brown, from thence a straight course to the Double Mill Pond joining upon the land of Gerrard Davis and Henry Asbury, thence down the said mill run to the mouth of Smith's Spring Branch, thence up the said branch to the beginning white oak; To have and to hold the said tract after the death of Ruth Read. In witness whereof the said Richard Read hath hereunto set his hand and seal the day month and year first above written.

Signed sealed and delivered in the presence of Richard Read

Willoughby Newton

John Berryman

John Norwood

Gerrard Hutt

Thomas Reynolds

Willington McKenney (his mark)

At a Court held for Westmoreland County the 29th day of May 1764 this indenture and the memo of livery of seizen and receipt endorsed or acknowledged by Richard Read party thereto and ordered to be recorded, previous to which, Elizabeth Read the wife of Richard Read being first privy examined as the law directs voluntary relinquished her right of dower in the lands conveyed by the said indenture or ordered to be recorded.

Page 263.

Hannah Tidwell's Will

In the name of God Amen, I Hannah Tidwell of the Parish of Cople and County of Westmoreland being of a perfect sense and memory do make and ordain constitute this to be my last will and testament in manner and form following.

Item I give and bequeath unto my granddaughter Hannah Tidwell daughter of John Tidwell my lands given me by my father to her and her heirs lawfully begotten, also my mare called Luke and for want of such heirs I give my said lands and mare to my granddaughter Elizabeth Tidwell and for want of such heirs begotten by her I give my said lands and mare to my granddaughter Barbary Tidwell and for want of such heirs of her body lawfully begotten I give the said lands and mare to my beloved daughter Elizabeth Tidwell.

Lastly, I appoint and constitute my beloved son William Carr Tidwell, executor of this my last will and testament. In witness whereof I have hereunto set my hand and affixed my seal this 27th day of January 1760.

Signed sealed published in presence of Hannah Tidwell (her mark)

Martha Lane

Elizabeth Walker (her mark)

William Lane Jr.

At a Court held for Westmoreland County the 29th day of May 1764 this last will and testament of Hannah Tidwell, deceased was proved according to law by the oath of Martha Lane and Elizabeth Walker witnesses thereto and ordered to be recorded and on the motion of William Carr Tidwell executor named in the said will who made oaths according to law and together with Gerrard Hutt Sr., and Jeremiah Jeffries his securities entered into and acknowledged bond with convention as the law directs, certificate is granted him for obtaining a probate thereof in due form. Teste

Page 265.

Mary Lee's Will

In the name of God Amen, I Mary Lee of Lee Hall in the Parish of Cople and County of Westmoreland, widow being of perfect sense and memory do make and ordain this to be my last will and testament in manner and form following.

Item I give and bequeath my beloved daughter Lettice Ball all my wearing apparel, books can whatever things of mine that may be in the house at the time of my death excepting the legacies hereafter mentioned.

Item I give and bequeath unto my dear son Richard Lee my chariot and horses and all my stocks upon his paying to my granddaughter Mary Ball 100 pounds current money of Virginia to be put out at interest on good security until my said granddaughter arrives at the age of 21 years or is married when she is to have the whole principal and interest.

Item I give and bequeath unto my daughter Lettice Ball all the money that my son Richard Lee may owe me at the time of my decease after deducting the price of the mourning rings hereafter mentioned and paying all my just debts which said money, I order to be paid to my said daughter as soon as possible after my decease.

Item I give to each of my children John Lee, Richard Lee, Lettice Ball and Henry Lee and my daughters in law Mary Lee and Lucy Lee and my granddaughter Mary Ball a mourning ring of a guinea value.

Item I given to my son John Lee my wedding ring.

Item I give unto my granddaughter Mary Ball my old mourning ring, my Bible and common prayer book.

Item I lend unto my said daughter Lettice Ball during her natural life to use them on whatever manner she thinks proper without paying any compensation for such use to any person whatsoever the following slaves; Phillis and her children, James, Abraham, John and girl Anne, Barshaba, Betty and her child Judy and their issue and increase together with all the rest and residue of my estate both real and personal not before given and after the death of my said daughter I give and bequeath unto my granddaughter Mary Ball and her heirs forever the following slaves; Phillis and her children, James, Abraham, John and girl Anne, Barshaba, with all their issues and increase provided the said Mary Ball shall marry with the consent of her mother Lettice Ball but if she should not marry with such consent then I give all the Negroes and their increase and all the rest of my estate to my grandsons William Ball and Henry Lee Ball in such parts and proportions as my daughter Lettice Ball shall direct by her last will and testament in writing or deed executed in her lifetime before two credible witnesses and if my said daughter should fail to make such will or deed then to be equally divided between the said William Ball and Henry Lee Ball after the decease of my said daughter.

Item after the decease of my said daughter Lettice Ball I give and bequeath to my two grandsons William Ball and Henry Lee Ball and their heirs forever the following slaves; Betty and her daughter Judy and all their issue and increase to be divided between or wholly given to either of my said grandsons William Ball and Henry Lee Ball as my said daughter Lettice Ball shall direct by her last will and testament in writing or deed executed and her lifetime before two credible witnesses and if my said daughter should failed to make such will or deed then to be equally divided between the said William Ball and Henry Lee Ball.

Item I constitute and appoint my son Richard Lee sole executor to this my last will and testament. In testimony whereof I have hereunto set my hand and seal this 19th day of October 1762. Signed sealed and declared and published in presence of us Mary Lee

Joseph Lane

Reuben Bennett

Anne Rogers (her mark)

At a court held for Westmoreland County the 29th day of May 1764 this last will and testament of Mary Lee: deceased was proved according to law by the oath of Joseph Lane a witness thereto and ordered to be recorded and on the motion of Richard Lee, Esq. the executors named in the said will who made oath according to law and together with Gerrard Hutt, Sr. , his security entered into and acknowledged bond with conditioned as the law directs, certificate is granted him for obtaining a probate thereof in due form. Teste

Page 267.

Butler Baker's Will

In the name of God Amen, I Butler Baker of Westmoreland County in Washington Parish am sick and weak in body but in perfect sense and memory do make and ordain and constitute this my last will and testament in manner and form following.

First, I give and bequeath my land to my son William Baker.

Second, I give and bequeath unto my son Samuel Baker: Negro girl Hannah.

Third, I leave Negro woman Pegg and her child to be sold and the money to be equally divided between my three daughters Elizabeth Baker, Frances Baker and Susannah Baker.

My will is that my three daughters shall have their choice of the three beds and furniture.

I give also to my [son] Samuel Baker one feather bed and furniture and he shall have 25 pounds current money to be raised out of my estate towards schooling and maintaining him.

My son William Baker shall have one cow and calf and two ewes and lambs.

All the rest of my estate shall be equally divided between my son Samuel Baker and my three daughters Elizabeth Baker, Frances Baker and Susannah Baker..

Samuel Dishman my whole and sole executor of this my last will and testament. In witness whereof I set my hand and seal this 21st day of January 1764.

Signed sealed and published in the presence of Butler Baker

John Weedon

Mary Davis

Esther Davis

At a court held for Westmoreland County the 26th day of June 1764 this last will and testament of Butler Baker, deceased was proved according to law by the oath of John Weedon, and Mary Davis witnesses thereto is ordered to be recorded and on the motion of Samuel Dishman the executor named in the same will who made oath according to law together with John Weedon, Jr., his security entered into and acknowledged bond which condition is law directs, certificate is granted him for obtaining a probate thereof in due form.

Test: James Davenport CCW

Page 268.

Goring & White to Blair Indenture

This indenture made the 14th day of June 1763 between William Goring, Goring White and Lettice White of the one part and James Blair of the other part. Witnesseth that William Goring, Goring White and Lettice White in consideration of 115 pounds current money to them has sold to James Blair a tract of land lying in Westmoreland County and Washington Parish containing by estimation 199 acres and bounded as follows; beginning at a marked red oak standing in the north side of the dam which spilleth out of Appomattox Creek extending thence, West 76 poles to a spanish oak standing on the north side of the said dam, thence South 3° West 52 poles to a marked white oak on the south side of the said dam, thence South 3° West 140 poles to a white oak corner tree of Randolph Davenport, thence southeast 80 poles to a spanish oak near the line of Robert Frank, thence North 58° East 67 poles to a Spanish Oak, thence North 87° East to a marked red Oak on the southwest side of the said dam thence North 15° East 60 one poles to a spanish oak standing in the said Frank's line, thence North 3° East 84 poles to a white oak standing on the East side of the said dam being near to the path called the Indian Path, thence North 65° West 64 poles to the beginning. In witness whereof the said William Goring, Goring White and Lettice White have hereunto set their hands and seals this 14th day of June 1763.

Signed sealed and delivered in presence of William Goring

Samuel Oldham Goring White

John Hurley Lettice White

William Berryman

Thomas Taylor

Page 270.

White's Wife to Blair Privy Examination

To Samuel Oldham, William Berryman and James Berryman, Gent. Whereas Goring White of the

County of Stafford and Lettice White his wife by their deed bearing date the 14th day of June 1763 have conveyed unto James Blair, Gent., Of the County of Westmoreland the fee simple estate of 199 acres of land in the Parish of Washington and County of Westmoreland and whereas the said Lettice White cannot conveniently travel to our court to make acknowledgment of the said conveyance therefore we do give you or any two of you power to receive the acknowledgment which she shall be willing to make. Witness James Davenport, clerk of our said court at the courthouse aforesaid the 14th day of June 1763.
At a Court held for Westmoreland County the 31st day of July 1763 this commission and the certificate of the execution thereof being returned are ordered to be recorded

Page 272.
Harding & Wife to Middleton Indenture
This indenture made the 31st day of July 1764 between Peter party of the Parish of Cople and County of Westmoreland and Mary Jeffries Harding his wife of the one part and Robert Middleton of the parish and county aforesaid of the other part. Witnesseth that whereas Thomas Walker grandfather to Mary Jeffries Harding, late of the Parish of Cople in the County of Westmoreland, deceased by virtue of a deed passed to him by Robert Middleton, late of the parish and county aforesaid, deceased dated the 25th day of August 1686 stood seized at his death of 150 acres of land and bounded as followeth; beginning at a red Oak by a path, being the corner and beginning tree of the said Robert Middleton, from thence extending South 32° East 20 poles to a corner red oak on a branch, from thence North 40° East 170 poles to a hickory corner tree of Richard Dunnahaugh [Dunahew], from thence South 75° East 48 poles to a red oak corner tree of the said Richard Dunnahaugh [Dunahew] in George Lamkin, from thence South 32° East 27 poles to a red Oak standing in the line of George Lamkin, from thence South 45° West bounding southeast on the land of Francis Clay, 232 poles to a red oak corner tree of the said Clay and Robert Middleton, from thence West 132 poles to a red oak standing in Robert Middleton's line, from thence along the said Middleton's line North 45° East 140 poles to the beginning tree which said 150 acres of land the said Thomas Walker gave and bequeath to his son Benjamin Walker, father to the said Mary Jeffries Harding as by his last will and testament dated the 27th day of January 1710, and that the said Benjamin Walker departed this life without making any will whereby the aforesaid 150 acres of land descended to the three daughters of Benjamin Walker; Seleashea Walker, Mary Jeffries Walker and Alice Walker as co-heirs. Now this indenture witnesseth that Peter Harding and Mary Jeffries Harding his wife in consideration of 40 pounds current money of Virginia has sold to Robert Middleton the said 150 acres of land. In witness whereof the parties aforesaid have to these presents interchangeably set their hands and seals the day and year above written.

Signed sealed and delivered in the presence of
George Simpson
George Rust
Henry Williams

Peter Harding
Mary Jeffries Harding (her mark)

At a Court held for Westmoreland County the 31st day of July 1764 this indenture of bargain and sale and receipt were acknowledged by Peter Harding and Mary Jeffries Harding his wife parties thereto and ordered to be recorded, previous to which, the said Mary Jeffries Harding being first privy examined as the law directs voluntarily relinquished her right of dower in the lands conveyed by the said indenture.

Page 275.
Eskridge to Eskridge Indenture
This indenture made this 25th day of June 1764 between Charles Eskridge and Hannah Eskridge his wife of the County of Loudoun and colony of Virginia of the one part and Samuel Eskridge of the County of Northumberland and colony of Virginia of the other part. Witnesseth that Charles Eskridge in consideration of the full sum and quantity of 280 pounds current money of Virginia has sold to Samuel Eskridge all that tract which the said Charles Eskridge hath in Westmoreland County in Yeocomico Neck which formerly belonged to Col. George Eskridge, deceased which he gave to his son Samuel Eskridge: deceased father to the said Charles Eskridge and on which Mrs. Jane Eskridge: mother to the said Charles Eskridge now lives on which said land or lands became

the right and property of the said Charles Eskridge by the death of his father the above said Samuel Eskridge who departed this life intestate which said lands is situated and bounded as followeth; beginning at a bridge near unto and adjoining the land of Capt. Peter Rust, deceased and Col. James Steptoe, deceased lands formerly Colemans which said bridge is over a branch falling into Yeocomico River being a corner to the said Charles Eskridge: Capt. Rust and Col. Steptoe, deceased and running from thence along the several watercourses and meanders of the said branch of Yeocomico River to or near the head of a cove called and known by the name of Self's Cove to the line of Capt. Peter Rust, deceased which he bought of the aforesaid Samuel Eskridge: deceased out of the aforesaid land of Col. George Eskridge, deceased and running from thence the meanders of the said cove to a marked red Oak, thence South 34° West 80 poles to a stake between three marked pine trees, thence 35° East to a pine on the head of a cove on the South West side of a plantation where William Allen formerly lived, thence down the said cove to the main Creek and running the meanders of the said Creek up towards Courtney's to a cove near the house of Robert Newberry, a tenement on the said court these land up to or near the head of the said cove and running from thence along a line of marked trees dividing the said land from James Courtney's land to Mr. George Rust's land and running thence along the said George Rust lines to the land and lines of Capt. Peter Rust, deceased and thence along said Capt. Peter Rust's lines to the beginning at or near the bridge; containing 280 acres. In witness whereof the said Charles Eskridge and Hannah Eskridge his wife have hereunto set their hands and seals the day and year above written.

Sealed and delivered in presence of — Charles Eskridge
Thomas Simpson — Hannah Eskridge
Robert Middleton
John Lewis
George Simpson
William Bailey
Matthew Neale
Robert Clarke

At a Court held for Westmoreland County 31st day of July 1764 this indenture and the receipt endorsed were proved by the oath of Robert Middleton, George Simpson and Matthew Neale witnesses thereto and ordered to be recorded. Teste

Page 277.

Butler to Butler Indenture

This indenture made the 30th day of July 1764 between Aaron Butler of the Parish of Washington and County of Westmoreland of the one part and Christopher Butler of the same parish and county of the other part. Witnesseth that Aaron Butler in consideration of a good and sufficient maintenance yearly and every year during the natural life of him to the value of 8 pounds to be paid by the said Christopher Butler each year as aforesaid has sold by these presents that tract or tenant of land with the appurtenances lying in the Parish of Washington and County of Westmoreland containing 101 acres it being part of a patent granted to Christopher Butler the elder for 600 acres now in the tenure or occupation of Thomas Finch and bounded on the lands of Daniel McCarty, George Payne and John Muse. In witness whereof the said parties to these presents have interchangeably set my hand and seal the day and year first above written.

Sealed and delivered in presence of — Aaron Butler (his mark)
Benjamin Weeks
Henry Williams
Benoney Williams
George Butler

At a Court held for Westmoreland County to 31st day of July 1764 this indenture and the memorandum endorsed were proved by the oath of Henry Williams: Benoney Williams and George Butler witnesses thereto and ordered to be recorded. Teste

Page 280.

Samuel Harrison's Will

In the name of God Amen, I Samuel Harrison of the County of Westmorland being sick of body but of sound and perfect memory do make this my last will and testament in manner and form following this 11th day of August 1763.

Imprimis, I give and bequeath to my son William Harrison all the land I live on that was ever in the possession of my father George Harrison with all improvements.

Item I give and bequeath to my son Jeremiah Harrison all the land I purchased of James Lane and Elizabeth Lane his wife with all improvements.

Item I give and bequeath to my daughter Ann Harrison the best feather bed in my estate except the double bed my wife and self commonly lye on and one good cow and calf to her disposal immediately after appraisement.

Item I give and bequeath to my daughter Hannah Harrison the next best bed and my will estate except as before excepted and one good cow and calf to be at her disposal immediately after my estate can be appraised.

Item I give unto My Lovely Wife Magdalene Harrison my double bed whereon we usually like together with the furniture thereunto belonging and further my will is said the furniture now used with the other two beds before mentioned shall go with and belong to the said two beds before given to my two daughters and further my will is that my son Jeremiah Harrison shall have his horse to his own immediate disposal and further my will is that my land and Negroes and James Cavinor and Sally Harper shall stay altogether until Dr. Nicholas Flood is paid the bond he has now against me and my will and desire is that my son Jeremiah Harrison's just accounts not including the present crop shall be accounted fully paid and satisfied by the legacy of land before mentioned to him and further my will is my whole estate together entire together with land orchards and all improvements to be applied to discharge my just debts by the profits that shall arise there from and further my will and desire is that my whole estate after my just debts are paid and legacies before mentioned complied with shall be equally divided between my loving wife and my four children.

Item I appoint ordain my two sons William Harrison and Jeremiah Harrison my sole and whole executors of this my last will and testament.

Signed and acknowledged in presence of Samuel Harrison
John Harrison
William Anderson
Thomas Walmoth (his mark)

At a court held for Westmoreland County the 31st day of July 1764 this last will and testament of Samuel Harrison, deceased was proved according to law by the oath of John Harrison and Thomas Walmoth, witnesses thereto and ordered to be recorded and on the motion of William Harrison and Jeremiah Harrison the executors named in the said will who made all according to law and together with Daniel Tebbs and Matthew Lamkin their securities entered into and acknowledged bond with condition as the law directs, certificate is granted them for obtaining a probate thereof in due form.
Teste

Page 281.
Anne Davis Will

In the name of God Amen, I Anne Davis of Westmoreland County in the Parish of Washington am weak in body but in perfect sound sense and memory do make this my last will and testament in the following manner.

I bequeath my negro woman Nell to my sister Esther Davis.

I bequeath my negro man Dick to my sister Katherine Davis.

I leave all the rest of my estate to Mary Davis be it whatsoever and appoint Butler Baker and Mary Davis my executors to this my last will and testament. In witness whereof I set my hand and seal this 9th day of January 1764.

Signed sealed published and delivered in the presence of Anne Davis (her mark)
John Weedon
Rebecca Weedon (her mark)
Butler Baker
Mildred Weedon (her mark)

At a court held for Westmoreland County the 28th day of August 1764 this last will and testament of

Anne Davis deceased was proved according to law by the oaths of John Weedon and Rebecca Weedon witnesses thereto and ordered to be recorded, and on the motion of Mary Davis the executrix named in the said will, who made oath according to law, and together with Thomas Taylor and John Weedon, her securities entered into and acknowledged bond with condition as the law directs, certificate is granted her for obtaining a probate thereof in due form. Teste

Page 283.

John Omohundro's Will

In the name of God Amen, I John Omohundro of Cople Parish in the County of Westmoreland, planter being weak of body but of sound sense and perfect memory do make and ordain and declare this to be my last will and testament in manner and form following.

I will that my body have Christian and decent burial at the plantation I now live.

Item I will that all my just debts be truly paid and as for my worldly goods I give and bequeath together with my lands as follows.

Item I give to my son Thomas Omohundro and his heirs forever the plantation whereon I now live to the swamp on the south side, also my still with everything belonging to it, and one cow and calf.

Item I give to my son William Omohundro and his heirs all my land on the north side of the swamp being part of the land whereon I now live and 1000 boards off the land that I have given to my son Thomas Omohundro.

Item I give to my son William Omohundro Negro boy Isaac, one calf, and one bed and furniture.

Item I give to my son John Omohundro two Negroes, Phillis and her increase and Frederick.

Item I give to my son Richard Omohundro, Negro James.

Item [I give to my] son in law Joseph Taylor, one shilling sterling.

Item I give to my daughter Jemima Weaver and her heirs Negro girl Sarah and her increase, one cow and calf, and one bed and furniture.

Item I lend to my daughter Elizabeth Davis: Negro man Harry during her natural life and after her decease to my grandson Jesse Davis.

It is my will and desire that my son John Omohundro shall have the use of all the negroes now on the plantation with me and the crops of tobacco and corn that shall be by then made on the said plantation for the present year and also all the corn and meat which I have laid in for this year's provision.

I do give unto my son Richard Omohundro the sum of five pounds current money to be paid him out of my estate on or before the 25th day of December next.

I give and bequeath all my estate not before given to be equally divided among my six children, Thomas Omohundro: William Omohundro: John Omohundro, Richard Omohundro, Elizabeth Davis: and Jemima Weaver.

Lastly, I constitute and appoint my two sons John Omohundro and Richard Omohundro, executors of this my last will and testament. In witness whereof I have hereunto set my hand affixed my seal this 16th of January 1765.

Signed sealed and published in the presence of us John Omohundro (his mark)

Thomas Chilton, Jr.
William Sanders
William Jenkins

At a court held for Westmoreland County the 26th day of February 1765 this las will and testament of John Omohundro, deceased was proved according to law by the oaths of William Sanders and William Jenkins witnesses thereto and ordered to be recorded and on the motion of John Omohundro and Richard Omohundro the executors named in the said will who made oath according to law and together with Richard Jenkins and William Jenkins their securities entered into and acknowledged bond with condition as the law directs, certificate is granted them for obtaining a probate thereof in due form. Teste

Page 285.

Triplett to Campbell Indenture

This Indenture made the 26th day of November 1764 between John Triplett of the parish of Hanover and County of King George, Gent., of the one part and Archibald Campbell of the Parish of

Washington and County of Westmoreland, clerk of the other part. Witnesseth that John Triplett in consideration of 25 pounds current money of Virginia has sold to Archibald Campbell in the Parish of Washington and County of Westmoreland containing 76 acres, 3 rods and 6 perches and bounded as follows; beginning at a marked red oak standing on the East side of the main road not far above the place where the road forks sending forth a road to the head of Mattox and running from thence along the meanders or turnings of the said main road which leads down to Mattox Bridge the several courses and distances following to wit;
South 7° East 14 poles thence
South 37° 30' East 10 poles, then
South 40° 15' East 24 poles, then
South 29° East 30 poles, then
South 43° East 14 poles, then
South 61° 30' East 34 poles, then
South 49° East 16 poles, then
South 57° East 44 poles, then
South 46° East 36 poles, then
South 36° 30' East 54 poles, then
South 57° East 40 poles, then
South 64° 30' East 8 poles, to a marked stooping red oak sapling, on the East edge of the road, then leaving the road and running through the woods
North 3° 20' West 82 poles to a scrubby red oak sapling corner to Mrs. Rachel Monroe's land and from thence to the beginning.
In witness and whereof the said John Triplett hath hereunto set his hand and seal the day and year above mentioned.
Signed sealed and delivered in presence of John Triplett
Daniel Fitzhugh
John Martin
John Monroe
John Bulger
Lawrence Washington
John Watts
William Nelson
At a court held for Westmoreland County the 26th day of February 1765, this indenture and the receipt endorsed were proved by the oaths of Daniel Fitzhugh, John Watts and William Nelson witnesses thereto and ordered to be recorded. Teste

Page 287.
Rust to Cox Indenture
This indenture made this 14th day of February 1765 between Samuel Rust of Cople Parish and Westmoreland County of the one part and Fleet Cox of the same parish and county of the other part. Witnesseth that Samuel Rust in consideration of 250 pounds current money of Virginia has sold to unto Fleet Cox that tract of land whereon my son Peter Rust now lives containing 250 acres and is bounded as followeth; bounded on the land of Samuel Walker, Magdalen Jackson, Michael Gilbert and James Lamkin and on the head of John Smith's mill pond to Walker's land. In witness whereof the parties to these presents have interchangeably set their hands and seals the day and year first above written.
Signed sealed and delivered in the presence of Samuel Rust
George Haborn
Peter Rust
William Morton
John Nicholas
John Alverson (his mark)
At a court held for Westmoreland County the 26th day of February 1765, this indenture together with the memorandum of livery of seizen and receipt endorsed was acknowledged by Samuel Rust party thereto and ordered to be recorded. Teste

Page 290.
Eskridge to Rust Indenture
This indenture made the 11th day of February 1765 between Samuel Eskridge and Mary Eskridge his wife of the county of Northumberland and colony of Virginia of the one part and Samuel Rust of the County of Westmoreland and said colony of the other part. Witnesseth that Samuel Eskridge and Mary Eskridge his wife in consideration of 400 pounds current money of Virginia has sold to Samuel Rust all those tracts together with all houses orchards woods and appurtenances thereunto belonging which the said Samuel Eskridge bought of Charles Eskridge lying in Yeocomico Neck in the County of Westmoreland, formerly belonging to Col. George Eskridge, deceased, which said lands he give to his son Samuel Eskridge, deceased, father to the said Charles Eskridge and on which Mrs. Jane Eskridge, mother to the said Charles Eskridge now lives on. Which said land or lands became the right and property of the said Charles Eskridge by the death of his father the above said Samuel Eskridge who departed this life intestate which said lands is situated and bounded as followeth; beginning at a bridge near unto and adjoining the land of Capt. Peter Rust, deceased and Col. James Steptoe, deceased lands formerly Colemans which said bridge is over a branch falling into Yeocomico River being a corner to the said Charles Eskridge, Capt. Rust and Col. Steptoe, deceased and running from thence along the several watercourses and meanders of the said branch of Yeocomico River to or near the head of a cove called and known by the name of Self's Cove to the line of Capt. Peter Rust, deceased which he bought of the aforesaid Samuel Eskridge: deceased out of the aforesaid land of Col. George Eskridge, deceased and running from thence the meanders of the said cove to a marked red oak, thence South 34° West 80 poles to a stake between three marked pine trees, thence 35° East to a pine on the head of a cove on the South West side of a plantation where William Allen formerly lived, thence down the said cove to the main creek and running the meanders of the said creek up towards Courtney's to a cove near the house of Robert Newberry, a tenant on the said land, thence up to or near the head of the said cove and running from thence along a line of marked trees dividing the said land from James Courtney's land to Mr. George Rust's land and running thence along the said George Rust lines to the land and lines of Capt. Peter Rust, deceased and thence along said Capt. Peter Rust's lines to the beginning at or near the bridge; containing 280 acres. In witness whereof the said Samuel Eskridge and Mary Eskridge his wife have hereunto set their hands and seals the day and year above written.
Signed sealed and delivered in the presence of — Samuel Eskridge
Davis Boyd — Mary Eskridge
John Ballantine [Ballendine]
George Simpson
Fleet Cox
Presley Hall

Page 293.
Eskridge's Wife to Rust Privy Examination and Release
To John Foushee, Charles Fallen [Fallin] and George Payne, Gent. Whereas Samuel Eskridge and Mary Eskridge by their indenture of bargain and sale bearing date the 11th day of February 1765 have sold and conveyed unto Samuel Rust the fee simple estate of 280 acres lying in the Parish of Cople and County of Westmoreland and whereas the said Mary Eskridge cannot conveniently travel to our court to make acknowledgement of the said conveyance, therefore we do give unto you or any two or more of you power to receive the acknowledgement which the said Mary Eskridge shall be willing to make. Witness James Davenport, clerk of our said court the 16th day of February in the 5th year of our reign.
Pursuant to the within condition to us directed met on Saturday the 23rd of February 1765 and examined Mary Eskridge wife of Samuel Eskridge who declared that she was willing and desirous the deed signed and passed from Samuel Eskridge and Mary Eskridge his wife to Samuel Rust should be recorded and that she did it without any threats of her husband. Given under our hands and seals the day and year first above written.
John Foushee

Charles Fallen
At a court held for Westmoreland County the 26th day of February 1765, this indenture together with the receipt endorsed were proved by the oaths of David Boyd, John Ballantine and Fleet Cox witnesses thereto and together with the commission annex for taking the acknowledgement and privy examination of Mary Eskridge wife of Samuel Eskridge and certificate of the execution thereof and ordered to be recorded. Teste

Page 294.
Gray to Monroe Indenture
This indenture made the 25th day of September 1764, between George Gray and Mary Gray his wife of the parish of St. Paul in the county of Stafford and Francis Gray of the Parish of Washington and parish of Westmoreland of the one part and Spence Monroe of the Parish of Washington and County of Westmoreland of the other part. Witnesseth that George Gray and Mary Gray his wife and Francis Gray in consideration 100 pounds current money of Virginia has sold to Spence Monroe all that tract being in the Parish of Washington and County of Westmoreland containing 100 acres being formerly possessed by Nathaniel Gray, father to the said George Gray and Francis Gray and by him conveyed to Job Sims by deed of exchange dated the 21st day of June 1735 and by Sims conveyed to George Gray by deed of sale, and which said land being recovered of the said George Gray by Francis Gray by ejectment brought against Spence Monroe tenant on the premises in the county court of Westmoreland on the 1st day of September 1763, and lying on the upper side of Monroe's Creek and now occupied by the said Spence Monroe and bounded as followeth; beginning on a point between two guts at the said creek at a marked persimmon two black oaks and a white oak on the line of Andrew Monroe, Sr., Gent., thence N.W. 300 pole along the said Monroe's line, thence
South 16 ½ ° West to Vivion's line, thence
South 27 ½ ° East 75 pole, thence
South 51 ½ ° East 49 pole, to the line of Spence Monroe's, thence bounded by the said Monroe to the line of Francis Gray and now in the tenure and occupied by John Boddington and bounded by the said Gray's line to the beginning.
In witness whereof the said George Gray, Mary Gray his wife and Francis Gray have hereunto set their hands and seals this 25th day of September 1764.
Signed sealed and delivered in the presence of — George Gray
James Bankhead — Francis Gray
Lovell Harrison
Charles Tyler
Lovell Massey
Nathaniel Gray
At a court held for Westmoreland County the 26th day of February 1765 this indenture together with a memorandum of livery of seizen and receipt thereon endorsed were proved by the oath of Lovell Harrison: Lovell Massey and Nathaniel Gray, witnesses thereto and ordered to be recorded. Teste

Page 298.
Gray to Monroe Indenture
this indenture made the 25th day of September 1764 between Francis Gray of the Parish of Washington in the County of Westmoreland, planter of the one part and Spence Monroe of the parish and county aforesaid, cabinetmaker of the other part. Witnesseth that Francis Gray in consideration of 100 pounds current money of Virginia has sold to Spence Monroe all that tract of land with the appurtenances lying in the Parish of Washington and County of Westmoreland containing 100 acres which's land being formerly possessed by Nathaniel Gray, father to the said Francis Gray, and by him conveyed to Job Sims by deeds of exchange dated 21st of June 1735 and by the said Simms conveyed to John Muse by deeds of lease and release bearing date the 28th and 29th of April 1745, which said land being recovered of John Muse by Francis Gray by ejectment in the County Court of Westmorland on the first day of September 1763 and lying on the upper side of Monroe's Creek and now in the tenure and occupation of John Boddington and bounded as followeth; beginning at a hickory near the creek aforesaid standing in the line that divides this land

from the land of Spence Monroe the party to this deed, running
North 72° West 47 poles and 19 links to a cedar, thence
North 10° East 54 poles 10 links to a large red Oak marked, thence
North 12° West 36 poles to a willow oak in a branch, thence running the several meanders of the said branch 153 poles to a large Spanish Oak marked which stands near the middle of the branch, thence
North 56° East 10 pole to a marked sweet gum, thence
North 53° East 28 pole to a marked white oak, thence
North 82° East 27 pole to a marked red oak, thence
North 81° East 8 pole 15 links to a red oak marked, thence
South 56° East 22 pole to a gum marked, thence
South 55° East 33 pole to a red oak marked at the head of a gully, thence
North 76° East 26 pole to the head of a gut, thence
South 64 E. to the creek, thence along the meanders of the said creek to the beginning.
In witness whereof the said Francis Gray has hereunto set his hand and seal this day 25th [blank] 1764.
Signed sealed and delivered in presence of Francis Gray
James Bankhead
Lovell Harrison
Charles Tyler
Lovell Massey
Nathaniel Gray
At a Court held for Westmoreland County the 26th day of February 1765 this indenture together with a memorandum of livery of seizen and receipt thereon endorsed were proved by the oath of Lovell Harrison: Lovell Massey and Nathaniel Gray witnesses thereto and ordered to be recorded. Teste

Page 301.
<u>Smith to Smith Indenture</u>
This indenture made the 20th day of December 1764 between Sarah Smith: Samuel Smith and John Smith the County of Westmoreland of the one part and Joseph Smith the said County of the other part. Whereas Joseph Smith, late of the County of Westmoreland, planter being seized and possessed of a tract of land in the said county and Parish of Washington and of sundry slaves and other personal estate be his last will and testament in therein did devise to his wife the said Sarah Smith during her widowhood his whole estate both real and personal and upon her intermarriage or death did direct that his son Samuel Smith should have his Negro boy Roger, his son Gideon Smith his Negro girl Will and her increase in after some other specific devises did direct that the residue of his estate should be equally divided between his sons Joseph Smith, Samuel Smith and Gideon Smith, and whereas the said Samuel Smith and Gideon Smith have received the two Negroes, Roger and Moll specifically devised to them in the will of their father in the said Sarah Smith their mother having contracted debts to a considerable amount in the maintenance and education of the said Joseph Smith Samuel Smith and Gideon Smith for the payment whereof or for the greatest part of them, the said Joseph Smith Samuel Smith and Gideon Smith have become securities which debts amount to the value of the residue of the estate of the said Joseph Smith the testator and whereas the said Joseph Smith, party to these presents at the request of the said Sarah Smith Samuel Smith and Gideon Smith has undertaken to pay and satisfy all sums of money due and owing from the said Sarah Smith is well those for which the said Samuel Smith and Gideon Smith are bounded securities as any other contracted by her. This indenture therefore witnesseth that in consideration thereof in the sum of five shillings to them in hand they the said Sarah Smith: Samuel Smith and Gideon Smith have in each of them hath granted bargained and sold by these presents unto the said Joseph Smith all their right title interest in property and that said tract of land, slaves and other personal state which they or either of them hath or may have, except their right and title to the said two Negroes, Roger and Moll and Jack son of Moll delivered to the said Samuel Smith and Gideon Smith as aforesaid. In witness whereof the said Sarah Smith Samuel Smith and Gideon Smith have hereunto set their hands and seals the day and year above mentioned.
Signed sealed and delivered in presence of us Sarah Smith

William Bernard
John Ashton
William Nelson
Samuel Smith
Gideon Smith

At a Court held for Westmoreland County the 26th day February 1765 this indenture was proved by the oaths of William Bernard, John Ashton and William Nelson the witnesses thereto and ordered to be recorded. Teste

Page 303.
Mary White Will

In the name of God Amen, I Mary White of Westmoreland County being sick and weak of body but of sound mind and memory do make and ordain this to be my last will and testament in manner and form following.
Item I give and bequeath unto my granddaughter Anne Porter one seal skin trunk and a Bible.
Item I give and bequeath unto my daughter Sarah Russell, Negro boy Joe during her life and after to return to my granddaughter Mary White daughter of Philip White.
Item I give and bequeath unto my son George White, Negro woman Alice.
Item I give and bequeath unto my granddaughter Mary White, daughter of Philip White 14 pounds current money to be raised out of my movable estate.
Item I appoint in constitute my friend Griffin Garland by executor, I also give him 6 pounds current money.
I desire that the rest of my estate if there be any, be divided between my daughter Anne Walker and my granddaughter Elizabeth Reynolds.
Given under my hand and seal this 20th day of October 1764.
Anne Davis (her mark)
Joanne Davis (her mark)
Mary White (her mark)

At a court held for Westmoreland County the 26th day of February 1765 this will was proved according to law by the oath of William Rochester and Anne Davis witnesses thereto and ordered to be recorded and on the motion of Griffin Garland the executor therein named who made oath according to law and together with Richard Parker and John Rust his securities entered into and acknowledged bond with conditioned as the law directs, certificate is granted him for obtaining a probate thereof in due form. Teste

Page 304.
Moxley to Moxley Deed of Gift

To all people to whom these presents shall come we Daniel Moxley and John Weaver do send greeting. Now know ye that we that Daniel Moxley and John Weaver of the Parish of Cople in the County of Westmoreland in consideration of the love good will and affection which we have and do bear towards their nephew Joseph Moxley: Jr., son of Joseph Moxley: Sr., of the Parish of Cople and County of Westmorland aforesaid have given to Joseph Moxley: Jr., after our deaths all our right to a still and worm which we the said Daniel Moxley, John Weaver and Joseph Moxley: Sr., bought in partnership of Adam Weaver the County of Westmoreland. In witness whereof we have hereunto set our hands and seals this 20th day of August 1764.
Signed sealed and delivered by the presence of us
Alexander Spark
Augustine Sanford
Daniel Moxley
John Weaver
Joseph Moxley

At a court held for Westmoreland County the 26th day of February 1765 this deed of gift was proved by the oath of Alexander Spark and Augustine Sanford the witnesses thereto and ordered to be recorded. Teste

Page 304.
Moxley to Sandford Deed of Gift

Know all men by these presents that I John Moxley of the Parish of Cople in the County of Westmoreland, planter's do give and grant unto my daughter Elenor Sanford for the natural love and affection I have been doth bear to her, Negro man Tom to her and her heirs forever only reserving my own natural life in the above Negro. As witness my hand and seal this 25th day of

February 1765
Signed sealed and delivered in the presence of us John Moxley (his mark)
Thomas Butler
At a court held for Westmoreland County the 26th day of February 1765 this deed of gift was acknowledged by John Moxley party thereto and ordered to be recorded. Teste

Page 306.
John Finch's Will
In the name of God Amen, I John Finch the County of Westmoreland being weak and sickly of body but in perfect sense and sound memory do make and ordain this my last will and testament in manner and form following.
Item I give and bequeath to my brother Nicholas Muse my silver watch and my silver shoe buckles in the buckles.
Item I give and bequeath to my sister Mary Randall 5 pounds current money to be paid her after this will is proved.
Item all the rest of my estate herein not given or otherwise bequeath it is my will and desire that it shall be equally divided between my brother Nicholas Muse and my two sisters Mary Randall and Ann Muse.
Confirmation whereof I have hereunto set my hand and seal the second day of January 1765.
Signed sealed and delivered in the presence of us John Finch
N.B. I appoint and ordain my brother Nicholas Muse and brother-in-law Thomas Randall whole and sole executors of this my last will and testament.
Augustine Sanford
Henrietta Sanford
Robert Sanford
At a court held for Westmoreland County the 26th day of February 1765 this will was proved according to law by the oath of Augustine Sanford and Henrietta Sanford: witnesses thereto and ordered to be recorded and on the motion of Nicholas Muse and Thomas Randall the executors therein named who made oath according to law and together with Nicholas Muse: Sr., their security entered into and acknowledged bond with condition as the law directs, certificate is granted them for obtaining a probate thereof in due form. Teste

Page 307.
Roe to Weeks Lease
This indenture made this 21st day of August 1764 between Henry Roe of the Parish of Washington and County of Westmoreland of the one part and Benjamin Weeks of the same parish and county of the other part. Witnesseth that Henry Roe in consideration of 10 pounds current money has sold to Benjamin Weeks all that tenement, plantation in tract of land lying in Westmoreland County containing 150 acres it being whereon Bunch Roe, the elder lived and now in the possession of George Johnston as tenant to the said Henry Roe. To have and to hold the said tract of land for and during the term of four years to commence on the first day of January next. In witness whereof I have to these presents set my hand and seal the day and year above written.
Signed sealed and delivered in presence of us Henry Roe
Nicholas Muse
Charles Weeks
John Bartlett
Jonathan Green (his mark)
At a court held for Westmoreland County the 26th day of March 1765 this indenture of lease was proved by the oath of Nicholas Muse: Charles Weeks and Jonathan Green witnesses thereto and ordered to be recorded. Teste

Page 308.
John Hilton's Will
In the name of God Amen, I John Hilton of Westmoreland County in the Parish of Washington being sick and weak in body but perfect sense and memory do make ordain constitute this to be my

last will and testament in manner and form.
I give and bequeath unto my son William Hilton by land and plantation to him and his heirs forever
I give unto my daughter Elizabeth Hilton 30 pounds cash to be paid to her at the day of her marriage or age of 21 years. If she is not married before that time my will and desire is that my wife shall have the use of the one-half personal estate widowhood then my will and desire is that all the rest of my estate of any kind whatsoever be equally divided between my son William Hilton and my two daughters Mary Hilton and Elizabeth Hilton.
I appoint my son William Hilton and John Weedon to be my executors to this my last will and testament. In witness whereof I set my hand and seal this 24th day of September 1764.
Signed sealed and acknowledged and published in presence of John Hilton
Jonathan Hilton
William Briggs
Judith Briggs
At a court held for Westmoreland County the 28th day of May 1765 this will was proved according to law by the oath of William Briggs a witness thereto and at a court held for the said County the 26th day of March last past the said will was proved by the oath of Jonathan Hilton one other witness thereto and ordered to be recorded and on the motion of William Hilton one of the executors named in the said will who made oaths according to law and together with Thomas Taylor his security entered into and acknowledged bond with condition as the law directs, certificate is granted him for obtaining a probate thereof in due form. Teste

Page 309.
Walker to Flood Indenture
This indenture made the 28th day of October 1764 between William Walker of the Parish of Cople and County of Westmoreland of the one part and William Flood, Gent., of same parish and county of the other part. Witnesseth that William Walker in consideration of 60 pounds current money of Virginia has sold to William Flood a tract of land lying in the County of Westmoreland and Parish of Cople containing 92 acres, bounded on the south by the land of John Short, on the west by the land of William Baley, on the north by the land of the said Flood and on the east by Yeocomico River. In witness whereof the parties to these presents have interchangeably set their hands and affixed their seals the day month and year above written.
Signed sealed and delivered in presence of William Walker
Mary Stone
James Knott
William Garrett (his mark)
Willoughby Newton
John Newton
To Willoughby Newton, John Newton and Thomas Chilton, Gent., Whereas William Walker by his indenture of bargain and sale bearing date the 28th day of September 1764 has sold and conveyed unto William Flood, Gent., The fee simple estate of 92 acres of land with the appurtenances, lying in the Parish of Cople in the County of Westmoreland and whereas Eleanor Walker wife to William Walker cannot conveniently travel to record of Westmoreland to make acknowledgment of the conveyance. Therefore, we do give unto you or any two of you power to receive the acknowledgment which the said Eleanor Walker shall be willing to make. Witness James Davenport, clerk of our said court the 14th day of November in the fifth year of our reign.
Westmoreland Sct. Pursuant to the above commission hereunto annexed we have examined Eleanor Walker the wife of William Walker separate from her husband concerning her acknowledgment of the deed passed by the said William Walker to Dr. William Flood for 92 acres of land which deed is also annexed which said deed she acknowledged and is desirous should be recorded. Given under our hands and seals the 17 November 1764.
Willoughby Newton
John Newton
To Willoughby Newton, John Newton and Thomas Chilton, Gent., Whereas William Walker by his indenture of bargain and sale bearing date the 28th day of September 1764 has sold and conveyed unto William Flood, Gent., The fee simple estate of 92 acres of land with the appurtenances, lying

in the Parish of Cople in the County of Westmoreland and whereas Anne Walker mother to William Walker cannot conveniently travel to record of Westmoreland to make acknowledgment of the conveyance. Therefore, we do give unto you or any two of you power to receive the acknowledgment which the said Ann Walker shall be willing to make. Witness James Davenport, clerk of our said court the 14th day of November in the fifth year of our reign.
Westmoreland Sct. Pursuant to the above commission hereunto annexed we have examined Anne Walker the mother of William Walker separate from her son concerning her acknowledgment of the deed passed by the said William Walker her son to Dr. William Flood for 92 acres of land which deed is also annexed which said deed she acknowledged and is desirous should be recorded. Given under our hands and seals the 17 November 1764.
Willoughby Newton
John Newton
At a Court held for Westmoreland County the 28th day of May 1765 this indenture in the receipt thereon endorsed were proved by the oaths of James Knott, Willoughby Newton in John Newton witnesses thereto and together with the commissions annexed for taking the acknowledgments and privy examinations of Eleanor Walker the wife and Anne Walker: mother of the said William Walker and the certificates of the execution thereof ordered to be recorded. Test

Page 314.
Lovell Massey's Will
In the name of God Amen, I Lovell Massey: Sr., of Westmoreland Co. and Parish of Washington being sick and weak do make this my last will and testament in manner and form as followeth.
Item I leave the use and occupation of my dwelling plantation to my loving wife Martha Massey during her widowhood and in case of her death or marriage, to my son Lovell Massey to the heirs of his body and for want of such heirs to my son James Massey in the lawful heirs of his body and for want of such heirs to my daughter Judith Massey and the heirs of her body and for want of such heirs to my daughter Mildred Massey.
Item I leave to my loving wife the use of Negroes Sam and Bess during her widowhood and in case of her marriage or death to my son James Massey.
Item I leave to my daughter Frances Spilman, Negro man Will to use him as her own during her natural life and after her decease to my daughter Judith Massey and the heirs of her body and for want of such heirs to my daughter Mildred Massey and her lawful heirs.
Item I give to my son Robert Massey 3 cows and calves, 8 head of sheep, and one breeding sow.
Item I give to my daughter Judith Massey my best bed and furniture (except that which my wife lies on) and 5 pounds cash with lawful interest till paid.
Item I give to my daughter Mildred my next best bed and furniture and 5 pounds cash with interest till paid.
Item I give to my son James Massey my young mare, my own riding saddle and bridle.
Item it is my will and desire that all my estate not before given wife's death or marriage be equally divided between my two sons Lovell Massey and James Massey.
Item I do constitute and appoint my loving wife Martha Massey my whole and sole executrix of this my last will and testament. In witness whereof I have hereunto set my hand and seal this third day of June 1764
Signed sealed and acknowledged in presence of us Lovell Massey (his mark)
Lovell Harrison
John Degge
James Degge
William Brown
At a court held for Westmoreland County the 28th day of May 1765 this will was proved according to law by the oaths of John Degge and James Degge: witnesses thereto and ordered to be recorded and on motion of Martha Massey: widow and executrix named in the same will who made oath according to law and together with James Degge and Spence Monroe her securities entered into and acknowledged bond with conditioned as the law directs, certificate is granted for obtaining a probate thereof in due form. Teste

Page 315.

Marye & Wife to Redman Lease

This indenture made the 13th day of October 1764 between James Marye of the Parish of St. Thomas in the County of Orange and Sarah Marye of the one part and Solomon Redman the Parish of Cople and County of Westmoreland, millwright of the other part. Whereas Robert Vaulx, late of the Parish of Washington and the County aforesaid, Gent., deceased did by his last will and testament bearing date the [blank] in the year 1750 [sic 8 Aug. 1754] did give and devise unto his two daughters Betty Vaulx and Sarah Vaulx his water grist mill lying on the main branch of Rappahannock Creek being near the dividing line of the Parish of Cople and the Parish of Washington in the County aforesaid. And whereas the said Sarah Vaulx has intermarried with the said James Marye. Now this indenture witnesseth that James Marye and Sarah Marye his wife in consideration of five shillings current money has sold unto Solomon Redman one moiety or half of the water grist mill aforesaid with all and singular the appurtenances to the same. To have and to hold the said moiety from the date next before the date of the date of these presence until the full-term of one whole year from thence next ensuing yielding and paying the rent of one pepper corn upon the feast day of Saint Michael the Archangel to the intent and purpose that by virtue of these presents and of the statute for transferring uses into possessions the said Solomon Redman may be in actual possession of the said moiety or half part of the water grist mill and be thereby enabled to accept and take a grant and release of the reversion and inheritance thereof. In witness whereof the parties to these presents have hereunto set their hands and seals the day and year first above written.

Signed sealed and delivered in presence of us — James Marye
Edward Ransdell — Sarah Marye
Edward Ransdell, Jr.
Richard Neale

At a Court held for Westmoreland County the 28th day of May 1765 this indenture of lease was proved by the oath of Edward Ransdell, Edward Ransdell, Jr., and Richard Neale the witnesses thereto and ordered to be recorded. Teste

Page 317.

Marye & Wife to Redman Privy Examination and Release

This indenture made the 24th day of September 1764 between James Marye of the Parish of St. Thomas in the County of Orange and Sarah Marye of the one part and Solomon Redman of the Parish of Cople and County of Westmoreland, millwright of the other part. Whereas Robert Vaulx, late of the Parish of Washington in the County aforesaid, Gent., deceased did by his last will and testament bearing date the 30th day of October 1764 [sic 8 Aug. 1754] did give and devise unto his two daughters Betty Vaulx and Sarah Vaulx his water grist mill lying on the main branch of Rappahannock Creek being near the dividing line of the Parish of Cople and the Parish of Washington in the County aforesaid. And whereas the said Sarah Vaulx has intermarried with the said James Marye. Now this indenture witnesseth that James Marye and Sarah Marye his wife in consideration of 60 pounds current money of Virginia has sold unto Solomon Redman in his actual possession now being by virtue of a bargain and sale by indenture bearing date the day next before the day of the date of the said indenture and by force of the statute for transferring uses into possession one moiety or half part of the water grist mill aforesaid with all and singular the appurtenances to the same.

In witness whereof the parties to these presents have hereunto set their hands and seals the day and year first above written.

Signed sealed and delivered in presence of us — James Marye
Edward Ransdell — Sarah Marye
Edward Ransdell, Jr.
Richard Neale

At a Court held for Westmoreland County the 28th day of May 1765 this indenture of lease was proved by the oath of Edward Ransdell, Edward Ransdell, Jr., and Richard Neale the witnesses thereto and ordered to be recorded. Teste

To Willoughby Newton, John Newton and John Augustine Washington, Justices of the Peace for

the County of Westmoreland in the colony of Virginia, Gent. Whereas James Marye and Sarah Marye by their indenture of bargain and sale bearing date the 30th day of October last past has sold and conveyed unto Solomon Redman the fee simple estate of half a water grist mill lying in the Parish of Cople in the County of Westmoreland and whereas the said Sarah Marye cannot conveniently travel to her court to make acknowledgment of the conveyance. Therefore, we do give unto you or any two of you power to receive the acknowledgment which the said Sarah be willing to make. Witness James Davenport, clerk of our said court the 10th day of November 1764.
Westmoreland Sct. In obedience to the above commission to us directed we the subscribers did attend on the above-named Sarah Marye and presented to her the indentures therein mentioned and the said Sarah saith that she doth freely and voluntarily acknowledge and transfer her right and title to the half of the said mill therein mentioned without any compulsion or persuasion of her husband. Certified under our hands this 11th day of November 1764.
Willoughby Newton
John Newton
At a court held for Westmoreland County the 28th day of May 1765 this indenture was proved by the oaths of Edward Ransdell, Edward Ransdell, Jr., and Richard Neale the witnesses thereto and together with the commission annexed for taking the acknowledgment and privy examination of Sarah Marye the wife of James Marye in the certificate of the execution thereof ordered to be recorded. Teste

Page 321.
Eskridge's Wife to Eskridge Privy Examination
To Fielding Turner, William Carr Lane and James Lane: Gentleman. Whereas Charles Eskridge and Hannah Eskridge his wife by their indenture of bargain and sale bearing date the 25th day of June 1764, have sold and conveyed unto Samuel Eskridge the fee simple estate of 280 acres of land with the appurtenances lying in the Parish of Cople in the County of Westmoreland and whereas the said Hannah Eskridge cannot conveniently travel to our court of Westmoreland County to make acknowledgement of the conveyance. Therefore, we do give unto your or any two or more of you power to receive the acknowledgement which the said Hannah Eskridge shall be willing to make. Witness James Davenport, clerk of our said court the 3rd day of October 1764.
Loudoun Sct. In obedience to the commission hereunto annexed, we the subscribers hath examined Hannah Eskridge: the wife of Charles Eskridge concerning her willingness of the sale of a tract of land in Westmoreland County as per indenture of feoffment bearing date June 25th, 1764, passed by Charles Eskridge and Hannah his wife to Samuel Eskridge: and she saith that she agreed to the sale of the said land without persuasions or threats of her said husband and that she is willing and desirous that the said deed should be recorded. Given under our hands and seals this 9th day of October 1764.
Fielding Turner
William Carr Lane
At a court held for Westmoreland County the 28th day of May, this commission for the privy examination of Hannah Eskridge the wife of Charles Eskridge and a certificate of the execution thereof being returned was ordered to be recorded. Teste

Page 323.
Corbin to Corbin Deed of Gift
To all to whom these presents shall come be it known that I Hannah Corbin, widow of the Parish of Cople in the County of Westmoreland in consideration of the natural love and affection which I have for my well beloved son Elisha Hall Corbin and for divers other good causes and considerations have given and granted and by these presents do give and grant the Negro slaves following: Phil, Cyrus, Ben, Lucey, Molley, Letty, Betty, Hannah, Nance, Alce, Lucy and Betty, together with their several increase; in manner as is hereafter set forth. That is to say, to my son Elisha Hall Corbin and heirs if he should arrive to the age of 21 years which will happen on the 26th day of March 1784, and if it should happen that I should depart this life before that time and my son should be living then he should immediately possess them after my decease. But if he should die under age then the said Negroes to be subject to such disposition as I shall make thereof to my last will and

testament. In witness whereof I have hereunto set my hand and seal this 29th day of May 1764.
John Montgomery
Jacob Allison (his mark)
At a court continued and held for Westmoreland County the 29th day of May 1765, this deed of gift was proved by the oaths of John Montgomery and Jacob Allison the witnesses thereto and ordered to be recorded. Teste.

Page 324.
White to Porter Lease
This Indenture made the 5th day of November 1764 between George White of the county of Lunenburg, late of the County of Westmoreland on the one part and William Porter, Jr., of the County of Westmoreland on the other part. Witnesseth that George White in consideration of the rents and covenants on the part of William Porter to be paid and performed hath granted and to farm let by these presents 100 acres of land with appurtenances lying in the County of Westmoreland and Parish of Cople on the head branches of Monacan Run and bounded as followeth: beginning at a marked white oak standing on the westward side of Edward Porter's plantation extending thence South West 147 poles to a marked white [oak] standing in a branch, thence North West 109 pole to a marked white oak standing near Payton's line, thence North East 147 pole to a marked red oak standing near the said Payton's line, thence South East 109 pole to the beginning. To have and to hold the land and premises during the space of 99 years from the date hereof, yielding and paying yearly and every year the full and just sum of 13 shillings and 3 pence current money to George White or his heirs and assigns, the first of which payment to be paid down at the signing of these presents and the next to be paid on the 5th day of November 1765. In witness whereof the said George White have to this lease affixed his hand and seal the day and year first above written.
Signed sealed and delivered in presence of George White
Griffin Garland
Thomas Newman
William Rochester
Joseph Redman
November the 5th 1764, then received of the within named William Porter, Jr., the sum of 65 pounds current money, it being the whole amount for the lease of all the land and plantation for the space of 99 years. As witness my hand this 5th day of November 1765. George White
Griffin Garland
Thomas Newman
William Rochester
Joseph Redman
At a court held for Westmoreland County the 25th day of June 1765, this indenture of lease and the receipt thereon endorsed were proved by the oaths of Griffin Garland: Thomas Newman and Joseph Redman: witnesses thereto and are ordered to be recorded.
Teste, James Davenport, Cl CW

Page 326.
Dameron & Wife to Redman Indenture
This indenture made the 3rd day of May 1765 between John Dameron of the Parish of Cople and County of Westmoreland and Ann Dameron his wife of the one part and Stuart/Stewart Redman of the same parish and county of the other part. Witnesseth that John Dameron and Ann Dameron his wife in consideration of the sum of 149 pounds current money has sold to Stuart Redman a tract of land lying part thereof in the parish and county aforesaid and partly in the parish of St. Stephen's in the county of Northumberland, being part of a patent formerly granted by the proprietors unto John Hartley of the aforesaid Parish of Cople and County of Westmoreland and bearing date 1697 and from him descended to his daughter Sarah Hartley who intermarried with James Smith and by the said James Smith and Sarah Smith his wife conveyed unto John Dameron containing 158 acres and bounded as followeth; beginning at a marked oak corner tree to the land of Capt. Benjamin Middleton which he purchased of John Hartley and in the line of John Cralle and from thence along

the said Cralle's line to the marsh and swamp and [xxxx] the said swamp to the aforesaid land of Capt. Middleton and so along the said Middleton's land to the first mentioned tree. In witness whereof the said John Dameron and Ann Dameron his wife have set their hands and affixed their seals the day and year above written.

Sealed and delivered in presence of — John Dameron
Samuel Allison Self — Ann Dameron (her mark)
Thomas Warmoth
William Hartley

At a court held for Westmoreland County this 25th day of June 1765, this indenture together with a memorandum of livery of seizen and receipt thereon were acknowledged by John Dameron and Ann Dameron his wife parties thereto and ordered to be recorded, previous to which the said Ann Dameron being first privy examined as the law directs voluntarily relinquished her right of dower in the lands conveyed by the said indenture. Teste

Page 328.

Michael Gilbert's Will

In the name of God Amen, I Michael Gilbert of the colony of Virginia and County of Westmoreland do make and ordain this to be my last will and testament in manner and form as followeth.

Item I give unto my loving wife the use of all my land and negroes and all my other estate during her natural life provided she makes no waste of it.

Item I give unto my son William Gilbert after the death of his mother, my plantation with all my land adjoining and further my will is after the death of my wife that all negroes and other estate except the land before given to William Gilbert: be equally divided between all my children, except Sarah Morton who has had her part before my death and except my son Francis Gilbert who I have sufficiently given to before my death.

I do hereby nominate and appoint my loving wife and my son William Gilbert: executors of this my last will and testament. As witness I have hereunto set my hand and seal this 13th day of February 1765.

Signed sealed and delivered in the presence of — Michael Gilbert (his mark)
Samuel Rust
John Baley
Charles Brown
William Morton
Agness Rust Gilbert (her mark)

At a court held for Westmoreland County the 25th day of June 1765, this last will was proved according to law by the oaths of Samuel Rust, Charles Brown and Agness Rust Gilbert witnesses thereto and ordered to be recorded and on the motion of Mary Gilbert and William Gilbert: the executors therein named who made oath according to law and together with Vincent Rust and George Rust their securities entered into and acknowledged bond with condition as the law directs, certificate is granted them for obtaining a probate thereof in due form. Teste

Page 329.

Courtney to Rust Indenture

This Indenture made the 13th day of June 1765, between James Courtney and Margaret Courtney his wife of the Parish of Cople and County of Westmoreland of the one part and Peter Rust of the same parish and county of the other part. Witnesseth that James Courtney and Margaret Courtney his wife in consideration of 100 pounds current money of Virginia has sold to Peter Rust all that tenement and farms of land whereon Robert Newberry and Jeremiah Courtney now lives and leased by the said James Courtney unto Ashton Hall and Jeremiah Courtney containing by estimation 110 acres lying in the Parish of Cople and county aforesaid being in Yeocomico Neck and bounded by the land of Samuel Rust that the said Samuel Rust purchased of Samuel Eskridge and by the creek known by the name of Earle's Creek and up a branch of said creek that runs up between the said James Courtney and Jeremiah Courtney's to the road that leads down into Yeocomico Neck and down the said road to the land of Samuel Rust's that was formerly Eskridge's and the reversions and remainders, rents, issues and profits thereof with the appurtenances. In witness whereof the parties first mentioned to these presents here hereunto set their hands and seals this day and year first above written.

Signed sealed and delivered in the presence of us — James Courtney, Margaret Courtney

Samuel Rust
Leonard Courtney
Samuel Courtney
Daniel Tebbs

Memorandum that Robert Newberry and Jeremiah Courtney, tenants in possession of the within granted lands and premises on the 15th day of June 1765, did atone to Peter Rust by force of the within grant and became tenants and paid him a shilling rent as an acknowledgement.

In the presence of us — Robert Newberry

Daniel Tebbs
Leonard Courtney
Samuel Rust

At a court held for Westmoreland County the 25th day of June 1765 this indenture together with a memorandum and receipt thereon were acknowledged by James Courtney party thereto and ordered to be recorded. Teste

Page 331.

Courtney to Rust Indenture

Know all men by these presents that I James Courtney in the parish Cople in County of Westmoreland am held and firmly bound unto Peter Rust of the parish and county aforesaid in the full and just sum of 200 pounds current money of Virginia which payment well and truly to be made I bind myself my heirs, executors, and administrators firmly by these presents as witness my hand and seal this 5th day of June 1765. Whereas Peter Rust hath this day purchased of the above bound James Courtney 110 acres of land lying in the Parish of Cople and County of Westmoreland and now in possession of Robert Newberry and Jeremiah Courtney in consideration of 100 pounds current money of Virginia that is to say 50 pounds part thereof on demand and the remainder on or before the 13th day of June next ensuing date hereof. Now the condition of the above obligation is such that if the above bound James Courtney Margaret Courtney his wife at the reasonable request of Peter Rust required in open court to acknowledge such deeds of writing as the Peter Rust shall think effectual for the conveying of the said land and premises then the above obligation to be void otherwise to stand and remain in full force power and virtue.

Signed sealed and delivered in presence of us — Samuel Courtney

Daniel Tebbs
Leonard Courtney
Samuel Courtney
Samuel Rust

At a Court held for Westmoreland County the 25th day of June 1765 this bond for the performance of covenants was acknowledged by James Courtney party thereto and ordered to be recorded. Teste

Page 332.

Lane & Wife to Jordan Lease

This indenture made the 9th day of May 1765 between William Carr Lane and Anne Lane his wife of Cameron parish and county of Loudoun of the one part and Robert Jordan of Cople parish and county of Westmoreland of the other part. Witnesseth that William Carr Lane and Anne Lane his wife in consideration of five shillings of good and lawful money of Virginia have sold all those tracts of lands lying in the Parish of Cople and County of Westmoreland containing 100 acres being part of a patent granted William Basely and Edward Hawley bearing date the 22nd day of March 1665 and by sundry conveyances was conveyed down to Elizabeth Baley and William Baley [her son] who sold the said land to William Lane: deceased and was given by him to his son William Carr Lane and is bounded as follows; beginning at a large gum standing at the head branch of Nominy River, thence along a line to the top of a hill dividing it in the land formerly Duncan's thence a Southwest course, thence southeast dividing it and the land formerly Madcass/Metcalfe's likewise it and the land formerly George Walker's, thence North East dividing it and Peter Smith's land, thence North West dividing it in another parcel of land formerly Walker's, thence North East again to a run down the several courses and meanders of the said run to the beginning dividing it and the Hon. Robert Carter's land. To have and to hold the aforesaid 100 acres of land with from the date hereof for and during the full term of one year from thence next ensuing yielding and paying the rent of one ear of Indian corn on the feast day of the birth of our Lord God next ensuing to the intent and purpose that by virtue of these presents and of the statute of transferring uses into possession the said Robert Jordan may be in actual possession of the premises and thereby enabled to accept a grant of the reversion and inheritance to him and his heirs forever. In witness whereof the parties to these presents have interchangeably set their hands and seals the day and year above written.

Signed sealed and delivered in the presence of — William Carr Lane, Anne Lane
Willoughby Newton
Thomas Chilton, Jr.
Daniel McKenney
Reuben Jordan

Page 334.

Lane & Wife to Jordan Indenture Lease & Release

This indenture made the 10th day of May 1765 between William Carr Lane and Anne Lane his wife of Cameron parish and county of Loudoun of the one part and Robert Jordan of Cople Parish and County of Westmoreland of the other part. Witnesseth that William Carr Lane and Anne Lane his wife in consideration of who Negro boys Tom and Phil and the sum of 10 pounds current money of Virginia have sold and released unto Robert Jordan being in the actual possession of the premises by virtue of a lease in the statue of transferring uses into possession all those tracts of lands lying in the Parish of Cople and County of Westmoreland containing 100 acres being part of a patent granted William Basely and Edward Hawley bearing date the 22nd day of March 1665 and by sundry conveyances was conveyed down to Elizabeth Baley and William Baley [her son] who sold the said land to William Lane: deceased and was given by him to his son William Carr Lane and is bounded as follows; beginning at a large gum standing at the head branch of Nominy River, thence along a line to the top of a hill dividing it in the land formerly Duncan's thence a Southwest course, thence southeast dividing it in the land formerly Madcass/Metcalfe's likewise it and the land formerly George Walker's, thence North East dividing it and Peter Smith's land, thence North West dividing it in another parcel of land formerly Walker's, thence North East again to a run down the several courses and meanders of the said run to the beginning dividing it and the Hon. Robert Carter's land. In witness whereof the parties to these presents have interchangeably set their hands and seals the day and year above written.

Signed sealed and delivered in the presence of — William Carr Lane, Anne Lane
Willoughby Newton
Thomas Chilton, Jr.
Daniel McKenney
Reuben Jordan

To Willoughby Newton, John Newton, Thomas Chilton and John of Augustine Washington, Gent. Whereas William Carr Lane and Anne Lane by their deeds of lease and release bearing date the 9th and 10th day of May 1765 have sold and conveyed unto Robert Jordan the fee simple estate of 100 acres of land lying in the Parish of Cople and whereas Anne Lane cannot conveniently travel to record of Westmoreland to make acknowledgment of the said convenience. Therefore, we do give unto you or any two or more of you power to receive the acknowledgment which the said Anne Lane shall be willing to make. Witness James Davenport, clerk of our said court the 10th day of May 1765.

Westmoreland Sct. By virtue of a writ issued from the County Court of Westmoreland bearing date the 10th day of May 1765 to us directed and hereunto annexed we have examined Mrs. Anne Lane the wife of Mr. William Carr Lane separately and she declared that she conveyed 100 acres of land as by deeds of lease and release bearing the date the 9th and 10th days of May 1765 freely and voluntarily without the threads or persuasions of her husband and that she is willing the said deeds of lease and release shall be recorded in the County Court of Westmoreland. Given under our

hands and seals this 11th day of May 1765
Willoughby Newton
Thomas Chilton, Jr.
At a Court held for Westmoreland County the 25th day of June 1765 These indentures of lease and release and the receipt endorsed on the said release were proved by the oath of Daniel McKenney a witness thereto and the same having been proved in May court last by the oath of Willoughby Newton and Reuben Jordan two other witnesses thereto are together with the commission annexed for taking the acknowledgment in privy examination of the within named Ann Lane and a certificate of the execution thereof were ordered to be recorded. Test

Page 338.
Crabb & Wife to Middleton Indenture
This indenture made the 25th day of June 1765 between John Crabb and Jane Crabb his wife of the County of Westmoreland and Parish of Cople of the one part and Robert Middleton, son of Thomas Middleton: deceased the county and parish aforesaid of the other part. Witnesseth that for as well for and in consideration of the sum of 140 pounds current money to John Crabb by the said Robert Middleton doth release acquit and discharge the said Robert Middleton as also for and in consideration of the council and advise already had received and retained and to be had received and retained by the said John Crabb of the said Robert Middleton they the said John Crabb and Jane Crabb his wife have sold by these presents unto Robert Middleton all that tract of land lying in the County of Westmoreland and Parish of Cople containing by estimation 152 acres bounded as followeth; beginning at a red oak corner to Garner and Crabb running thence North 17° West 118 poles to a small red oak in the back line, thence with the said line West by South 194 poles to a red oak in Alderton's line, thence South 20° East 100 poles to a large white oak in the said Alderton's line, thence South 27° East 135 poles to a white oak by the creekside, thence up the several meanders of the said creek to where trees formerly stood a white oak in the fork of the said creek, thence North 69° East 114 pole to the beginning.. In witness whereof they the said John Crabb and Jane Crabb his wife have hereunto set their hands and seals the day and year above written.
Sealed and delivered in presence of us — John Crabb
John S. Chilton — Jane Crabb
William Templeman
Griffin Garland
At a Court held for Westmoreland County the 25th day of June 1765 this indenture and receipt thereon endorsed was acknowledged by John Crabb party thereto and ordered be recorded. Teste

Page 341.
Thomas Delozier Will
In the name of God Amen, I Thomas Delozier of the County of Westmoreland being very weak and sickly in body but at this present time in perfect sense and sound memory do make and ordain this my last will and testament in manner and form following.
To item I lend to my beloved wife Susannah Delozier, Negro boys Selah and Moses for and during her natural life.
Item I give and bequeath unto my son Richard Davis Delozier, Negro boy Moses after the decease of my loving wife and in case that he should die without heirs it is my will and desire that my daughter Molly Randall Delozier shall have an equal part in the said Negro with my son Daniel Delozier.
Item I give and bequeath unto my son Daniel Delozier, Negro boy Selah after the decease of my loving wife and in case that he should die without heirs it is my will and desire that my daughter Molly Randall Delozier shall have an equal part in the said Negro with my son Richard Davis Delozier.
Item all the rest of my estate herein not given or otherwise bequeath it is my will and desire that it shall be equally divided amongst my three children; Richard Davis Delozier: Daniel Delozier and Molly Randall Delozier.
Lastly, I appoint and ordain my beloved wife Susannah Delozier whole and sole executrix of this my last will and testament. In confirmation whereof I have hereunto set my hand and affixed my seal

this 24th day of December 1764.

Signed sealed and delivered in the presence of us Thomas Delozier (his mark)

Augustine Sanford

James Bryed

Henrietta Sanford

At a Court held for Westmoreland County the 30th day of July 1765 this will was proved according to law by the oath of Augustine Sanford and Henrietta Sanford: witnesses thereto and ordered to be recorded and on the motion of Susanna Delozier the executrix named in the said will who made oath according to law and together with Solomon Redman and Thomas Randall her securities entered into and acknowledged bond with condition has along directs, certificate is granted her for obtaining a probate thereof in due form. Test

Page 342.

Neale to Redman Indenture

This indenture made this 13th day of July 1765 between Edward Ransdell, Gent and guardian to the orphans of Daniel Neale of the County of Westmoreland County deceased the one part and Solomon Redman: millwright and carpenter of the aforesaid County of Westmoreland of the other part. Witnesseth that Edward Ransdell doth bind unto the said Solomon Redman, Richard Neale an orphan of Daniel Neale, deceased, to serve him the said Solomon Redman from the day and date of these presents until he shall arrive to the full the age of 21 years and to be taught and instructed the art and trade of a millwright and carpenter and at the expiration of his servitude the said Solomon Redman to pay unto Richard Neale the freedom dues that is by law allowed for indented servants. In witness whereof the parties to these presents have hereunto set their hands and seals the day month and year first above written.

Signed sealed and delivered in the presence of us Richard Neale

Diar Jackson [?]

Joseph Redman

At a Court held for Westmoreland County the 31st day of July 1765 this indenture was acknowledged by the parties thereto and with the of approbation of the court is ordered to be recorded. Teste

Page 343.

Gill to Gill Deed of Gift

to all people to whom this present writing shall come, I Edward Gill of the County of Westmoreland and Parish of Cople send greeting. Know ye that the said Edward Gill for the natural love and affection I do hold to my son Edward Gill, George Gill, Spencer Gill, James Gill and to my daughter Lettice Self &c, have given and granted and sold by these presents as follows;

I give to my son Edward Gill, Negro boy Jack, one bed and furniture, three head of cattle, one chest and one pot.

I give to my son George Gill, Negro boy Sampson, one horse, one feather bed and furniture, one pot, three head of cattle.

I give to my son Spencer Gill, Negro girl Jenny, one feather bed and furniture, three head of cattle, one part.

I give to my son James Gill, Negro girl Patty, one feather bed and furniture, three head of cattle, one pot.

I give to my daughter Lettice Self, Negro girl Nanny, four head of cattle, one pot, one chest, one dish, two bason's, three plates, and one side saddle.

I give the remaining part of my goods not mentioned to be equally divided between all my children.

In witness whereof I have hereunto set my hand and seal this 26th day of August 1765.

Witness Edward Gill (his mark)

Thomas Newman

John White

At a court held for Westmoreland County the 27th day of August 1765 this deed of gift was proved by the oath of Thomas Newman and John White the witnesses thereto and ordered to be recorded. Teste

Page 345.
John Kirk's Will
In the name of God Amen, I John Kirk of the Parish of Cople and County of Westmoreland, being sick and weak in body but of perfect sense and memory do make this my last will and testament in the manner and form following.
I give and bequeath to my wife Sarah Kirk who I make my executrix all that I have during her life except the gun who I freely give to my son John Kirk and after her death that all may be equally be divided amongst all my children lawfully begotten.
Signed sealed and delivered in presence of us this 11th day of December 1764
James Walker John Kirk (his mark)
Randell Kirk
John Kirk (his mark)
At a court held for Westmoreland County the 27th day of August 1765 this will was proved according to law by the oath of Randell Kirk and John Kirk witnesses thereto and ordered to be recorded and on the motion of Sarah Kirk the executrix named in the same will who made oath according to law who together with Thomas Boyd and Randall Kirk her securities entered into and acknowledged bond with condition as the law directs, certificate is granted her for obtaining a probate thereof in due form. Teste

Page 346.
Crabb's Wife to Middleton Privy Examination
To Willoughby Newton, Richard Lee and John Newton, Gent. Whereas John Crabb and Jane Crabb his wife by their indenture of bargain and sale bearing date the 25th day of June 1765 conveyed unto Robert Middleton the fee simple estate of 152 acres of land with the appurtenances lying in the Parish of Cople and County of Westmoreland and whereas the said Jane Crabb cannot conveniently travel to record of Westmoreland County to make acknowledgment. Therefore, we do give unto you or any two or more of you power to receive the acknowledgment which the said Jane Crabb shall be willing to make. Witness James Davenport, clerk of our said court the 22nd day of August in the fifth year of our reign.
Westmoreland Sct. By virtue of and in obedience to a commission to us directed, we the subscribers did go to the said June Crabb and privy examined her apart from her husband concerning her willingness for conveying her right of the said land and premises who saith that she doeth the same freely and of her own voluntary will in court without any persuasions or threats of her husband, certified under our hands this 24th day of September 1765.
Willoughby Newton
John Newton
At a court held for Westmoreland County this 24th day of September 1765 this commission further privy examination of Jane Crabb the wife of John Crabb and a certificate of the execution thereof being returned was ordered to be recorded. Test

Page 347.
Thomas Chilton's Will
In the name of God Amen, I Thomas Chilton of the Parish of Cople in the County of Westmoreland being of sound and disposing mind and memory do make and ordain this my last will and testament in manner and form following.
Item I give and devise to my son Thomas Chilton and to his heirs all my lands, tenements and hereditaments in the County of Westmoreland and 18 Negroes; Whitehaven, Nan, Jack, Tom, Suckey, Black, Will, Grace, Cate, at home Jeany young child Lucey, Suckey's young child, Jone, Guy, Cupid, Osborn, Ben, Little Moll, Boson, Monkey and Orange and their issue.
Item I give and bequeath unto my son Thomas Chilton, the great couch in the hall, the great escrutore and chest of drawers, the two gilt cooking glasses, the clock, my riding saddle and bridle, pistols and holsters, my silver kilted gun.
Item whereas my daughter Mary Ransdell is possessed of Negro wench Nan and her child and three other Negroes, all George, Rose and Solly, which I before this time lent her hath, in

confirmation of the said gift I do now bequeath the same Negroes to my said daughter Mary Ransdell and her heirs forever. I also lent to my said daughter a Negro girl Ealle the daughter of old Sarah for her life and at her decease I did give it to my grandson Chilton Ransdell.

If item I give to my daughter Mary Ransdell five shillings sterling in full of her part of my estate.

Item whereas my daughter Hannah Sturman is possessed of Negroes, Millly, Anthony and Lester, which I before this time lent her have in confirmation of the said gift I do now bequeath the said Negroes to my daughter Hannah Sturman and her heirs forever. I also lent to my said daughter Negro girl Nan the daughter of Jeany for her life and at her decease I then give it to my granddaughter Jemima Sturman and her heirs forever.

I give to my daughter Hannah Sturman five shillings sterling in full of her part of my estate.

Item I give and devise to my three sons William Chilton, John Chilton and Charles Chilton the land in Fauquier County that I bought of the executors of Robert Vaulx and William Elliott to be equally divided between them, my will and desire is that my son John Chilton shall have that part of the land he now lives on.

Item I give to my son Stephen Chilton and heirs of his body lawfully begotten forever the land in Prince William County which I bought of William Hawley and of .

Item I give and bequeath all the rest of my Negroes that are not herein before given away, and all the rest of my estate, unto my four sons William Chilton: John Chilton: Charles Chilton: and Stephen Chilton to be equally divided amongst them.

Lastly, I nominate and appoint my said son Thomas Chilton my sole executor of this my last will and testament. In testimony whereof I have hereunto set my hand and seal this fourth day of September 1765.

Signed sealed and acknowledged to be the last will and testament of Thomas Chilton in the presence of us who have subscribed thereto in his presence and at his request.

William Booth — Thomas Chilton
William Walker (his mark)
James Sanford

This will was proved according to law by the oath of William Booth and James Sanford witnesses thereto and ordered to be recorded and on the motion of Thomas Chilton the executor in the said will named who made oath according to law and together with Richard Henry Lee and John Newton, Gent., his securities entered into and acknowledged bond with conditioned as the law directs, certificate is granted him for obtaining a probate thereof in due form. Teste

Page 349.

Robert Washington Will

I Robert Washington at this time in perfect health and disposing sense and memory make this my last will and testament in manner following.

Imprimis, I given to my daughter Sukey Washington: 18 Negroes; Frank, Tom, Lucey, Judy, Nan, Cate, Ben, Nel, the five Negroes following children of Judy; Ann, Suckey, Franke, Jenny and Tom, the four following children of Lucey; Rachael, Beck, Liddy and Ben, and a Negro child Will the son of Cate. Of the said Negroes the three following live at my son John Washington's; [xxxxxxxxxxx] Nan, Cate and her child Will which are above mentioned. I give the said 18 Negroes and their increase to my daughter Sukey Washington and her heirs forever.

Item I give unto my grandson Robert Townshend Washington Negro girl Alice and her increase forever.

Item I give unto my granddaughter Sarah Washington Negro girl Sall and her increase.

Item I given to my son John Washington all the rest of my estate both real and personal the pain all my just debts.

Item I appoint my friend William Bernard, guardian to my daughter Sukey Washington and my son John Washington executor of this my will.

Lastly, it is my desire that my estate may not be appraised. In witness whereof I have hereunto set my hand and seal this 11th day of February 1763.

Signed sealed and published in presence of — Robert Washington
William Craighill
William Monroe, Jr.

William Bernard
Richard Bernard
At a court held for Westmoreland County the 24th day of September 1765 this will was approved according to law by the witnesses thereto and ordered to be recorded and on the motion of John Washington executor therein named who made oath according to law it together with William Bernard his security entered into and acknowledged bond with conditioned as the law directs, certificate is granted him for obtaining a probate thereof in due form. Teste

Page 350.
Triplett to Monroe Indenture
This indenture made the 23rd day of September 1765 between John Triplett of the Parish of Hanover in the County of King George of the one part and George Monroe, Jr., of the County of Westmoreland of the other part. Witnesseth that John Triplett in consideration of 100 pounds current money of Virginia have sold to George Monroe, Jr., a parcel of land containing by estimation 200 acres lying in Westmoreland County in Washington Parish and bounded as followeth; beginning at Piper's Road running North 3° West 55 poles to a small branch of the said branch North 75 ¾° East 30 pole, thence 10 ¼° West 48 pole, thence South 76 ½° West 20 pole, thence South 56 ¾° West 6 pole, South 47 ¾° West 52 pole, thence North 52 ¾° West 40 pole, thence North 83° West 78 pole to the new road, thence down the said road to Stephen Smith's corner, thence North 79° West to Spillman's line, thence down the said Spillman's line to Peter Jett's line, thence down the said line to a path, thence along the path to Piper's Road, thence along the said road to the beginning. In witness whereof the said John Triplett have hereunto set his hand and seal the day and year first above written.
Signed sealed and delivered in the presence of John Triplett
William Peirce
John Atwell
At a Court held for Westmoreland County the 24th day of September 1765 this indenture together with the memorandum of livery of seizen and receipt thereon endorsed were acknowledged by John Triplett party thereto and ordered to be recorded. Teste

Page 353.
Rust to Rust Deed of Gift
I Peter Rust of the Parish of Cople and County of Westmoreland send greeting. Know ye that I the said Peter Rust in consideration of the natural love and affection which I have and do bear to my father Samuel Rust of the same parish and county and also for other good causes and considerations me thereunto moving have given and granted by these presents unto the said Samuel Rust all my right title and interest of Negro woman Sarah and her two children Mime and Let. In witness here unto I have set my hand and seal this 24th day of June 1765.
Signed sealed and delivered in the presence of us Peter Rust
John Crabb, Jr.
Mary Beale (her mark)
At a court held for Westmoreland County the 24th day of September 1765 this deed of gift together with the memorandum livery of seizen were acknowledged by Peter Rust party thereto and ordered to be recorded. Teste

Page 354.
Lee & Wife to Lee Indenture & Commission
This indenture made the 27th day of March 1765 between the Hon. Philip Ludwell Lee L.L.D. of Stratford in the County of Westmoreland, Esq. and Elizabeth Lee his wife of the one part and Richard Lee of Lee Hall in the said County of Westmoreland, Esq. of the other part. Witnesseth that Philip Ludwell Lee and Elizabeth Lee his wife in consideration of £300 money of Great Britain has sold to Richard Lee all that dividend tract of land lying in the Parish of Cople and County of Westmoreland containing by estimation 204 acres and 13 poles being part of a tract of land late in the tenure and occupation of James Steptoe, late of the said county deceased, commonly known by the name of Hominy Hall tract which said dividend or parcel of land was allotted to the said

Elizabeth Lee by order and decree of the court of the County of Westmoreland bearing date the 25th day of July 1758. In witness whereof the parties to these presents have hereunto set their hands and seals the day and year first within written.
Sealed and delivered in the presence of us Philip Ludwell Lee
Francis Lightfoot Lee Elizabeth Lee
George Simpson
Thomas Lee Taylor
John Bulger
Ebeneazer Fisher
Thomas Logan
Samuel Washington
To John Martin, Richard Henry Lee, and John Newton, Gent. Whereas the Hon. Philip Ludwell Lee, Esq., L.L.D. in Elizabeth Lee his wife by their indenture of bargain and sale bearing date the 27th day of March 1765 sold and conveyed unto Richard Lee, Esq. the fee simple estate of 240 acres and 13 poles of land with the appurtenances lying and being in the Parish of Cople and County of Westmoreland and whereas the said Elizabeth Lee cannot conveniently travel to her court of Westmoreland County to make acknowledgment. Therefore, we do give unto you or any two of more of you power to receive the acknowledgment which the said Elizabeth Lee shall be willing to make. Witness James Davenport, clerk of our said court the 28th day of March 1765.
Westmoreland Sct. By virtue of a writ of dedimus from the County Court of Westmoreland bearing date the 28th day of March 1765 two us directed in hereunto annexed we have examined Mrs. Elizabeth Lee who wife of the Hon. Philip Ludwell Lee, Esq. L.L.D. separate and apart from him and she declared that she conveyed the land with her husband to Richard Lee, Esq. as by indenture of bargain and sale bearing date the 27th day of March 1765 freely and voluntarily without any threats or persuasion of her husband and that she is willing the said indenture of bargain and sale shall be recorded in in the said County Court of Westmoreland. Given under our hands and seals this fifth day of April 1765.
John Martin
Richard Henry Lee
At a court continued and held for Westmoreland County the 25th day of September 1765 this indenture and receipt thereon endorsed were proved by the oaths of Francis Lightfoot Lee, Ebeneazer Fisher and Thomas Logan, witnesses thereto and together with the commission annexed for the acknowledgment and privy examination of Elizabeth the wife of the said Philip Ludwell Lee, Esq. and a certificate of the execution thereof ordered to be recorded. Teste James Davenport

Page 359.
Gallahaugh to Seacock Deed of Gift
I Thomas Gallahaugh the County of Westmoreland Parish of Cople, planter, send greetings this 10th day of September 1765. Now know ye that I the said Thomas Gallahaugh for diverse good causes you by these presents give unto Thomas Seacock of the parish and county aforesaid one horse, eight head of cattle, 14 head of hogs, two feather beds and furniture, and all the rest of my estate of what nature or kind soever. In witness whereof I have hereunto set my hand and seal the day and year first above written.
Signed sealed and delivered in presence of us Thomas Gallahaugh (his mark)
James Rust
Samuel McCave
William Harris (his mark)
At a court continued in held for Washington County the 25th day of September 1765 this deed of gift was proved by the oaths of James Rust and Samuel McCave witnesses thereto and ordered to be recorded. Teste

Page 360.
Black to Payne Indenture
This indenture made the 14th day of October 1765 between William Black and Frances Black his

wife of the County of Prince George [Maryland] of the one part and George Payne of the County of Westmoreland of the other part. Witnesseth that William Black and Frances Black his wife in consideration of 233 pounds 7 shillings current money of Virginia have sold to George Payne a tract of land lying in the Parish of Washington and County of Westmoreland containing by estimation 179 acres and 28 poles and bounded as follows; beginning at a marked chestnut tree standing at the head of a valley, a line tree to this land in the land of Matthew Bayne extending nigh and by two locust posts, thence down the said valley to a small red Oak corner tree to this land in the land of the said Bayne and lying of the land of Col. Lee's, thence to a great chestnut a line which divides this land and land of James Naughty, thence to the main run part of the aforesaid that divides the said land in the land of William Quisenbury, thence down the several meanders of the said run to the mouth of another great run, thence up the said run to the mouth of a small branch, thence with the said branch to the beginning, being the land purchased by William Black of Humphrey Pope. In witness whereof the said William Black and Frances Black his wife hath hereunto set their hands and affixed their seals the day and year first above written.
Signed sealed and delivered in the presence of William Black
Edward Ransdell, Jr.
Alexander Spark, Thomas Redman Robinson (his mark)
William Peirce, Richard Buckner, Thomas Chilton (his mark)
At a Court held for Westmoreland County the 31st day of December 1765 this indenture and the receipt thereon endorsed was proved to be the act and deed of the said William Black by the oath of Alexander Spark, William Pierce and Thomas Chilton witnesses thereto and ordered to be recorded. Test
Memorandum Mrs. Black personally acknowledged this deed and relinquished her right of dower June 30, 1767 (see order book that date)

Page 362.
Black to Pierce Indenture
This indenture made this 24th day of June 1766 between William Black of the County of Prince George [Maryland] and Frances Black his wife of the one part and William Peirce of the County of Westmoreland of the other part. Witnesseth that said William Black and Frances Black his wife in consideration of 97 pounds 11 shillings and 3 pence current money of Virginia has sold to William Peirce all that tract of land lying in the Parish of Cople and County of Westmoreland the same being part of a tract of land formerly purchased by the said William Black from William Hardwick as by deed bearing date the 3rd day of April 1753, containing by estimation 111 ½ acres and bounded as followeth; beginning at a small, corner tree to William Sturman running
South 27° West 15 pole to the mouth of a small branch and up the said branch
North 56° West 13-4/10 poles,
North 50° West 13-2/10 poles
thence North 31½° West 27-6/10 poles to the head of a gully thence,
North 51° West 50 pole thence,
North 89° West 20 8/10 poles to the head of another branch thence, down the said branch it several meanders to the main run of Rappahannock Creek and up the said run it several meanders to Vaulx's Mill Dam, thence along a line of your regular marked trees dividing this land and their of William Sturman's southeasterly to the gum at the first station. In witness whereof the said William Black and Frances Black his wife hath hereunto set their hands and affixed their seals the day and year first above written.
Signed sealed and delivered in the presence of William Black
John Turberville Frances Black
John Ballantine, Jr.
Jeremiah Rust
At a Court held for Westmoreland County the 24th day of June 1766 this indenture and the receipt thereon endorsed were acknowledged by William Black party thereto and ordered to be recorded. Test James Davenport
Memorandum Mrs. Black personally acknowledged this deed and relinquished her right of dower June 30, 1767 (see order book that date)

Page 364.
Black to Turberville Indenture
This indenture made the 14th day of June 1766 between William Black of the County of Prince George [Maryland] and Frances Black his wife of the one part and George Turberville of the County of Richmond of the other part. Witnesseth that William Black and Frances Black his wife in consideration of 87 pounds 8 shillings and 6 pence current money of Virginia have sold to George Turberville all that tract of land lying in the Parish of Lunenburg in County of Richmond the same being a tract of land purchased from William Hardwick as by deed bearing date the 3rd day of April 1753 containing by estimation 81 acres 1 rod and 6 poles and bounded as followeth; beginning at a small marked gum standing on the south side of a swamp and running South 32 ½° East 59 pole along a line of marked trees dividing this land from other lands belonging to the said George Turberville to a marked red oak corner tree thence along a row of irregular marked trees which being reduced to a straight line is South 8° West 59 pole to a marked red oak corner tree of this land in the aforesaid Turberville's land, thence along another of the said Turberville's lines South 14° West 80 pole to a marked red oak corner to this land the said Turberville's land and that now held by Edmund Bulger, thence along the said Bulger's line being reduced straight is North 34° West 161 ½ poles to a small gun marked for a corner between the said Bulger and this land standing on the side of the above swamp, then up the several windings and meanders of the said swamp to the first beginning gum. In witness whereof he the said William Black and Frances Black his wife have hereunto set their hands and affixed their seals the day and year first above written.
Signed sealed and delivered in the presence of William Black
Thomas Thomson
Alexander Spark
William Porter
William Bruer
At a Court held for Westmoreland County the 24th day of June 1766 this indenture in the receipt thereon endorsed were acknowledged by William Black party thereto and ordered to be recorded. Teste
Memorandum Mrs. Black personally acknowledged this deed and relinquished her right of dower June 30, 1767 (see order book that date)

Page 367.
Campbell & Degge Property Line Agreement & Bond
Know all men by these presents that we Archibald Campbell of the Parish of Washington and County of Westmoreland, clerk and William Degge of the said parish and county, planter to prevent future disputes and to perpetuate a good neighborhood have agreed and do hereby agree for ourselves and for our heirs and assigns that the following lines which we have marked shall be the fixed boundaries between our respective lands in the White Oak Swamp forever, we mean between the tract of land which the said Archibald Campbell purchased from Thomas Bowcock on the West side and the land now possessed by the said William Degge on the East side of these lines; beginning at a white oak and small sweet gum along marked trees North 43° 45 minutes West 85 poles thence along marked trees North 8° 45 minutes West 60 poles to a marked white oak thence along marked trees North 13° 15 minutes East 100 poles to a small marked white oak. In witness whereof we have hereunto set our hands and seals this 23rd day of June 1766.
Archibald Campbell
William Degge
At a court held for Westmoreland County the 24th day of June 1766, this bond for performance of covenants were acknowledged by the parties thereto and ordered to be recorded. Teste.

Page 368.
Strother to Price Lease
This Indenture made the 28th of October 1765 between William Strother of the Parish of Washington and County of Westmoreland, planter of the one part and John Price of the aforesaid parish and county of the other part. Witnesseth that William Strother in consideration of 5 shillings

current money of Virginia has sold a tract of land containing 50 acres unto John Price it being part of John Beard's patent for 490 acres dated [blank] the said 50 acres being bought of John White by George Blackmore by deeds bearing date [blank] and given by the last will and testament of George Blackmore: deceased to Lovell White and by the said White conveyed to William Strother, deceased which he the said William Strother claims as heir at law and binding on the lands of Francis Williams, Samuel White and the said John Price. To have and to hold the said tract of land unto the said John Price from the day next before the day of the day of these presents for the full term of one whole year from thence next ensuing, yielding and paying unto William Strother the rent of one pepper corn upon the feast of St. Michael the Archangel next coming to the intent and purpose that by virtue of the statute for transferring uses into possession the said John Price may be in actual possession of the premises and be thereby the better enabled to accept and take a grant and release of the reversion and inheritance indented to be made between him and the said William Strother and Winifred Strother his wife. In witness whereof the said William Strother hath to this present indenture set his hand and seal the day month and year first above written.

Sealed and delivered in presence of — William Strother
James Degge — Winifred Strother (her mark)
Charles Weeks
William Diggs/Degge
John Degge

Page 368.

Strother & Wife to Price Privy Examination & Release

This Indenture made the 29th of October 1765 between William Strother and Winifred Strother his wife of the Parish of Washington and County of Westmoreland, planter of the one part and John Price of the aforesaid parish and county of the other part. Witnesseth that William Strother and Winifred Strother his wife in consideration of 40 pounds current money has sold and released a tract of land containing 50 acres unto John Price: being in his actual possession by virtue of the statute for transferring uses into possession, it being part of John Beard's patent for 490 acres dated [blank] the said 50 acres being bought of John White by George Blackmore by deeds bearing date [blank] and given by the last will and testament of Georg Blackmore: deceased to Lovell White and by the said White conveyed to William Strother, deceased which he the said William Strother claims as heir at law and binding on the lands of Francis Williams, Samuel White and the said John Price. In witness whereof the parties aforesaid have put their hands and seals the day and year first above written.

Sealed and delivered in presence of — William Strother
James Degge — Winifred Strother (her mark)
Charles Weeks
William Diggs/Degge
John Degge

To William Berryman, John Martin, Archibald Campbell and James Blair, Gent., Whereas William Strother and Winifred Strother his wife by their indenture of lease and release bearing date respectively the 28th and 29 days of October 1765 sold and conveyed unto John Price the fee simple's estate of 50 acres of land with appurtenances lying in the Parish of Washington and County of Westmoreland and whereas the said Winifred Strother cannot conveniently travel to record to make acknowledgment of the said conveyance. Therefore, we do give unto you or any two of you power to receive the acknowledgment which the said Winifred Strother shall be willing to make. Witness James Davenport, clerk of our said court the 23rd day of June in the sixth year of our reign.

Westmoreland Sct. Agreeable to the above commission we have taken the relinquishment of Winifred Strother's dower to a certain tract of land above mentioned and apart from her husband who freely relinquishes. Given under our hands and seals this 23rd day June 1766.
William Berryman
John Martin

At a Court held for Westmoreland County the 24th day of June 1766 these indentures of lease and release and the receipt endorsed on the said release were proved by the oaths of Charles Weeks,

William Diggs/Degge and John Degge witnesses thereto and together with the commission annexed for taking the acknowledgment and privy examination of the within named Winifred Strother and a certificate of the execution thereof are ordered to be recorded. Test James Davenport Cl Cur

Page 374.
Chandler to Callis indenture
I Frances Chandler of the Parish of Cople and County of Westmoreland in consideration of the good will and affection which I have and do bear towards my friend Francis Callis guardian to my son Thomas Chandler and [daughter] Elizabeth Chandler of the same Parish and County aforesaid and in order to indemnify and secure him for being my security for the administration and execution of my deceased husband Joseph Chandler, deceased and his being bound to pay to Judith Kenner the sum of 5000 pounds of crop tobacco and the casks due to her for rent in the sum of 45 pounds current money of Virginia due to the said Francis Callis as guardian to Thomas Chandler and Elizabeth Chandler have given and granted and by these present do freely give and grant to my friend Francis Callis his heirs executors and administrators all and singular my goods and chattels and the crop of corn and tobacco now growing in all my third part of my deceased husband's estate consisting in Negroes, Frank and Isaac and third part of a Negro Billey and George now being in my present possession and allotted to me by order of Court bearing date the 24th day of September 1765 in the parish aforesaid by these presents I have delivered to my friend Francis Callis inventory signed with my own hand in bearing even date with these presents for the indemnification of the said Callis payment of all my debts due or that may become due to my son Thomas Chandler and Elizabeth Chandler and to my friend Francis Callis their guardian and himself his heirs executors and administrators from henceforth as his proper goods and chattels. In witness whereof I have hereunto set my hand and seal this 26th day of October 1765.
Signed sealed and delivered in the presence of Frances Chandler (her mark)
Thomas Atwell
George Monroe
At a court held for Westmoreland County the 24th day of June 1766 this deed was proved by the oath of Thomas Atwell and George Monroe the witnesses thereto and ordered to be recorded. Teste

Page 375.
Jonathan Piper's Will
In the name of God Amen, I Jonathan Piper of the County of Westmoreland being sick and weak but of disposing sense and memory do make constitute and ordain this to be my last will and testament.
Item my will is that if my fathers will should entitle my son John Piper to all my Negroes that then I give to my daughter Mary Piper 100 acres of land given by a deed of gift by my father.
Item if my son John Piper should get but his equal part of the Negroes that then I give the above mentioned hundred acres to John Piper and his heirs.
Item I give to my daughter Mary Piper a dark mare colt two years old branded "IP."
Item I give to my son John Piper the colt that my black mare is with fold with all the rest of my estate Negroes stocks and household furniture to be equally divided between my five children; Mary Piper, John Piper, Susanna Piper, Jenny Piper, and Rachael Piper.
Lastly, I appoint my wife sole executor of this my last will and testament. As witness I have hereunto set my hand and seal this 18th day of September 1763
Signed sealed and delivered in presence of Jonathan Piper
John Smith
William Piper
Rachel Monroe
At a court held for Westmoreland County the 29th day of July 1766 this will was proved according to law by the oaths of John Smith: William Piper and Rachel Monroe the witnesses thereto and ordered to be recorded and on the motion of Anne Piper, widow and executrix named in the said will who made oath according to law and together with John Smith and George Johnston her

securities entered into and acknowledged bond with conditioned as the law directs, certificate is granted for obtaining a probate thereof in due form. Teste

Page 376.
William Hodgson Will
In the name of God Amen, I William Hodgson the Parish of Washington and County of Westmoreland being in perfect health and of sound mind and memory do make and ordain this to be my last will and testament in manner and form following.
I leave and bequeath my body to the earth to be buried in the Round Hill Church yard. It is also my will and desire that the sermon be preached in the above church from the following words; Job: Chapter 24, Verse 19th and part of the 20th, As the drought and heat consume the snow waters: so doth the grave those which have sinned. The womb shall forget him; the worm shall feed sweetly on him; he shall be no more remembered;
As for my personal state in Virginia I leave and bequeath unto Katherine Baker and her heirs as a testimony of the sincere love I have for her. I also do constitute and appoint the said Katherine Baker sole executrix of this my last will and testament desiring that she will pay all my lawful debts. Written with my own hand and seal this 31st day of July in the year of our Lord 1765.
In presence of William Hodgson
Thomas Taylor
John Chancellor
William Jackson
At a court held for Westmoreland County the 29th day of July 1766 this will was proved according to law by the oaths of Thomas Taylor and William Jackson witnesses thereto and ordered to be recorded and on the motion of Katherine Baker the executrix named in the said will who made oath according to law and together with Thomas Taylor her security entered into and acknowledged bond with conditioned as the law directs, certificate is granted her for obtaining a probate thereof in due form. Teste

Page 377.
Hume & Wife to Turberville Indenture
This indenture made the 1st day of July 1766 between James Hume and Elizabeth Hume his wife of the parish of St. George and County of Spotsylvania and town of Fredericksburg, merchant the one part and John Turberville of the Parish of Cople and County of Westmoreland, Gent., of the other part. Witnesseth that James Hume and Elizabeth Hume his wife in consideration of 537 pounds 10 shillings current money of Virginia have sold to John Turberville a tract of land which descended to the aforesaid and Elizabeth Hume from the will of her father Chandler Awbrey which is situated and being in the Parish of Cople and County of Westmoreland containing by estimation 183 acres and being the land whereon Chandler Awbrey, deceased father to Elizabeth Hume lived and adjoining to the land of the said John Turberville on Machodoc River and to the land of the Hon. Philip Ludwell Lee, Esq. known by the name of Baxter's. In witness whereof the first parties to these presents interchangeably set their hands and seals the day and year first above written.
Signed sealed and delivered in the presence of James Hume
Francis Lightfoot Lee Elizabeth Hume
George Turberville
William Brown
John Redman
Westmoreland Sct. To Charles Dick, Charles Yates, Fielding Lewis, Benjamin Grymes and John Stewart, Gent. Whereas James Hume and Elizabeth to his wife in the County of Spotsylvania aforesaid by their deed of bargain and sale bearing date the first day of July 1766 have conveyed unto John Turberville of the County of Westmoreland, Gent., 183 acres of land lying in the Parish of Cople and County of Westmoreland and whereas the said Elizabeth Hume can conveniently travel to her said County Court to make acknowledgment. Witnesses James Davenport, clerk of our said Courthouse the 25th day of June 1766.
Spotsylvania County Sct. By virtue of a commission to us directed bearing date the 25th day of June 1766 to take the privy examination of Elizabeth Hume wife to James Hume of the County of

Spotsylvania aforesaid touching her relinquishment of her right and also the right of dower to a tract of land containing 183 acres in the Parish of Cople and County of Westmoreland conveyed by them to John Turberville, Gent., as by deed of bargain and sale bearing date the first day July 1766. We have examined the said Elizabeth Hume privately and she acknowledged all her right and title to the said land and declared that she did the same of her own free will and consent without the threats or persuasions affairs assessment and that she is willing that the same should be recorded in Westmoreland court. Given under our hands and seals this first day July 1766.
Charles Dick
Charles Yates
At a Court held for Westmoreland County the 29th day of July 1766 this indenture and receipt thereon endorsed were proved by the oath George Turberville, William Brown and John Redman witnesses thereto and together with the commission annexed for taking the acknowledgment and privy examination of Elizabeth Hume the wife of James Hume and the certificate of the execution thereof ordered to be recorded. Test

Page 380.
Rice to Peirce Deed
This indenture made the 29th day of July 1766 between William Rice of the Parish of Cople and County of Westmoreland of the one part and Joseph Pierce, Gent of the said County the other part. Witnesseth that William Rice the good and valuable consideration of 60 pounds current money has sold unto Joseph Pierce the parcel of land containing 130 acres being in Cople Parish in Westmoreland County and bounded as followeth; beginning at a marked white oak corner to land held by Mr. Edward Ransdell in the said Pierce and running along a line dividing this land from the said Ransdell's North 58 ½° East 174 pole to a marked red Oak standing near the side of a road the same being a corner tree to a parcel of land before sold out of this tract by the said William Rice to William Hazlerigg, then along the said Hazlerigg's line South 6 ½° East 94 pole to another marked red Oak standing by the side of the said road near the aforesaid Hazlerigg's dwelling house, thence South 35° West 80 pole to a red oak standing in a valley being corner to land lately belonging to the estate of Thomas Templeman, deceased and now held by the said Pierce, then North 29 ½° West 20 pole to a small mark gun standing at the side of a run then down the said run to where a branch falls into it from Rice's plantation, then down the aforesaid run or swamp the several meanders thereof to the line dividing this land from that formerly patented by Col. Pierce then along that line to the first beginning white oak. In witness whereof I have hereunto set my hand and affixed my seal the day and year first above written.
Sealed and delivered in presence of William Rice
Edward Sanford
Edward Ransdell, Jr.
John Rust
At a court held for Westmoreland County the 29th day of July 1766 this indenture and receipt were acknowledged by William Rice party thereto and ordered to be recorded, previous to which, Jemima Rice the wife of William Rice personally appeared and being first privy examined as them all voluntary relinquished her right of dower in the lands conveyed by the said indenture. Teste James Davenport Cl Cur

Page 383.
Self to Self Performance Bond
Know all men by these presents that we Thomas Self and Elizabeth Self his wife of the County of Loudoun and colony of Virginia are held and firmly bound to John Self of this County of Westmoreland and colony aforesaid in the full and just sum of 200 pounds current money of Virginia to which payment will and truly to be made. Seal with our seals and dated the 8th day of October 1765. The condition of the above obligation is such that if Thomas Self and Elizabeth Self his wife shall in no ways concern themselves in any manner or form or touching a certain parcel of land lying in Westmoreland County the property of Henry Self, deceased father to the said Thomas Self and John Self but shall in all things that the said John Self quietly and peacefully hold use occupy and assess his part allotted to him by his father's will then this present obligation to be void

and of non-effect otherwise to remain in full force power and virtue.
Signed sealed and delivered in the presence of Thomas Self
Susanna Douglass Elizabeth Self
Martha Self
At a Court held for Westmoreland County the 26th day of August 1766 this bond for performance of covenants was passed by the oath of Susanna Douglass and Martha Self the witnesses thereto and ordered to be recorded. Test

Page 384.
Wright to Wright Deed of Gift
I Francis Wright of the Parish of Cople and County of Westmoreland for the natural love and affection that I have and do bear unto my two sons Richard Wright and Presley Wright and my daughter Nancy Wright. I Francis Wright being in perfect memory have given and granted and confirmed by this my present writing do freely grant (after my decease) unto the said Richard Wright, Presley Wright and Nancy Wright, six Negro slaves and their increase from the date of this present writing namely Negroes; Lettice, Winney, Sukey, Jack, Hannah, Nell. In witness whereof I have here unto set my hand and seal this 26th day of August 1766.
Sealed and delivered in presence of Francis Wright
Fleet Cox
Benedict Middleton
John Ballantine
John Sinclair
At a Court held for Westmoreland County the 26th day of August 1766 this deed of gift was acknowledged by Francis Wright party thereto and ordered to be recorded. Teste James Davenport Cl Cur

Page 385.
Butler to Butler Deed of Gift
I Thomas Butler: Sr., of Yeocomico Neck in the Parish of Cople and County of Westmoreland in consideration of the love and goodwill and affection which I have and do bear towards my loving son William Butler have given and granted by these presents a tract of land lying in Yeocomico Neck and bounded as followeth; beginning at a small cedar on the south side of a small marsh which makes up to the little well and running from thence easterly to another small cedar near the little well, thence to a poplar in the edge of the old field, thence southerly along a line of marked trees to a pine near an old path that leads from my house to Thomas Gallahaugh, from thence along a line of marked trees on the south side of the said path to a white oak which is the corner tree, thence along the line South East between Richard Lowe and me to a marked mahogany tree, thence to a dogwood tree being on a branch between George Eskridge and me, thence down the said branch to the creek, thence down the several meanders of the said creek to the south side of a little marsh and so [xxxxxxxxxx] marsh to the beginning cedar containing by estimation 60 acres including the houses wherein the said William Butler now liveth with all the fencing on the said land and plantation with all other appurtenances whatsoever belonging. In witness whereof I have hereunto set my hand and seal this fourth day of June 1765.
Sealed and delivered in the presence of Thomas Butler
John Norwood
Robert Newberry
Jeremiah Courtney
George Christie
At a Court held for Westmoreland County the 26th day of August 1766 this deed of gift was proved by the oath of Jeremiah Courtney a witness thereto and the same having been proved on June court 1765 by the oath of two other the witnesses thereto is ordered to be recorded. Teste

Page 386.
Christie's Nuncupative Will
Westmoreland Sct. This date came John Threlkeld , Jesse Price and Samuel McCave and made

oath that on Saturday the 11th instant, George Christie of this county and Parish of Cople, weaver did make his will in the form following.
My will and desire is that George Courtney, the son of Leonard Courtney may have my silver shoe buckles, my silver sleeve buttons and my blue serge coat, also I give all the remainder and residue of my estate of what kind so ever together with all debts due to me to Jeremiah Courtney.
Sworn to before me this 13th day of January 1766
John Newton
At a Court held for Westmoreland County the 26th day of August 1766 this writing purporting to be the nuncupative will of George Christie, deceased being proved according to law by the oath of the witnesses thereto is ordered to be recorded and on the motion of Jeremiah Courtney who made oath according to law and together with Matthew Partridge his security entered into and acknowledged bond with condition as the law directs, certificate is granted him for obtaining letters of administration of the estate of the said decedent with the said will the next in due form. Teste

Page 387.
Jarvis Wife to Tidwell Privy Examination
To John Martin, John Monroe and Archibald Campbell: Gent. Whereas John Jarvis and Sarah Jarvis by their indenture of bargain and sale bearing date the 27th day of June 1763 have sold and conveyed unto William Carr Tidwell the fee simple estate of 147 acres of land lying in the Parish of Cople and County of Westmoreland and whereas the said Sarah Jarvis cannot conveniently travel to our court to make acknowledgment. Therefore, we do give unto you or any two or more of you power to receive the acknowledgment which she the said Sarah Jarvis shall be willing to make. Witness James Davenport, clerk of our said court the 29th day of January 1764.
Westmoreland Sct. In obedience to the annexed commission, we have (apart from her husband) examined Sarah Jarvis and do hereby certify that she doth voluntarily and without his threats or persuasions acknowledge all her right and title of the land mentioned in the said commission and that she is willing the same should be recorded. As witness our hands and seals this 31st day of January 1764. John Martin
John Monroe
At a Court held for Westmoreland County the 27th day of March 1764 this commission and the certificate of the execution thereof being returned are ordered to be recorded. Teste

Page 388.
William O'Bryan Goff Will
In the name of God Amen, I William O'Bryan Goff of the County of Westmoreland and colony of Virginia being in perfect sense and memory do make publish and declare this to be my last will and testament.
Item I give and bequeath to my daughter Frances Johnston 100 acres of my land lying in Prince William County to be laid off at the north east end of my tract of land joining to Hornsby's and Brown's line to go square as the land runs to Neabsco Run and the heirs of her body forever and failing such issue to my son Benjamin Goff.
Item I give and bequeath to my daughter Frances Johnston 60 pounds current money to be paid to her by my beloved wife Jane Goff within the term of three years after my decease.
Item I give and bequeath to my son Benjamin Goff three Negroes; Sample, Jeffrey, and Hester.
Item I give and bequeath to my son Benjamin Goff all my lands that I hold in Yeocomico Neck in Westmoreland County.
Item I give and bequeath to my son Benjamin Goff 100 acres of my land in Prince William County.
Item I give and bequeath to my beloved wife Jane Goff all the remaining part of my land lying in Prince William County not before devised for and during her natural life and after her decease to my son Benjamin Goff.
Item I give and bequeath to my beloved wife Jane Goff Negro man Charles, Negro woman Winney, and Negro woman Lucey with all their increase from and after the 17th day of last April, and Negro lad Jack for and during my wife's natural life and after my wife's decease I give the said Negroes to my son Benjamin Goff.
Item all the rest and residue of my personal estate not heretofore devised I give and bequeath to

my beloved wife Jane Goff upon condition that the said estate to be appraised as soon as conveniently may be after my decease and that my said wife do when required by my executor give sufficient security to the executor for the payment or half the value according to the appraisement price to my son Benjamin Goff when he arrives at the age of 21 years, otherwise I give and bequeath the whole of my said residual estate to my son Benjamin Goff.
Item my will and intention is that the several legacies and bequests hereby devise to my beloved wife Jane Goff shall be considered as given her in lieu of her dower.
Item I give and bequeath to my son William Goff one shilling sterling to be paid out of my estate.
Item my will and desire is that my executors shall have my son Benjamin Goff virtuously and industriously brought up that he may be time arithmetic, to read and to write and that they may bind to some trade or profession at the discretion of my executors, and further that my son Benjamin Goff shall be maintained in educated out of the profits of my whole estate according to the discretion of my executors till he arrives at the age of 21 years.
Item I constitute and ordain and appoint my beloved wife Jane Goff and William Lee, Esq. of Westmoreland County, executrix and executor or of this my last will and testament and guardian to my son Benjamin Goff.
In witness whereof I have hereunto set my hand and seal this 19th day of July 1766.
Item Signed sealed and published in the presence of William O'Bryan Goff
George Curtis
John Askins
Daniel Minor
At a court held for Westmoreland County the 30th day of September 1766 this will was proved according to law by the oath of George Christie, John Askins and Daniel Minor the witnesses thereto and ordered to be recorded and on the motion of Jane Goff and William Lee the executors named in the said will who made oath according to law and together with George Rust, Daniel Bennett: Philip Ludwell Lee and Francis Lightfoot Lee their securities entered into and acknowledged bond with condition as the law directs, certificate is granted them for obtaining a probate thereof in due form. Teste

Page 390.
Goff to Goff Deed of Gift
I Jane Goff of Cople Parish in Westmoreland County and colony of Virginia, widow in consideration of my natural affection and regard and for diverse other good causes and considerations me thereunto moving have given and granted by these presents unto my beloved son Benjamin Goff and his heirs forever all those Negroes devised and bequeath to me by my late beloved husband William O'Bryan Goff in his last will and testament bearing date the 19th day of July 1766; Negro man Charles, Negro woman Winney, and Negro woman Lucey and all her increase from and after the 17th day of the last April always excepting and reserving to myself during my natural life or so long as the said Negroes shall be kept in the colony aforesaid. In witness whereof I have hereunto set my hand and seal this 10th day of September 1766
Signed sealed and delivered in presence of Jane Goff (her mark)
William Lee
Daniel Minor
At a court held for Westmoreland County the 30th day of September 1766 this deed of gift was acknowledged by Jane Goff party thereto and ordered to be recorded. Test

Page 391.
Cossum Bennett's Will
In the name of God Amen, Cossom Bennett of the County of Westmoreland being sick and weak but in perfect and sound memory do ordain this my last will and testament in manner and form as follows.
Item I give unto my eldest son William Bennett his horse, saddle and bridle at my death.
Item I give unto my son Bunbury Bennett his mare, saddle and bridle at my death.
Item I give to my dear beloved wife all the rest of my whole estate lands Negros and all other things belonging to my estate during her life and after her death the whole estate to be sold and equally

divided among my children.
I do make my wife and my son William Bennett and Thomas Bunbury my executors to fill this my last will and testament.
Signed with my hand and seal with my seal this 14th day of July 1765
Signed sealed and delivered in the presence of us Cossom Bennett
Calvert Jones
David Jones
James Cuthbertson
At a court held for Westmoreland County the 30th day of September 1766 this will was proved according to law by the oaths of Calvert Jones and James Cuthbertson witnesses thereto and ordered to be recorded and on the motion of Catherine Bennett: William Bennett and Thomas Bunbury the executors named in the said will who made oath according to law and together with Joseph Sanford and Richard Neale their securities entered into and acknowledged bond with condition as the law directs, certificate is granted them for obtaining a probate thereof in due form.

Page 392.
John Hurley's Will
In the name of God Amen, I John Hurley of Washington Parish in the County of Westmoreland being much indisposed and sick but of sound mind and memory do make this my last will and testament in manner and form following.
I give and bequeath unto my son John Hurley all my wearing clothes.
Item I give and bequeath unto my wife Behethelem Hurley all my estate that it be it of what nature or property whatever and I appoint my said wife to be my soul and whole executrix of this my last will and testament. In witness whereof I have hereunto set my hand and seal this 31st day of January 1766.
John Atwood John Hurley
Sarah Atwood (her mark)
William Wroe
At a court held for Westmoreland County this 30th day of September 1766 this will was proved according to law by the oath of John Atwood and William Wroe witnesses thereto and ordered to be recorded and on the motion of Behethelem Hurley the executrix named in the said will who made oath according to law and together with John Atwood her security entered into and acknowledged bond with condition as the law directs, certificate is granted for obtaining a probate thereof in due form. Test

Page 393.
Presley Cox's Will
In the name of God Amen, I Presley Cox of Cople Parish in Westmoreland County in Virginia being at this time in health both of body and mind do make this my last will and testament in the following manner and form.
I give and bequeath to my son Fleet Cox my great Bible and large looking glass which hangs in the hall and Negro man Dick.
Item I give and bequeath to my grandsons Richard Wright and Presley Wright and my granddaughter Nancy Wright 10 pounds current money of Virginia each to be paid out of my estate by my executors when they arrive to the age of 21 years for the day of marriage.
Item I give to my grandsons Fleet Cox and Presley Cox and my granddaughter Molly Cox 10 pounds current money each to be paid out of my estate by my executors when they arrive to the age of 21 years or day of marriage.
Item I give to my son William Cox Negro man Phil, Tom, and Isac, Negro woman Jenney, Negro woman named Nan and her three children; Will, Lett and Nan, with all the future increase.
Item after my just debts and the legacies already given and bequeath fully satisfied and paid then I give the remainder of my estate both real and personal of what nature or kind whatsoever both within doors and without to my son William Cox and his heirs forever.
Lastly, I constitute and appoint my son Fleet Cox and my son William Cox and Francis Wright to be my whole and sole executors of this my last will and testament. In witness whereof I have hereunto

set my hand and affixed my seal this 18th day of February 1766.

Witness: Presley Cox

George Lamkin
John Baley
Winifred Baley (her mark)

At a court held for Westmoreland County the 30th day of September 1766 this will was proved according to law by the oaths of George Lamkin, and John Baley witnesses thereto and ordered to be recorded and on the motion of William Cox the executor named in the said will who made oath according to law him together with Fleet Cox his security entered into and acknowledged bond with condition as the law directs, certificate is granted him for obtaining a probate thereof in due form. Test

Page 395.

Goff to Askins Lease

This indenture made the 22nd day of July 1766 between William O'Bryan Goff of the Parish of Cople and County of Westmoreland of the one part and John Askins and Mary Askins his wife and Elizabeth Askins their daughter of the parish and county aforesaid of the other part. Witnesseth that in consideration of the rents and covenants hereafter reserved on the part in behalf of the said John Askins and Mary Askins his wife and Elizabeth Askins their daughter to be performed the said William O'Bryan Goff has granted leased and to farm let by these presents a tract of land in Yeocomico Neck in the parish and county aforesaid and bounded by the lands of Jeremiah Garland Bailey, William Jeffries and Samuel Rust, deceased being the lands I bought of Farnifold Knott containing 100 acres. To have and to hold the said land unto John Askins and Mary Askins his wife and Elizabeth Askins their daughter during their natural life or the longest liver of them yielding and paying yearly and every year during the term aforesaid unto the said William O'Bryan Goff the just and full sum of 600 pounds of crop tobacco the first of which rent is to become due on the first day of January next ensuing and the said John Askins and Mary Askins his wife and Elizabeth Askins their daughter doth covenant that they will build a dwelling house 20 feet long and 16 foot wide on the said lands this present year and other necessary houses as they shall be in want of afterwards. In witness whereof the said William O'Bryan Goff and John Askins for himself his wife and their daughter To this present indenture set their hands and seals the day month and year first written.

Sealed and delivered in presence of William O'Bryan Goff

John Norwood John Askins

Daniel Minor
Gerrard Ball (his mark)

At a court held for Westmoreland County the 30th day of September 1766 this indenture of lease was proved by Gerrard Ball he witness thereto and the same having been before proved by the oaths of two other of the witnesses thereto and ordered to be recorded. Teste

Page 397.

Morton & Wife to Muse Lease

Indenture made the 30th day of September 1762 between Thomas Morton of Lunenburg parish in Richmond County and Ann Morton his wife of the one part and Richard Muse of the County of Westmoreland and Parish of Washington of the other part. Witnesseth that Thomas Morton and Ann Morton in consideration of five shillings current money of Virginia has sold to Richard Muse a tract of land containing 200 acres lying in the Parish of Washington and County of Westmoreland and bounded as followeth; beginning at a marked white oak standing on a point between the main Swamp in a branch called Vaughan's branch extending North West by West 80 poles, Northwest by North 60 poles to a white Oak, then North East 160 poles to a certain oak on a knoll, thence South South East 200 poles unto the said main Swamp, finally down the said Swamp to the beginning. To have and to the said tract from the day before the date hereof during the term of one whole year next ensuing yielding and paying the rent of one ear of Indian corn on the last day of the year to the intent and purpose that by virtue of these presents and of the statute made for transferring uses into possession the said Richard Muse may be in actual possession of the premises and be thereby enabled to accept a grant of the reversion and inheritance thereof to him which is intended to be granted and release by them the said Thomas Morton and Ann Morton. In witness whereof the parties to these presents have interchangeably set their hands and seals the day and year above written.

Signed sealed and delivered in the presence of us Thomas Morton
Ann Morton

At a Court held for Westmoreland County the 30th day of September 1766 this indenture of lease was acknowledged by Thomas Morton and Ann Morton his wife parties thereto and ordered to be recorded. Teste

Page 399.

Morton & Wife to Muse Release

This indenture made the 30th day of September 1766 between Thomas Morton of Lunenburg parish in the County of Richmond and Ann Morton his wife of the one part and Richard Muse of the Parish of Washington and County of Westmoreland of the other part. Witnesseth that Thomas Morton and Ann Morton his wife in consideration of 112 pounds 1 shilling current money of Virginia has sold unto Richard Muse in his actual possession by virtue of an indenture of bargain and sale made for the term of one year and by virtue of the statute for transferring uses into possession a tract of land containing 200 acres lying in the Parish of Washington and County of Westmoreland and bounded as followeth; beginning at a marked white oak standing on a point between the main Swamp in a branch called Vaughan's branch extending North West by West 80 poles, Northwest by North 60 poles to a white Oak, then North East 160 poles to a certain oak on a knoll, thence South South East 200 poles unto the said main Swamp, finally down the said Swamp to the beginning. In witness whereof the said parties to these presents have hereunto set their hands and seals the day and year above written.

Signed sealed and delivered in the presence of us Thomas Morton
Ann Morton

At a Court held for Westmoreland County the 30th day of September 1766 this indenture of release was acknowledged by Thomas Morton and Ann Mortonhis wife parties thereto she being first privy examined as the law directs and ordered to be recorded. Teste

Page 401.

Burtch [Burch] & Wife to Nelson Lease

This indenture made this 28th day of September 1766 between Baynham Burch and Elizabeth Burch his wife of the Parish of Washington and the County of Westmoreland of the one part and William Nelson of the aforesaid parish and county of the other part. Witnesseth that Baynham Burch and Elizabeth Burch his wife in consideration of two young negroes hath sold by these presents to William Nelson a tract of land containing 100 acres where they now dwell lying in the parish and county aforesaid, beginning at the corner of this land, the land of Francis Triplett's and the land of John Nelson's, from thence running a straight course to the head of a branch called the First Pond branch, thence down the said branch to the Old Mill now in possession of Peter Bashaw, thence down the said mill run to the line of Burditt Ashton's, thence along the said Ashton's line to the line of George Hale's, thence along the said Hale's line to the line of John Nelson, thence along the said Nelson's line to the beginning. To have and to hold the plantation from the day of the date of these presents for and during the term of one whole year from thence next ensuing paying one ear of Indian corn on the last day of the said term to the intent that by virtue of these presents and of the statute for transferring uses into possession that the said William Nelson may be in actual possession of the premises and thereby be the better enabled to accept and take a release of the reversion and inheritance thereof to him and his heirs forever. In witness whereof the said parties to these presents have hereunto set their hands and seals the day and year above written.

Sealed and delivered in presence of Baynham Burch
George Stone Elizabeth Burch (her mark)
Peter Jett
William Craighill

At a court held for Westmoreland County the 30th day of September 1766 this indenture of lease was acknowledged by Baynham Burch and Elizabeth Burch his wife parties thereto and ordered to be recorded. Teste

Page 402.
Burtch [Burch] & Wife to Nelson Release
This indenture made this 29th day of September 1766 between Baynham Burch and Elizabeth Burch his wife of the Parish of Washington and the County of Westmoreland of the one part and William Nelson of the aforesaid parish and county of the other part. Witnesseth that Baynham Burch and Elizabeth Burch his wife in consideration of two young negroes hath sold by these presents to William Nelson in his actual possession now being by virtue of a bargain and sale by force of the statute for transferring uses into possession, a tract of land containing 100 acres where they now dwell lying in the parish and county aforesaid, beginning at the corner of this land, the land of Francis Triplett's and the land of John Nelson's, from thence running a straight course to the head of a branch called the First Pond branch, thence down the said branch to the Old Mill now in possession of Peter Bashaw, thence down the said mill run to the line of Burditt Ashton's, thence along the said Ashton's line to the line of George Hale's, thence along the said Hale's line to the line of John Nelson, thence along the said Nelson's line to the beginning. In witness whereof the parties have hereunto set their hands and seals the day the month and year above written.
Sealed and delivered in presence of Baynham Burch
George Stone Elizabeth Burch (her mark)
Peter Jett
William Craighill
At a court held for Westmoreland County the 30th day of September 1766 this indenture of Release and receipt was acknowledged by Baynham Burch and Elizabeth Burch his wife parties thereto (she being first privy examined as the law directs) and ordered to be recorded. Teste

Page 406. Hambrick [Hamrick] to McKenny [McKinny/McKenne] Indenture
This indenture made the 27th day of October 1766 between Isaac Hamrick and Anna Hamrick his wife of the parish of Dettingen and County of Prince William of the one part and John McKenney of the aforesaid parish and county of the other part. Witnesseth that Isaac Hamrick and his wife in consideration of 20 pounds current money has sold to John McKenney all that plantation containing 50 acres lying in the Parish of Cople and County of Westmoreland being part of a tract of land whereon Samuel Garner formerly lived now vested lawfully in ye said Isaac Hamrick and Hannah Hamrick his wife, the said land adjoining to the land of Henry Asbury, deceased. In witness whereof the said parties above mentioned to these presents have interchangeably set their hands and seals the day and year above mentioned.
Signed sealed and delivered in presence of us Isaac Hamrick
John Hutt Hannah Hamrick
William Brown
George McKenney
At a court held for Westmoreland county the 28th day of October 1766 this indenture and the memorandum of livery of seizen was acknowledged by Isaac Hamrick and Hannah Hamrick his wife parties thereto (she being first privy examined and ordered to be recorded. Teste

Page 408.
Jeremiah Jeffries Will
In the name of God Amen, I Jeremiah Jeffries of the parish of Cople and County of Westmoreland being sick and weak of body but of good and perfect sense and memory do make and ordain this to be my last will and testament.
Imprimis, I give unto my brother Robert Jeffries my still and all my wearing apparel.
Item I give to Leasure Hall the use of the houses and land he has in his possession for his natural life if he chooses to live on it and then to return to the owner of my other lands.
Item I give unto my wife Sarah Jeffries, Negro man Tom and all the remainder of my moveable estate to her and her heirs and I do constitute and appoint my wife and my friend George Rust to be executors of this my last will and testament. In witness whereof I have hereunto set my hand and seal this 1st day of May 1766.

Signed sealed in the presence of us Jeremiah Jeffries
Fleet Cox
Peter Rust
William Edwards (his mark)
Samuel Rust
This will was proved according to law by the oaths of Peter Rust and Samuel Rust witness thereto and ordered to be recorded and on the motion of Sarah Jeffries, widow and executrix named in the said will who made oath according to law and together with George Rust her security entered into and acknowledged bond with condition as the law directs, certificate is granted her for obtaining a probate thereof in due form. Teste

Page 410.
Winifred Sanford's Will
In the name of God Amen, I Winifred Sanford of the Parish of Cople and the County of Westmoreland being weak and sickly of body, but of perfect sense and sound memory do make this my last will and testament in manner and form following
Item I give and bequeath unto my son William Sanford, a bed and furniture, two mares, 7 hogs, 8 head of cattle, 5 pound 10 shillings current money, 1 pewter dish, 6 plates, 1 small bason, one [xxxxxxxxxxx] parcel leather, five [xxxxxxx] flesh fork, ladle, egg slice and sarch.
Item I give and bequeath unto Ann South 1 fur hat and cloke, 1 pair of pumps and buckles.
Item I give and bequeath to Elizabeth Walker, the wife of Peter Walker my side saddle.
Item I give and bequeath unto Ann Moxley my sister all my wearing clothes and 5 pound yarn and 2 pound cotton.
Lastly, I appoint John South and Joseph Moxley whole and sole executor of this my last will and testament, in confirmation whereof I have hereunto set my hand and affixed my seal this 27th day of September 1766.
Signed sealed and delivered in presence of Winifred Sanford (her mark)
Robert Sanford
Peter Walker (his mark)
At a court held for Westmoreland County the 28th day of October 1766, this will was proved according to law by the oaths of Robert Sanford and Peter Walker the witnesses thereto and ordered to be recorded and on the motion of Joseph Moxley one of the executors in the said will named who made oath according to law and together with Robert Sanford and John South his securities entered into and acknowledged bond with condition as the law directs, certificate is granted him for obtaining a probate thereof in due form. Teste

Page 411.
Triplett to Fitzhugh Indenture
This Indenture made the 17th day of December 1762 between John Triplett of King George County of the one part and Daniel Fitzhugh of Westmoreland County of the other part. Witnesseth that John Triplett for diverse good considerations him hereunto moving and also in consideration of 5 shillings paid by Daniel Fitzhugh has sold a tract of land lying in the County of Westmoreland on the upper side of Mattox Creek containing 63 acres, bounded by the lines of the land of John Martin, Doctor James Bankhead, the tract commonly called Wilford's Neck and the said Mattox Creek which tract John Triplett purchased of John Vicars of Prince William County. To have and to hold the tract to the said Daniel Fitzhugh for the uses intents and purposes and upon the tracts after mentioned and for no other use intent or purpose whatsoever, that is to say one equal part of the said 63 acres to the use of Sarah Lovell wife of Robert Lovell, daughter of the said John Triplett and formerly the wife of William Hore, deceased during the term of her natural life and to permit her to hold occupy and peaceably enjoy the same during the said term and to take the rents and profits thereof to her own proper use in the same manner as if her said former husband had died seized thereof and after the death the said Sarah to the use of the said Daniel Fitzhugh and Catherine Fitzhugh his wife granddaughter of the said John Triplett and heirs of their bodies lawfully begotten and failing heirs of the body of the said Catharine by the said Daniel to the said Daniel Fitzhugh and his heirs forever. And the other two thirds parts of the 63 acres to the said Daniel Fitzhugh and

Catharine his wife and the heirs of the body of the said Katherine and failing such heirs to the said Daniel Fitzhugh and his heirs forever and the said John Triplett for himself his heirs executors and administrators doth hereby covenant and promise to and with the said Daniel Fitzhugh his heirs and assigns that he or they will at any time hereafter at the request of the said Daniel his heirs or assigns may do execute and acknowledge any such further and other deed act or conveyance in law for the better securing the premises to the said Daniel Fitzhugh and his heirs for the uses intents and purposes aforesaid us by the said Daniel Fitzhugh his assigns for their council learned in the law shall be reasonably devised or required.

Lastly, that he the said John Triplett his heirs, administrators will warrant and defend the premises to the said Daniel Fitzhugh and his heirs for the uses aforesaid against him the said John Triplett and every person or person claiming by from or under him. In witness whereof the said John Triplett hath hereunto for his hand and seal the day of written.

Signed and delivered in presence of [xxxxxxxx]

John Lovell

George Carmichael

John Burnside

[xxxxxxxx]

[xxxxxxxx]

[xxxxxxxx]

At a Court held for Westmoreland County the 24th day of February 1767 this indenture was proved by the oath of George Carmichael, John Burnside and Johnson Bulger witnesses thereto and ordered to be recorded. Teste

Page 412.

John Lee's Will

In the name of God, Amen. I John Lee of the County of Essex, gentleman, being sick and weak in body but of sound memory and understanding (praise God for it) do make this my last Will and Testament hereby revoking and disannulling all former Wills by me heretofore made first and principally I commend my soul into the hands of Almighty God my Creator hoping for free pardon and remission of all my Sins and to enjoy Everlasting Happiness in his Heavenly kingdom through the sole merits of Jesus Christ my Saviour. My body I commit to the Earth at the discretion of my Executors hereinafter named and as to such worldly estate as it hath pleased God to in trust me I dispose of as followeth:

Item, I lend unto my wife Mary Lee all my estate both real and personal excepting the lands purchased by me of John Miller and Thomas Ayres, during her life.

Item, I lend unto John Lee Jr., and Susanna Lee his wife, during their lives, my land purchased of John Miller and Thomas Ayres aforesaid, and I give and devise the remainder of the said lands to my cousin Hancock Lee (son of the said John Lee Jr.) to him and his heirs forever.

Item, I give and bequeath unto the said Hancock Lee all the rest of my lands in the County of Essex to him and his heirs forever.

Item, I lend (after the death of my wife) unto my brother Henry Lee for and during his life my lands in Westmoreland County called King Capsicoe, which my father purchased of John Wright, William Chandler and Deliverance Chandler, his wife, and Susanna Appleyard and the lands I purchased of Francis Wright and Molly Wright, his wife, and after the death of my said brother Henry Lee: I give and devise the said Lands unto my nephew Henry Lee and his heirs forever, provided my said nephew live to the age of twenty-one years, remainder to my said brother Henry and his heirs forever.

Item, after the death of my wife, I lend all the rest of my lands in Westmoreland unto my brother Richard Lee for and during his natural life, the remainder I give and devise to the issue male of my said brother Richard Lee but for want of such issue I give and devise the said lands to my nephew Henry Lee and his heirs, provided my said nephew lives to the age of 21 years, remainder to my brother Henry and his heirs.

Item, I lend unto my sister Lettice Ball during her life the negroes I purchased of Col. William Ball's estate, Vizt. Letty and her child Frank, George and Betty and their increase and after the death of my sister I give the said negroes and their increase to my niece Mary Ball and nephew Henry Lee

Ball to be equally divided between them and their heirs forever.
Item, I give unto my wife Mary Lee my negro fellow Abel, Moll (the daughter of Yellow Nan) my chariot harness and six chariot horses to her and her heirs forever.
Item. After the payment of my debts, I give unto Mary Smith and Fanny Smith daughters of Baldwin Mathews Smith one young negro woman each to them and their heirs forever.
Item. After the life of my wife my will is that my negroes be divided into three equal parts, one third whereof I lend to my brother Henry Lee during his life and after his death I give the same to my nephew Henry Lee and his heirs, provided he live to the age of 21 years, otherwise I give the same to my brother Henry Lee and his heirs.
Item, I lend one other third part of my said negroes to my brother Richard Lee during his life, the remainder to the issue of my said brother Richard Lee but for want of such issue, I give the same to my brother Henry Lee and his heirs.
Item, I give the other third and residue of my slaves to in manner following, that is to say, one moiety thereof to Hancock Lee: son of John Lee Jr., and his heirs, the other moiety I give to be equally divided amongst Lettice Lee, Philip Lee, Mary Lee and Elizabeth Lee, the other children of the said John Lee and their heirs.
Item, I give and bequeath unto my nephew Hancock Lee my negro fellow Peter (carpenter) exclusive of his part of the other slaves aforesaid.
Item, I give unto the said Hancock Lee my desk, book case, and clock.
Item, I give to my brother Henry Lee my picture and those of my father and mother [xxxx]. . .
Item I give unto my brothers [xxxxxxxxxxxxxxx] sheep, horses and hogg in Westmoreland after [xxxxxxxxxxxx] stocks of horses, cattle, sheep and hogs in Essex.
Item, my will is that my wife do sell any timber from the lands lent her for her own use or for the payment of my debts.
Item I give my wearing clothes to my neighbor Robert Farmer excepting my linens.
Item for the regard I have for Mr. Robert Greer, I lend unto him the lodging room over my chamber or the school house which ever he chooses with a good bed and furniture to it, a small table and 4 chairs and likewise my will is that he be provided with cloathing and victuals in my house during his life.
Item, I do hereby appoint and constitute my wife Mary Lee executrix, my brothers Richard Lee and Henry Lee: and my kinsman John Lee Jr., executors of this my last will and testament. In Witness whereof I have hereunto set my hand and affixed my seal the 23rd day of September 1765.
Signed sealed published in the presence of us John Lee
John Matthews
Robert Greer
John Gillon
Alexander Parker
At a court held for Westmoreland County the 24th day of February 1767 this will was proved according to law by the oaths of John Gillon and Alexander Parker witnesses thereto and ordered to be recorded. Richard Lee, Esq., the heir at law being present and consenting thereto, and at a court held for the said county the 25th day of August 1767, on the motion of Mary Lee: widow and executrix named in the said will who made oath according to law and together with Thomas Smith, clerk, John Augustine Washington, Richard Henry Lee and Richard Parker, Gent., her securities entered into and acknowledged bond with condition as the law directs, certificate is granted her for obtaining a probate thereof in due form, liberty being reserved to Richard Lee, Henry Lee and John Lee the other executors to join in the probate when they shall think fit. Teste

Page 415.
John Newton's Will
In the name of God Amen, I John Newton of the County of Westmoreland being sick and weak of body but of sound understanding and memory do make this my last will and testament in manner and form following.
Item I give to my son Willoughby Newton all the lands and slaves I have in expectation from my father to him and his heirs.
Item I give to my son Willoughby Newton Negroes; Diana the daughter of Moll, Jemmima the

daughter of Beck, Rachel and Hannah.
Item I give to my son Willoughby Newton all the stock of cattle and sheep left by my fathers will.
Item I give to the child my wife now goes with my plantation in Yeocomico Neck where I lately lived to him or her heirs.
I give to the said child my wife now goes with all the residue and remainder of my negroes not heretofore mentioned.
Item I give to my wife the plantation where I now live bounded from Fall Hall Marsh or Swamp up to the branch that leads to Oldham's Ole House, from thence to the road leading to Bradley Garner's including Long's, Caddeen's, & James McCluskey's thereunto. I likewise give to my said wife the use of the mill and the corn field over the said mill during her natural life.
Item I give to my wife 8 slaves such as she may choose out of all the slaves, I die possessed of including those left me by my father during her natural life.
Item I also give to my wife all the furniture now in my house.
Item I give to my son Willoughby Newton all the furniture and plate left me by my father.
Item I give to my wife 20 head of cattle, 20 head of sheep and the half of all my hoggs.
Item I give to the poor of Cople Parish the sum of 20 pounds to be paid to them at the rate of 5 pounds per year.
My will further is that in case both my aforesaid children should die before they are married or without issue in the life time of my wife, that she my said wife shall have and enjoy the use of all my estate both real and personal during and also shall have full and absolute power to give and dispose of the aforesaid estate to and amongst my sisters and their children or any one or more of them or their heirs.
Item I devise all my land in Loudoun County to my executors hereafter named in trust and to be by them sold and the money applied [xxxxxxxxxx]
Lastly, I do constitute and appoint my friend Richard Lee, Esq., Mr. David Boyd and Mr. William Flood, executors as also my wife executrix.
Signed sealed published & declared this 8th day of January 1767 in the presence of
Richard Caddeen John Newton
Mary Stone (her mark)
John McDormer (his mark)
William Flood
At court held for Westmoreland County the 24th day of February this will was proved according to law by the oaths of Richard Caddeen and John McDormer witnesses thereto and ordered to be recorded and on the motion of Richard Lee, Esq., and William Flood, Gent., the executors named in the said will who made oath according to law and together with William Price and Gerrard Hutt their securities entered into and acknowledged bond with condition as the law directs, certificate is granted them for obtaining a probate thereof in due form. Teste

Page 417.
Walker & Wife to Lane Indenture & Privy Examination
This Indenture made the 4th day of October 1766 between James Walker and Elizabeth Walker his wife of the county of Granville in the province of North Carolina, planter in consideration of 85 pounds current money of Virginia have sold to Joseph Lane a tract of land in Nominy Forrest in the parish Cople and County of Westmoreland containing by estimation 140 acres and bounded by the lands of the said Joseph Lane, the heirs of the Reverend Mr. Joseph Simpson, deceased, the heirs of Miss Elizabeth Turberville: deceased and the land of Mr. Gerrard Hutt now in the possession of Gerrard Hutt, Jr., (it being the land whereon Vincent McKenney now liveth as a tenant, which said land was given to Lydia Hardwick (who intermarried with Thomas Walker, father to the said James Walker) by her father James Hardwick as by his last will and testament bearing date the [xx] day of December 1726; which said land descended to James Walker as eldest son and heir at law to his mother Lydia Walker who likewise intermarried with William Plunkett, her second and last husband & died the 7th day of January 1766. In witness whereof the first parties to these presents have interchangeably set their hands and seals the day and year first above written.
Signed sealed in the presence of James Walker
Richard Lee Elizabeth Walker (her mark)

Reuben Jordan
John Rice
Lewin Bennett Garlick
To Robert Munford, John Speed, Edmond Taylor: Benjamin Baird and Thomas Anderson of the county of Mecklenburg, Gent. Whereas James Walker and Elizabeth Walker his wife of the county of Granville in the province of North Carolina by their indenture of bargain and sale bearing date the 4th day of October 1766 have sold unto Joseph Lane of the County of Westmoreland in the colony of Virginia, Gent., the fee simple estate of 140 acres of land lying in Nominy Forrest in the county of Cople and County of Westmoreland, and whereas Elizabeth Walker cannot conveniently travel to our court of Westmoreland to make acknowledgement of the conveyance. Therefore, we do give unto you or any two of you power to receive the acknowledgement that the said Elizabeth Walker shall be willing to make. Witness James Davenport, clerk of our court the 7th day of October 1766.
By virtue of a commission to us directed from the county court of Westmoreland we have caused Elizabeth Walker, wife of James Walker personally to appear before us and received her acknowledgement of the indenture annexed to the said commission and then examined her apart from her husband when she freely and voluntarily relinquished her right of dower and assented that the indenture should be recorded in the county court of Westmoreland. Certified under our hands and seals this 17th day of October 1766.
Robert Munford
Thomas Anderson
At a court held for Westmoreland County the 24th day of February 1767 this [indenture] together with a memorandum of livery of seizen and receipt thereon endorsed and a bond for performance of covenants were proved by the oaths of Richard Lee, Esq., Reuben Jordan and Lewin Bennett Garlick witnesses thereto and together with the commission and privy examination of Elizabeth Walker, the wife of James Walker and the certificate of the execution thereof ordered to be recorded. Teste

Page 421.
Garner & Wife to McKenny Indenture & Privy Examination
This indenture made the 27th day of October 1766 between Samuel Garner and Isabel Garner his wife of the parish of Overwharton and county of Stafford, planter of the one part and John McKenney of the Parish of Cople and County of Westmoreland, planter of the other part. Witnesseth that Samuel Garner and Isabel Garner his wife in consideration of 5 pounds current money of Virginia paid by Isaac Hamrick on behalf of John McKenney has sold to the said John McKenney 1/3rd part of a tract lying in Nominy Forrest in the Parish of Cople and County of Westmoreland containing by estimation 50 acres and bounded by the lands of James Gregory, the heirs of Thomas Asbury, deceased and the land whereon Mary Connelly now lives which said 17 acres Samuel Garner holds in the right of his wife Isabel Garner who claims the same for her right of dower as widow and relict of George [xxxxxxxxxxxxxx] {Haughlcom} of all the said 50 acres of land and which said [xxxxxxxxxx] more or less goes to his daughter [xxxxxxxxxxx] of the said Isaac Hamrick after the decease of the said Isabel Garner wife of Samuel Garner. In witness whereof the first parties to these presents have interchangeably set their hands and seals the day and year first above written

Signed sealed and delivered in presence of	Samuel Garner
Francis Lightfoot Lee	Isabel Garner

Joseph Lane
Reuben Jordan
Stuart Redman
To Richard Lee, John Turberville, John Augustine Washington and Thomas Chilton of the County of Westmoreland, Gent. Whereas Samuel Garner and Elizabeth [sic Isabel] Garner by their indenture of bargain and sale bearing date the 27th day of October 1766 have sold and conveyed unto McKenney the fee simple estate of 17 acres of land lying in the Parish of Cople in the County of Westmoreland being 1/3rd part of a tract containing by estimation 50 acres and whereas Isabel Garner cannot conveniently travel to our court to make acknowledgement. Therefore, we do give unto your or any two of you power to receive the acknowledgement which the said Isabel Garner is

willing to make. Witness James Davenport, clerk the 31st day of October in the 7th year of our reign. Westmoreland County, Sct. By virtue of the within writ to us directed, we did personally go to Isabel Garner the wife of Samuel Garner and she acknowledged the indenture hereunto annexed to be her act and deed and that she did the same freely and voluntarily without the persuasions or threats from her husband and was willing that the same should be recorded in the county court of Westmoreland all which we certify in his said court under our hands and seals this 31st day of 1766.
John Turberville
John Augustine Washington
At a court held for Westmoreland County the 24th day of February 1767 this indenture and receipt thereon endorsed were proved by the oaths of Joseph Lane, Reuben Jordan and Stuart Redman witnesses thereto and together with the commission annexed for taking the acknowledgement and privy examination of Isabel Garner the wife of Samuel Garner and the certificate of the execution thereof ordered to be recorded. Teste

Page 425.
William Viguar [Vigour] Will (Joiner)
I William Viguar being in a low state of health at this time although in my perfect senses and memory.
Item I give to my wife Sarah Viguar all my estate within doors and without doors real and personal during her natural life and after her life to be divided between my six sons.
Item I give to my daughter Frances Viguar one shilling sterling and no more.
I leave my wife Sarah Viguar to be my executor during her life and Matthew Bayne: Jr., unto which I have set my hand and seal.
In the presence of William Viguar
Matthew Bayn
William Bayn
Elizabeth Bayn
Matthew Bayn, Jr.
At a Court held for Westmoreland County the 31st day of March 1767 this will was proved according to law by the oaths of Matthew Bayn and William Bayn and Elizabeth Bayn witnesses thereto and ordered to be recorded and on the motion of Sarah Viguar and Matthew Bayne: Jr. the executors named in the said will who made oath according to law and together with Matthew Bayn, Sr., their security entered into and acknowledged bond with conditioned as the law directs, certificate is granted them for obtaining a probate thereof in due form. Teste

Page 425.
Courtney to Smith Indenture
This indenture made the 17th day of November 1766 between Dorcas Courtney, widow of the County of Westmoreland and colony of Virginia of the one part and Spence Smith of the County of Northumberland in colony aforesaid of the other part. Witnesseth that Dorcas Courtney for the consideration of the natural love and affection which he hath in the unto her son the said Spence Smith and likewise for the sum of 56 pounds current money of Virginia has sold unto Spence Smith (after her death) all that tract of land lying in the County of Westmoreland and bounded as followeth; beginning at or near the mouth of a small gut adjoining the land Capt. John Newton formerly the land of Daniel Bonum's and the land of Mr. Daniel McCarty's and the said Spence Smith land and the land of Capt. Willoughby Newton's formally the land of the Hon. Thomas Lee, deceased and the Hon. Philip Ludwell Lee, Esq. and Potomack River all which said tract of land is containing by estimation 73 acres. In witness whereof the said Dorcas Courtney hath hereunto set her hand and seal in Westmoreland the day and year aforesaid.
Sealed and delivered in the presence of Dorcas Courtney
John Rust
William Barecroft
Jesse Price
Samuel McCave
Thomas Claytor (his mark)

At a court held for Westmoreland County the 31st day of March 1757 this indenture together with a memorandum and receipt thereon endorsed proved by the oaths of John Rust, William Barecroft, and Samuel McCave witnesses thereto and ordered to be recorded. Teste

Page 427.
Minor & Wife to Redman Lease
This indenture made this 31st day of March 1766 between John Minor and Kesiah Minor his wife of the Parish of Cople in the County of Westmoreland of the one part and Solomon Redman of the parish and county aforesaid of the other part. Witnesseth that John Minor and Kesiah Minor his wife in consideration of 26 pounds current money of Virginia has sold to Solomon Redman a tract of land containing 100 acres bounded as followeth; joining upon Mrs. Edward Ransdell and on the lands of Richard Lee, Esq. of Maryland and Mrs. Daniel McCarty. To have and to hold the said plantation from the day of the date of these presents for and during term of one whole year from hence next ensuing yielding and paying thereof one ear of Indian corn on the last day of said term to the intent that by virtue of these presents and of the statute for transferring uses into possession that the said Solomon Redman may be in actual possession of the premises and thereby be the better enabled to accept and take a release of the reversion and inheritance thereof to him and his heirs. In witness whereof the said parties to these presents have hereunto set their hands and seals the day and year above written.
Sealed and delivered in the presence of
William Chilton John Minor
Benjamin Middleton

Page 429.
Minor & Wife to Redman Release
This indenture made this 31st day of March 1766 between John Minor and Kesiah Minor his wife of the Parish of Cople in the County of Westmoreland of the one part and Solomon Redman of the parish and county aforesaid of the other part. Witnesseth that John Minor and Kesiah Minor his wife in consideration of 26 pounds current money of Virginia has sold to Solomon Redman a tract of land containing 100 acres being in his actual possession by virtue of a bargain and sale to him bearing the date the day next before the date of these presents for the term of one year and by force of the statute for transferring uses into possessions and bounded as followeth; joining upon Mrs. Edward Ransdell and on the lands of Richard Lee, Esq. of Maryland and Mrs. Daniel McCarty. In witness whereof the parties have hereunto set their hands and seals the day the month and year first above written.
Sealed and delivered in the presence of
William Chilton John Minor
Benjamin Middleton
At a court held for Westmoreland County the 31st day of March 1766 these indentures of lease and release and the receipt endorsed on the said release were acknowledged by John Minor party thereto and ordered to be recorded. Test

Page 432.
Gray to Williams Indenture
This indenture made the 12th day of September 1766 between Francis Gray of the Parish of Washington and County of Westmoreland of the one part and Arthur Williams of the parish and county aforesaid. Witnesseth that Francis Gray in consideration of 150 pounds current money to him has sold unto Arthur Williams a tract of land in the Irish Neck bounded as followeth; beginning at a marked pine standing on the bank of Monroe's Creek corner to the land of the late Thomas Butler: thence North 65° East 95 ½ pole to Potomack River thence down the several meanders of the said river to the mouth of Monroe's Creek, thence up the several meanders of the said creek to the beginning containing 112 acres being the same tract purchased by the said Francis Gray of Benjamin Tyler late of the parish and county aforesaid. In witness whereof the said Francis Gray to these presents have hereunto set his hand and seal the day and date above mentioned.
Signed sealed and delivered in presence of Francis Gray

Sarah Davis (her mark)
Alvin Mothershead (his mark)
Benjamin Settle (his mark)
William Settle
Spence Monroe
William Weathersby
James Boddington
At a Court held for Westmoreland County this 31st day of March 1767 this indenture together with a memorandum of livery of seizen and receipt thereon endorsed were proved by the oath of Spence Monroe: William Weathersby and James Boddington witnesses thereto and ordered to be recorded. Test

Page 434.
Brenum [Brannan] to Stowers Apprentice Agreement
This indenture made the 31st day of March 1767 between Joseph Brenum in Washington County of the one part and Samuel Stowers of the County of Richmond, carpenter of the other part. Witnesseth that Joseph Brenum has bound himself an apprentice to the said Samuel Stowers to the said Joseph shall come to the age of 21 years. In witness whereof the parties to these presents have hereunto interchangeably set their hands and seals the day and year first above written.
Sealed and delivered in presence of us Joseph Brenum (his mark)
Samuel Stowers
At a Court held for Westmoreland County the 31st day of March 1767 this indenture was acknowledged by the parties thereto and with the approbation of the court is ordered to be recorded. Teste

Page 435.
Burrus to Stower Apprentice Agreement
This indenture made the 31st day of March 1767 between Michael Burrus of the Parish of Lunenburg in the County of Richmond one part and Samuel Stowers of the County of Richmond, carpenter of the other part. Witnesseth that the said Thomas Williams [sic Michael Burrus] has bound himself an apprentice to the said Samuel Stowers to the said Williams [sic Burrus] shall come to the age of 21 years. In witness whereof the parties to these presents have hereunto interchangeably set their hands and seals the day and year first above written.
Sealed and delivered in presence of us Michael Burrus (his mark)
Samuel Stowers
At a Court held for Westmoreland County the 31st day of March 1767 this indenture was acknowledged by the parties thereto and with the approbation of the court is ordered to be recorded. Teste

Page 436.
Walker to Spark Indenture
This indenture made the 31st day of March 1767 between Samuel Walker of the County of Amelia, planter and Sarah Walker his wife of the one part and Alexander Spark of the County of Westmoreland, merchant of the other part. Witnesseth that Samuel Walker and Sarah Walker his wife in consideration of 35 pounds current money of Virginia has sold to Alexander Spark a tract of land lying in the Parish of Cople in the County of Westmoreland containing 100 acres and bounded as followeth; beginning at a chestnut tree standing near Solomon Redman's mill run, thence up the said run to the mouth of a branch making into the said run, thence up the said branch to Minor's line, thence along the said line to the main road, thence up the said road to the beginning which said tract was sold and conveyed to the said Samuel Walker by Valentine Sturman late of the County of Westmorland by indenture bearing date the 8th day July 1752. In witness whereof the parties to these presents have hereunto set their hands and seals the day and year above written.
Sealed and delivered in presence of Samuel Walker
Richard Neale Sarah Walker (her mark)
Daniel Muse, Jr.

At a Court held for Westmoreland County the 31st day of March 1767 this indenture in the receipt thereon endorsed were acknowledged by Samuel Walker and Sarah Walker his wife parties thereto (she being first privily examined as the law directs) and ordered to be recorded. Teste

Page 438.
Griffin & Daniel to Bailey Lease
This indenture made the 25th day of December 1766 between John Griffin and Edmond Daniel of the County of Caroline and parish of St. Mary's of the one part and John Bailey of the County of Westmoreland and Parish of Washington of the other part. Witnesseth that John Griffin and Edmond Daniel in consideration of five shillings Sterling has sold to John Bailey a parcel of land containing 100 acres in the Parish of Washington in County of Westmorland line on the branches of Appomattox Creek being formerly sold by Francis Wright, Gent unto Thomas Robins in the said Robins having sold the said land unto Robert Frank, Sr., of the aforesaid County in the said Robert Frank, Sr., acknowledged the above said land unto Robert Frank, Jr., as per a deed of gift bearing the date 12th day of August 1714 it being the land where John Backus lived on in the year 1766 and bounded as follows; beginning at a white oak corner to James Hardwick's land, thence along his line South to a corner of Piper's in a branch, thence East and eastwardly to a forked locust in the corner of the said Piper's line standing on a ditch, thence along the said Piper's line in the ditch North to a corner white oak of Robert Frank's line standing on a knoll by the dam, thence West along the said Frank's line to a locust post corner to [xxx] said Frank and Bailey: thence along the said Bailey to the first mentioned beginning. To have and to hold the said land from the day of the date hereof for and during the full term of one whole year from thence yielding and paying the rent of one ear of Indian corn at the expiration of the said term to the intent and purpose that by virtue of these presents and of the statute for transferring uses into possession the said John Bailey may be in the actual possession of the said piece of land and premises hereby bargained and sold and thereby be the better enabled to accept intake a grant and release of the reversion and inheritance thereof to them the said John Griffin and Edmond Daniel hath to this present indenture set their hands and affixed their seals the day and year first above written.

Sealed and delivered in presence of us — John Griffin
William Piper — Edmond Daniel
Peter Jett
Jeremiah Garland Bailey
Francis Jett

At a Court held for Westmoreland County the 28th day of April 1767 this indenture of lease was proved by the oaths of William Piper, Peter Jett and Jeremiah Garland Bailey witnesses thereto and ordered to be recorded. Teste

Page 440.
Griffin & Daniel to Bailey Release
This indenture made the 26th day of December 1766 between John Griffin and Sarah Griffin his wife and Edmond Daniel and Martha Daniel his wife of the County of Caroline and Parish of St. Mary's of the one part and John Bailey of the County of Westmoreland and Parish of Washington of the other part. Witnesseth that John Griffin and Sarah Griffin his wife and Edmond Daniel and Martha Daniel his wife in consideration of 6000 pounds of tobacco has sold to John Bailey in his actual possession now being by virtue of a sale and bargain to him and force of the statute for transferring uses into possession all that parcel of land containing 100 acres in the Parish of Washington and County of Westmorland lying on the branches of Appomattox Creek being formerly sold by Francis Wright, Gent unto Thomas Robins in the said Robins having sold the said land unto Robert Frank, Sr., of the aforesaid county in the said Robert Frank, Sr., acknowledged the above said land unto Robert Frank, Jr., as per a deed of gift bearing the date 12th day of August 1714 it being the land where John Backus lived on in the year 1766 and bounded as follows; beginning at a white oak corner to James Hardwick's land, thence along his line South to a corner of Piper's in a branch, thence East and eastwardly to a forked locust in the corner of the said Piper's line standing on a ditch, thence along the said Piper's line in the ditch North to a corner white oak of Robert Frank's line standing on a knoll by the dam, thence West along the said

Frank's line to a locust post corner to [xxx] said Frank and Bailey: thence along the said Bailey to the first mentioned beginning. In witness whereof the said John Griffin and Sarah Griffin his wife, Edmond Daniel and Martha Daniel his wife to this present indenture set their hands and affixed their seals the day and year first above written.

Sealed and delivered in presence of us — John Griffin
William Piper — Sarah Griffin
Peter Jett — Edmond Daniel
Jeremiah Garland Bailey — Martha Daniel (her mark)
Francis Jett

At a Court held for Westmoreland County the 28th day of April 1767 this indenture of release and a receipt thereon endorsed and a bond for the performance of covenants were proved to be the act and deed of the said John Griffin and Edmond Daniel by the oath of William Piper, Peter Jett and Jeremiah Garland Bailey witnesses thereto and ordered to be recorded. Teste James Davenport Cl Cur

Page 444.

Triplett to Smith Indenture

This indenture made the 17th day of March 1766 between John Triplett of King George County of the one part and Stephen Smith of Westmoreland County of the other part. Witnesseth that John Triplett in consideration of a Negro boy Will, has sold unto Stephen Smith a parcel of land containing 200 acres lying in Westmoreland County in Washington Parish and bounded as followeth; beginning at "A" a Spanish Oak running North 70° West 146 ½ pole to Spillman's path, North 3° West 34 pole to "C" corner of George Monroe's, thence down Bailey's road to "D" corner to the said Monroe: thence South 140 pole to the new road at "E", thence down the said road., South 30 ½° West 103 pole, thence North 79° West to Spillman's line, thence along the said line to the beginning. In witness whereof the said John Triplett hath hereunto set his hand and seal the day and [year] first above written.

Sealed and delivered in presence of — John Triplett
John Bailey
George Marshall
William Piper
James Frank

At a court held for Westmoreland County the 28th day of April 1767 this indenture and the receipt thereon endorsed were proved by the oaths of John Bailey: George Marshall and William Piper witnesses thereto and ordered to be recorded. Teste

Page 445.

William Flemming's Will

In the name of God Amen, I William Flemming of the Parish of Cople and County of Westmoreland being sick and weak of body but of sound and perfect memory do make this my last will and testament in manner and form following.

Item my will is that my loving wife have the use of all my estate during her natural life or widowhood she making no willful waste of the same and if she marry my will is she have no more of my estate than the law allows.

Item I give and bequeath (after the marriage or death of my loving wife Abigail Flemming) to my beloved son John Fleming Negro woman Frank, Negro man Ned, Negro boys Tom and James.

Item I give and bequeath to my beloved son William Flemming Negro man Abbo, Negro woman Bess (or young Negro Frank if he chooses in lieu) and Negro boys Daniel and Adam.

Item I give and bequeath to my beloved daughter Elizabeth Jackson and her husband Thaddeus Jackson the use of my Negro girl Winne during their natural life and afterwards my will is the said Negro go to the heirs begotten and born of the said Thaddeus Jackson and my daughter Elizabeth.

Item I give and bequeath to my beloved daughter Peggy Pritchett and her husband Rodham Pritchett the use of my Negro girl Hannah during her natural life and afterwards my will is the said Negro go to the heirs begotten and born of the said Rodham Pritchett and my daughter Peggy.

Item I give and bequeath to my beloved daughter Martha Fleming Negro girl Nan and in case either

of my said daughters die without heir my will is the survivor of the deceased have the Negroes.
Item my will is my daughter Martha Fleming have 7 pounds current money paid out of my estate to make her estate equal to her two sisters who have each of them had a horse a piece.
Item my will is that my two daughters Peggy Pritchett and Martha Fleming have each of them made out of my estate one feather bed and furniture a piece.
Item my will is after my son William Flemming has taken his choice of my aforesaid Negroes, Bess and Frank that the others not chosen and Negro George be the property of my grandchildren by Thaddeus Jackson and my daughter Elizabeth Jackson and Rodham Pritchett and my daughter Peggy Pritchett after the marriage or death of my loving wife on condition the said Thaddeus Jackson and Rodham Pritchett or their heirs purchase a Negro for my daughter Martha Fleming in proportion to that legacy.
Item I give and bequeath to my beloved son John Fleming my still.
Item my will is after the marriage or death of my loving wife that the remainder of my estate not yet given be equally divided between all my children.
Lastly, my will is that my loving wife Abigail Flemming my beloved sons John Fleming and William Flemming be the executors of this my last will and testament. In witness whereof I the said William Flemming have hereunto set my hand and seal the seventh day of January 1767.
Signed sealed and delivered in the presence of William Flemming (his mark)
James Bailey
Peter Smith: Jr.
Hugh Thomas, Jr.
At a court held for Westmoreland County the 28th day of April 1767 this will was proved by the oaths of Peter Smith: Jr., and Hugh Thomas, Jr., witnesses thereto and ordered to be recorded and on motion of John Fleming and William Flemming the executors named in the said will who made oath according to law and together with James Bailey and Peter Smith their securities entered into and acknowledged bond with conditioned as the law directs, certificate is granted them for obtaining a probate thereof in due form. Teste

Page 447.
Edward Sears Will
In the name of God Amen, I Edward Sears of the County of Westmoreland and Parish of Cople, planter being weak in body but of perfect sense and memory do make this my last will and testament.
Item I desire that 100 pounds currency be laid out in land which my wife Mary Sears is to inherit during her natural live and then to my son William Sears and all the rest of my estate to my wife Mary Sears during her time of her living my widow and if she marries, I desire she may have no more than what the law allows and if my wife should marry or at her death, I desire that the remainder of my estate be equally divided amongst my children.
Lastly, to conclude I nominate my wife Mary Sears and my son William Sears sole executors of this my last will and testament. In witness whereof I have hereunto set my hand and seal this 4th day of July 1766.
Signed sealed and delivered in presence of Edward Sears
Absalom Blundell
James Walker
At a court held for Westmoreland County the 28th day of April 1767 this will was proved according to law by the oaths of Absalom Blundell and James Walker witnesses thereto and ordered to be recorded and at a court held for the said county the 26th day of May 1767 on the motion of Mary Sears, widow and executrix named in the said will who made oath according to law and together with Richard Lee, Esq., Thomas Attwell and John Self her securities entered into and acknowledged bond with condition as the law directs, certificate is granted her for obtaining a probate thereof in due form, liberty being reserved to William Sears the other executor to join in the probate when he should think proper. Teste

Page 448.
Jeffries to Hall Lease

This indenture made the 20th day of December 1766 between Robert Jeffries of the County of Westmoreland and Parish of Cople of the one part and Leasure Hall of the same place, planter of the other part. Witnesseth that the said Robert Jeffries in consideration of the rents and covenants on the part of Leasure Hall to be paid and performed has demised and to farm let by these presents a tenement and tract of land containing 1 acre lying in the county and parish aforesaid being part of a tract of land that fell to the said Robert Jeffries by the death of his brother Jeremiah Jeffries near Rust's will and bounded as followeth; beginning a a red oak on the West side of a branch, thence along the hillside to Rust's line, thence up the said line to a hickory that stands in the head of a bottom that runs up from the mill pond from the said hickory running near South East to a white oak, from thence running a straight course to the red oak at the beginning. To have and to hold the tenement and tract of land with the appurtenances to the said Leasure Hall for and during his natural life after the 29th day of December and paying thencefore yearly and every year on the 25th day of December the full and just sum of 2 shillings sterling money. In witness whereof the parties above mentioned have set their hands and seals the day and year first above written.

Signed sealed and delivered in the presence of us — Robert Jeffries
William Lewis — Leasure Hall
Samuel Beale
Thomas Beale (his mark)
Jeremiah Hall

At a court held for Westmoreland county the 26th day of May 1767 this indenture was proved by the oaths of William Lewis: Samuel Beale and Jeremiah Hall witnesses thereto and ordered to be recorded. Teste

Page 450.
<u>Jeffries to Hall Lease</u>

This indenture made the 24th day of December 1766 between Sarah Jeffries, widow and relict of Jeremiah Jeffries, deceased of the Parish of St. Stephen's in County of Northumberland of the one part and Jeremiah Hall of the Parish of Cople and County of Westmoreland of the other part. Witnesseth that the said Sarah Jeffries in consideration of 35 pounds current money has demised and to farm let by these presents to Jeremiah Hall all her dower of the lands which lately along to her deceased husband lying in the Parish of Cople and County of Westmoreland. To have and to hold the said quantity of land as shall be her dower for and during the natural life of the said Sarah Jeffries yielding and paying yearly and every year during the term aforesaid unto Sarah Jeffries on the 25th day of December 1 grain of Indian corn if the same shall be lawfully demanded. In witness whereof I have hereunto set my hand and seal the day month and year first above written.

Signed sealed and delivered in the presence of — Sarah Jeffries (her mark)
James Knott
William Lewis
Samuel Rust Doun (his mark)
Eleanor Knott (her mark)
Charles McCully

At a Court held for Westmoreland County the 26th day of May 1767 this indenture was proved by the oath of James Knott, William Lewis and Samuel Rust Doun witnesses thereto and ordered to be recorded. Teste

Page 452.
<u>Bashaw to Nelson Lease</u>

This indenture made the 28th day of October 1766 between Peter Bashaw and Percilia [Priscilla] Bashaw of the Parish of Washington and County of Westmoreland of the one part and William Nelson in the parish and county aforesaid of the other part. Witnesseth that Peter Bashaw and Priscilla his wife in consideration of five shillings has sold unto William Nelson a tract of land containing 55 acres lying in the County of Westmoreland in Parish of Washington and bounded as follows; beginning at the dividing line between this land in the land of Warner Bashaw and from thence to the line of John Payton's and along the said Payton's line to the line of Francis James and from the land of Francis James to Burditt Ashton's line from the line of the said Ashton to the great run and thence running down the said run to the line of Warner Bashaw and thence along the said Bashaw's line to the beginning. To have and to hold the said tract unto William Nelson from the day next before the day of the date of these presents for the term of one year yielding and paying one pepper corn upon the first of St. Michael the Archangel next coming to the intent and purposes that by virtue of these presents and of the statue for transforming uses into possession the said William Nelson may be in the actual possession and be the better enabled to accept and to take a grant and release of the reversion and inheritance thereof. In witness whereof the said Peter Bashaw and Priscilla Bashaw his wife have hereunto set their hands and seals the day month and year first above written.

Sealed and delivered in the presence of — Peter Bashaw
John Nelson — Priscilla Bashaw (her mark)
John Jerdon [Jordan] (his mark)
Francis James

Page 453.

Bashaw to Nelson Release

This indenture made the 29th day of October 1766 between Peter Bashaw and Percilia [Priscilla] Bashaw of the Parish of Washington and County of Westmoreland of the one part and William Nelson in the parish and county aforesaid of the other part. Witnesseth that Peter Bashaw and Priscilla his wife in consideration of 51 pounds has sold unto William Nelson a tract of land in his actual possession now being by virtue of a bargain and sale and by force of the statue of transferring uses into possessions a tract containing 55 acres lying in the County of Westmoreland in Parish of Washington and bounded as follows; beginning at the dividing line between this land in the land of Warner Bashaw and from thence to the line of John Peyton's and along the said Payton's line to the line of Francis James and from the land of Francis James to Burditt Ashton's line from the line of the said Ashton to the great run and thence running down the said run to the line of Warner Bashaw and thence along the said Bashaw's line to the beginning.. In witness whereof the parties hereunto interchangeably set their hands and seals the day month and year first above written.

Sealed and delivered in the presence of — Peter Bashaw
John Nelson — Priscilla Bashaw (her mark)
John Jerdon [Jordan] (his mark)
Francis James

At a court held for Westmoreland County the 26th day of May 1767 these indentures of lease and release and receipt endorsed on the said release were proved to be the act and deed of the said Peter Bashaw by the oaths of John Nelson, John Jordan, and Francis James the witnesses thereto and ordered to be recorded. Teste

Page 457.

Crabb to Hutt Indenture and Privy Examination

This indenture made the 19th day of May 1767 between John Crabb and Jane Crabb his wife of the Parish of Cople in the County of Westmoreland of the other part and Gerrard Hutt of the aforesaid parish and county of the other part. Witnesseth that John Crabb and Jane Crabb his wife in consideration of 200 pounds current money of Virginia has sold to Gerrard Hutt all that plantation containing 300 acres lying in the Parish of Cople and colony of Westmoreland that did belong to Coleman Read adjoining to the land of Gerrard Hutt, likewise to the land that formerly belonged to Thomas Blundell and the land that formerly belonged to John Wright and bounded by these lines. In witness whereof the said parties first above mentioned to these presents have interchangeably set their hands and seals the day and year above written.

Sealed and delivered in the presence of us — John Crabb
Joseph Lane — Jane Crabb
Richard Lee
Reuben Jordan
John Turberville

To Richard Lee, John Turberville and John Augustine Washington of the County of Westmoreland,

Gent. Whereas John Crabb and Jane Crabb his wife by their indenture of bargain and sale bearing date the 19th of May 1767 have sold unto Gerrard Hutt the fee simple estate of 300 acres of land in the Parish of Cople in the County of Westmoreland and whereas the said Jane Crabb cannot conveniently travel to our court to make acknowledgement. Therefore, we do give unto you or any two or more of you power to receive the acknowledgement which the said Jane Crabb shall be willing to make. Witness James Davenport, clerk of our said court the 21st day of May in the seventh year of our reign. Joseph Lane D.C.C.W.

Westmoreland County Sct. By virtue of the above writ to us directed we did personally go to the said Jane Crabb the wife of John Crabb and she did acknowledge the indenture hereunto annexed to be her act and deed and that she did the same freely and voluntarily and was willing the same should be recorded in the county court of Westmoreland. Given under our hands and seals this 22nd day of May 1767

Richard Lee

John Turberville

At a court held for Westmoreland County the 26th day of May 1767 this indenture and the memorandum of livery of seizen and receipt endorsed was acknowledged by John Crabb party thereto and together with the commission annexed for taking the acknowledgment and privy examination of Jane Crabb the wife of John Crabb and certificate of execution thereof ordered to be recorded. Teste, James Davenport Cl Cur

Page 461.

Willoughby Newton's Will

In the name of God Amen, the 27th day of December 1766, I Willoughby Newton of the Parish of Cople in the County of Westmoreland in the colony of Virginia do make this my last will and testament in manner and form following;

Item I give and bequeath and devise to my son John Newton my mill and all my lands in Westmoreland County except the land I bought of Philip Ludwell Lee, Esq., Also my cherry tree desk and bookcase with glass door together with all my books, one silver tankard and silver salver [tray], the new case of knives and forks with the dozen of silver spoons in the case, 4 silver salts and ladles, 2 beds and furniture belonging to the rooms upstairs, one dozen chairs made by Spence Monroe: three tables in the new house, 20 head of cattle in the neck at Bonum's and 6 Negroes; Neck, Akey, Narvin, Caezar, Saul, Little George and Isaac the blacksmith: also Daniel Kanady the smith and the smiths tools.

Item I give and bequeath to my grandson Richard Jackson 1 feather bed and furniture, and [the following items I bought from his father's estate] the desk and book case with the corner cupboard, the large silver tankard with the large soup spoon, a dozen silver spoons and the clock.

Item I give and bequeath to my daughter Judith Brent the land and plantation I leased to George Haden in Loudoun County on Great Rocky Run together with all the land I now hold above the said Haden's on the said run to and along the line of the land I made a deed of gift of to my son John Newton and along his line to the land I gave to William Jett and Katherine Jett his wife, and along their line to the said Great Rocky Run, being about 500 acres. I also confirm my gift of all the slaves now in the possession of my daughter Judith Brent which I give her when she married Mr. Brereton Kenner.

Item I give and devise to my daughter Katherine Lane the land where Demsey Carroll lived, also the land where John Goddard lived and along John Newton's line to the Mountain Road near Lane's store including the land between that and Thomas Brown's line, also the plantation and lands I leased to Thomas Brown, being about 350 acres. I also confirm the deed of gift to Mr. William Jett and Katherine Jett his wife for 500 acres of land in Loudoun County where they built their house and the 6 negroes in their possession.

Item I give and devise to my son in law Mr. Thomas Lawson and Lettice Lawson his wife, 6 cows, 12 sheep to be paid out of my stock at home. I also confirm my gift of the negroes now in their possession when they went to housekeeping. I also give them two more negroes; Phillis and her child Milley and their increase.

Item I give to my son in law Mr. John Berryman and Martha Berryman his wife, 7 Negroes that are now at my quarter in Loudoun County; Aron, George, White, George, Denney, Pompy, Toney, Judy and her child Isaac, and their increase.

Item I give to my son in law Mr. Benjamin Berryman and Sarah Berryman his wife, 1 feather bed and furniture, 6 cows and 12 sheep. I also confirm my gift of the negroes I delivered them when they went to housekeeping that are now in their possession and their increase.

Item I give and devise to my daughter Elizabeth Newton the use of my now dwelling house and plantation together with all the land from Corbin's Mill Swamp down the small run by the old place where Capt. Oldham lived, including the said plantation and from thence up the said branch to the Cool Spring, thence up the valley to the road that leads to Bradley Garner's including the plantations where William Grace lived, also the land leased to the said William Grace and the plantation where Rose Brannan [Brenum] lives for and during the natural live of my daughter Elizabeth Newton and after her decease to my son John Newton. I also give to my daughter Elizabeth Newton and her heirs 10 Negroes with their increase; Akey the carpenter, Jack King, Darkey, Simon, Jack the churchman, Little Jenney and her children Alice, Charlott, Venus and Joe. Also four mullatos; Thomas Clark, Abraham Clark, Lawrence Clark and John Clark to serve until they arrive to the age of 31 years old. Also, servant woman Hester Madden, servant man John Cole the weaver and the two looms. I also give my daughter Elizabeth Newton my chariot and harness with four of my best horses , all my kitchen furniture, one silver tankard, one silver cup with two handles, a large silver soup spoon, one dozen of plate tablespoons with all the tea spoons, tongs and all the china, three of the best beds and furniture, her choice all the tables and chairs in my dwelling house, one desk in the chamber and two corner cupboards, one chest of drawers and all the table linen and earthenware, also 4 yoke of the best oxen with cart yokes, 20 cows and 1 bull, 4 sheep, her choice of my stock at home and also 20 of her choice of my hogs.

Item I give and devise unto my daughter Mary Newton, the following 21 Negroes and their increase; Dick, Moll and their children, Jack, Amey, Phillip, Nelly, Solomon, Billey, Neck Jenney and her children, Quamina, Nan, Nell, Joan, Darby, Frank, Richard, Gumby, Venus and her children, Adam and Jude, and Neck Jack. I also give to my daughter Mary Newton two feather beds and furniture, the desk in the hall closet. It is also my will and desire that my daughter Mary Newton do continue with my daughter Elizabeth Newton and live with her till she marries which I desire shall not do without the consent and advice of my executors.

It is my will and desire that my lands in Loudoun and Fairfax County not before devised or given away together with all my stocks of cattle, hogs &c on these lands and all the rest of my estate in Westmoreland County or elsewhere not before given or devised be sold by my executors to the best advantage in money, I also devise that the land I bought of the Honble Philip Ludwell Lee, Esq., be sold for money and the money arising from such sales to be equally divided between my daughters Elizabeth Newton, Judith Brent, Catherine Lane, Lettice Lawson, Martha Berryman, Mary Newton and Sarah Berryman and my granddaughter Elizabeth Ashton and Ann Jackson.

Item my will and desire is that each of my nurses; Ann Eskridge and Jane Durell be paid 10 pounds current money each out of my estate.

Lastly, I constitute and appoint my good friend Richard Lee, Esq., and my son John Newton, executors of this my last will and testament to execute and do all things therein contained.

In witness whereof I have hereunto set my hand and seal the day month and year first above written.

Signed sealed and acknowledged in the presence of us Willoughby Newton
John Norwood
William Anderson
Ann Eskridge
Jane Durell
George Hull
John J. Williams (his mark)
William Flood
Thomas Smith
Joseph Lane

I Willoughby Newton of the County of Westmoreland do make this codicil to be annexed to and made part of my last will and testament made by be bearing date the 27th day of December 1766, as my son John Newton has departed this life since the making and publishing my last will and testament and has by his last will and testament made several devises and bequeaths which would be wholly void unless confirmed by me, I do hereby give and devise to my grandson Willoughby Newton, son of my son John Newton all the estate I have by my said son John Newton to him and the heirs of his body, but in case my said grandson Willoughby Newton should die without heir I give and devise the said estate unto and to be equally divided among my seven daughters; Elizabeth Newton: Judith Brent, Catherine Lane: Lettice Lawson, Martha Berryman, Mary Newton and Sarah Berryman.

It is also my will and I do hereby order and direct that in case my grandson Willoughby Newton or his heirs should claim or recover the lands I hold in Loudoun county and which by said will I have ordered to be sold that my said grandson shall have no part of my estate. And I devise such part of my estate given to my grandson to be equally divided among my seven daughters.

Item I do hereby give and devise and confirm unto Mrs. Betty Newton, widow of my son John Newton all the devises and bequeaths made to her by my son John Newton in his last will and testament of such parts of my estate as I had by my last will and testament devised to my said son and which are become void by his dying before me. In case the said Betty Newton shall fully comply with and agreement made by her said husband John Newton with William Bernard of the County of Westmoreland and for the sale of the lands my said son held in the said county in right of the said Betty Newton his wife, but in case she shall not comply with the said agreement and complete the said sale to William Bernard, then in that case I give and devise what part of my estate my son John Newton has by his said will devised to her and what I have hereby devised and confirmed to her to my grandson to my seven daughters. And I do hereby declare that the said Betty Newton: widow shall not have or enjoy my water grist mill or cornfield over the said mill but devise the same to my grandson Willoughby Newton and for want of heirs to my seven daughters.

I give and devise my lands in Loudoun County mentioned in my said will and also the tract of land purchased by me of Col. Philip Ludwell Lee and the said County of Westmoreland Richard Lee, Esq. my surviving executor mentioned in my said will to be sold in fee simple to the purchasers and the money arising by such sale to be applied as directed by my said last will and testament.

I hereby order and it is my will and desire that the said Richard Lee, Esq. shall have the care and direction and management of what estate I have given to my grandson Willoughby Newton until he shall arrive at the age of 21 years.

It is also my will and desire and I hereby order my Negroes remain upon my several plantations this present year and that the crops made by them be after paying the charges and expenses attending making the said crop supplied in the discharge of my debts.

I also give to my daughter Elizabeth Newton all the provisions provided this year for my family and I further order and direct that the fence rails shall be used in fencing in the cornfield I have ordered to be taken in the forest this present year which extends partly on the lands given to my said son's widow shall at the end of this year be brought upon the lands I have given my said daughter Elizabeth Newton and remain for the use of the same.

In witness whereof I have hereunto set my hand and seal this 28th day of January 1767.

Signed sealed and published for a codicil in the presence of Willoughby Newton

William Flood

John J. Williams (his mark)

David Boyd

Ann Eskridge

At a court held for Westmoreland County the 26th day of May 1767 this will and the codicil annexed or approved according to law by the oath of John Williams and David Boyd witnesses thereto and ordered to be recorded and on the motion of Richard Lee, Esq. the surviving executor named in the said will who made oaths according to law and together with William Bernard, Richard Parker and Fleet Cox, Gent his securities entered into and acknowledged their bond with condition as the law directs, certificate is granted him for obtaining a probate thereof in due form. Teste

Page 467.

Jackson to Kelley Apprentice Agreement

This indenture made the 26th day of May 1767 between Newman Jackson of Cople Parish for the time being of the one part and James Kelley of Lunenburg parish, joiner of the other part.

Witnesseth that Newman Jackson doth bind himself unto James Kelley of the county of Richmond to serve him, his lawful commands, gladly obey, he shall do no damage to his master nor suffer any to be done, he shall not frequent ordinaries but behave himself as a true and faithful apprentice ought to do until he shall arrive to the age of 21 years in consideration of which service the said James Kelley to instruct the said Newman Jackson in the art trade and mystery of a carpenter and joiner.

Sealed and delivered in presence of Newman Jackson
Richard Parker James Kelley

At a court held for Westmoreland County the 26th day of May 1767 this indenture was acknowledged by the parties thereto and with the approbation of the court is ordered to be recorded. Teste.

Page 468.

Tebbs to Tebbs Indenture

This indenture made this 10th day of December 1766 between Mary Ann Tebbs of King and Queen County of the one part and Daniel Tebbs of Westmoreland County of the other part. Witnesseth that Mary Ann Tebbs in consideration of 125 pounds current money of Virginia has sold to Daniel Tebbs all my right of dower of and in the lands wherein Ashton Hall, John Norwood and William Kirk now lives on which I claim as my dower of the said Daniel Tebb's part of the land he claims from his deceased father Daniel Tebbs, my late husband. In witness whereof I have hereunto set my hand and seal the day and year above written.

Signed Sealed and delivered in presents of Mary Ann Tebbs
Samuel Rust
Fleet Cox
John Ballantine

At a court held for Westmoreland County the 26th day of May 1767 this indenture and the receipt thereon endorsed were proved by the oaths of Samuel Rust, Fleet Cox and John Ballantine the witnesses thereto and ordered to be recorded. Teste

Page 469.

Lamkin to Cox Indenture

I Ann Lamkin of the Parish of Cople in the County of Westmoreland, widow in consideration of 65 pounds current money of Virginia have sold and relinquished unto Fleet Cox of the parish and county aforesaid all my right of dower of in and to those two several tracts of land which Matthew Lamkin and Frances Lamkin his wife by deed bearing date with these presents sold to the said Fleet Cox. In witness whereof I have hereunto set my hand and seal the 10th day of June 1767.

Sealed and delivered in the presence of us Ann Lamkin
Richard Parker
John Ballantine, Jr.
George Simpson
Joseph Lane
Benedict Middleton
Charles Bennett

At a court held for Westmoreland county the 30th day of June 1767 this indenture was acknowledged by Ann Lamkin party to thereto and ordered to be recorded. Teste

Page 470.

Weeks to Steel Indenture

This indenture made the 30th day of June 1767 between Benjamin Weeks of the Parish of Washington in the County of Westmoreland, Gent., of the one part and Charles Weeks Steel of the said parish and county of the other part. Witnesseth that Benjamin Weeks in consideration of 20 pounds current money of Virginia has sold to Charles Weeks Steel all that tract of land in the said parish and county of Westmoreland containing by estimation 200 acres which said land was devised by the last will and testament of Charles Kill, deceased bearing date the 4th day of January 1749 unto the said Benjamin Weeks for and during his natural life and after his decease to the said

Charles Weeks Steel. In witness whereof the parties to these presents have hereunto set their hands and seals the day and year first above written.
Sealed and delivered in presence of us Benjamin Weeks
At a court held for Westmoreland County the 30th day of June 1767 this indenture and receipt thereon endorsed was acknowledged by Benjamin Weeks, Gent., party thereto and ordered to be recorded. Teste

Page 471.
Jeffries Plot, Division and Allotment of Dower Lands
At a court held for Westmoreland County the 28th day of October 1766, ordered that Willoughby Newton, John Newton, Samuel Rust and Fleet Cox or any three of them, allot to Sarah Jeffries her dower in the lands of her late husband Jeremiah Jeffries, deceased and make report thereof to the court. James Davenport Cl Cur
[Plot follows on page 471]
Westmoreland County Sct. Pursuant to an order of the said county court bearing date the 28th of October 1766, I went in company with Willoughby Newton, Samuel Rust and Fleet Cox, Gent., appointed to allot to Sarah Jeffries her dower in the lands of her late husband Jeremiah Jeffries, deceased; and began at the letter "A" a stake corner to Mr. Samuel Rust and Obediah Moss [Morse] and run South 3° East 8 pole to another stake by the side of Mr. Rust's Mill Pond a branch of Yeocomico River, thence down the said branch and up another branch of the said river to "C", a stake in the swamp in Mr. Samuel Rust's line, thence along the said line South 45° West to the beginning which includes 159 acres of land, then by the directions of the said gentlemen, I began at the letter "D", a stake near a white oak on the water side and run North 26 ½° East to "E" another stake in the swamp, the widows thirds is included by the letter, A, B, D, E, C which includes 64 acres of land with the area that Leasure Hall holds within that bounds. Survey and completed the 11th day of November 1766.
Presley Hall Griffin Garland S.W.C
and
Joseph Keen
Chain carriers
11th November 1766, Pursuant to the above order we have allotted Sarah Jeffries her dower in the lands of her late husband Jeremiah Jeffries, deceased agreeable to the surveyor's plot annexed to which we refer. Willoughby Newton
Samuel Rust
Fleet Cox
At a court held for Westmoreland County the 30th day of June 1767 this allotment of dower and plot of the lands of Jeremiah Jeffries, deceased being returned was ordered to be recorded. Teste

Page 473.
Strother to Weedon Indenture
This indenture made the 30th day of June 1767 between William Strother of the County of Westmoreland and Winifred Strother his wife of the one part and Capt. George Weedon of the town of Fredericksburg in the County of Spotsylvania of the other part. Witnesseth that William Strother and Winifred Strother his wife in consideration of [30] pounds has sold to George Weedon (in his actual possession and occupation now being) all that tract of land being in the County of Westmoreland (being that tract of land which the said William Strother bought of Daniel Ford by deeds of lease and release bearing date the 28th and 29 days of August 1749 whereupon the said Daniel Ford then dwelt) containing by estimation 50 acres and bounded as follows; beginning on the north side of Attopin Creek otherwise called Rozier's Creek at the north side of the swamp by Potomack River and bounded by the lands of William Strother party to these presents formerly belonging to Mr. Lawrence Washington, extending South West 320 poles to a red oak corner tree dividing the land of the said Washington: Francis Gray, and Gerard Foard, thence North West 128 poles to a white Oak by a path, thence northerly along a line of marked trees to the main run of the line of Mr. William Tyler, thence along the said Tyler's line crossing a point of land on the north side of the said branch to a marked gum on the said branch, thence down the said branch according to

the several meanders thereof to the first beginning. In witness whereof the said William Strother and Winifred Strother his wife have hereunto set their hands and affixed their seals the day and year first above written.

Signed sealed and delivered in presence of William Strother
Thomas Muse
Daniel Fitzhugh
Edward Ransdell, Jr.

At a Court held for Westmoreland County that 30th day of June 1767 this indenture and receipt thereon was acknowledged by William Strother party thereto and ordered to be recorded. Test

Page 475.

Black to Spark Deed

This indenture made the 30th day of June 1767 between William Black and Frances Black his wife of the County of Prince George [Maryland] of one part and Alexander Spark of the County of Westmoreland of the other part. Witnesseth that William Black and Frances Black his wife in consideration of 300 pounds lawful money of Virginia have sold to Alexander Spark all that tract of land lying in the Parish of Cople and County of Westmoreland containing by estimation 110 acres and bounded as follows; beginning at a small red oak standing near a branch which divides this land from the land of William Stewart Minor and extending down branch to the great swamp and up the said swamp to the junction of the spring branch and up the Spring Branch to a gum thence South West 86 poles to a small red oak the beginning. Purchased by the said William Black of John Spence.

We said William Black and Frances Black his wife for the consideration before mentioned to likewise bargain and sell another small tract of land to Alexander Spark being and lying in the parish and county aforesaid containing by estimation 17 acres and beginning at a small gum tree standing by William Sturman's Spring Branch from thence along a row of marked trees along the lane of William Stewart Minor to a branch on which was formerly a mill which belonged to Dr. William Flood and at this time belonging to George Turberville, and along the said branch to the junction of Sturman's Spring Branch and at the said branch to the beginning place. In witness whereof William Black and Frances Black his wife have hereunto set their hands and seals the day and year first above written.

Signed sealed and delivered in presence of William Black
Francis Lightfoot Lee Frances Black
Thomas Muse
Jeremiah Rust

At a Court held for Westmoreland County does 30th day of June 1767 this indenture was acknowledged by William Black and Frances Black his wife parties thereto and ordered to be recorded previous to which the said Frances Black being first privily examined as the law directs voluntarily relinquished her right of dower in the lands conveyed by the said indenture. Teste

Page 478.

Jean Weedon's Nuncupative Will

Westmoreland County, December 15, 1763, these are to certify that Elizabeth Weedon and Rebecca Weedon within 24 hours after the death of their sister Jean Weedon made oath before me that the said Jean Weedon deceased desired that all the estate to be possessed should be divided betwixt her three sisters, Elizabeth Weedon, Rebecca Weedon, Sarah Weedon. Given under my hand the day and year above mentioned. James Blair

At a Court held for Westmoreland County the 28th day of July 1767 this writing purporting the nuncupative will of Jean Weedon: deceased was proved according to law by the oaths of Elizabeth Weedon and Rebecca Weedon the witnesses who in court relinquished all benefit that they may claim hundred the said will in the said will thereupon ordered to be recorded and on the motion of Thomas Taylor who made oaths according to law and together with William Hilton is security entered into and acknowledged bond with condition as the law directs, certificate is granted him for obtaining letters of administration of the said Jean Weedon with the said will and next in due form. Teste

Page 478.
Massey to Peirce Lease
This indenture made the 28th day of July 1767 between Robert Massey of the County of King George of the one part and Copeland Peirce of the County aforesaid of the other part. Witnesseth that Robert Massey in consideration of five shillings current money of Virginia the sell unto Copeland Peirce all that tract of land lying in the Parish of Washington and County of Westmoreland containing 200 acres, 100 acres of which tract was purchased by the said Robert Massey of John Ashton as will appear by deed bearing date the 28th day of November 1762, the remainder of the said tract was formerly the property of John Rollings [Rawlings] who died without will and the said land descended to his daughter Ann Rollings [Rawlings] with whom the said Robert Massey intermarried. To have and to hold the said tract unto Copeland Peirce from the day of the date hereof for and during the full term of one whole year from thence next ensuing yielding and paying yearly the rent of one ear of Indian corn at the expiration of said term to the intent and purpose that by virtue of these presents and of the statute of transferring uses into possession the said Copeland Peirce may be in the actual possession of the said tract and be the better enabled to accept and take a grant and release of the reversion and inheritance thereof. In witness whereof the said Robert Massey have to this indenture set his hand and seal the day month and year first above written.
Signed sealed and delivered in presence of Robert Massey
Thomas Taylor
John Martin
Peter Jett

Page 478.
Massey & Wife to Peirce Release
This indenture made the 28th day of July 1767 between Robert Massey and Ann Massey his wife of the Parish of Hanover in County of King George of the one part and Copeland Peirce of Parish and County aforesaid of the other part. Witnesseth that Robert Massey and Ann Massey his wife in consideration of 220 pounds current money of Virginia has sold and released unto Copeland Peirce a tract of land in his actual possession now being by virtue of a bargain and sale to him by force of the statute for transferring uses into possession all that tract of land containing 200 acres, 100 acres of which tract was purchased by the said Robert Massey of John Ashton as will appear by deed bearing date the 28th day of November 1762, the remainder of the said tract was formerly the property of John Rollings [Rawlings] who died without will and the said land descended to his daughter Ann Rollings [Rawlings] with whom the said Robert Massey intermarried. In witness whereof the said Robert Massey and Ann Massey his wife have hereunto interchangeably set their hands and seals the day month and year first above written.
Signed sealed and delivered in presence of Robert Massey
Thomas Taylor Ann Massey
John Martin
Peter Jett
At a Court held for Westmoreland County the 28th day of July 1767 these indentures of lease and release and the receipt endorsed on the said release for acknowledged by Robert Massey and Anne Massey his wife parties thereto and are ordered to be recorded, previous to which, the said Anne Massey being first privily examined as the law directs voluntarily relinquished her right of dower in the lands conveyed by the said release. Teste

Page 482.
Bulger & Randall's marriage Contract
This indenture contract and marriage agreement concluded and agreed on the 21st day of November 1766 between John Bulger of the County of Westmoreland and Parish of Washington, planter of the one part and Jane Randall of the County of King George in the Parish of Hanover of the other part. Witnesseth that John Bulger and Jane Randall are agreed on a marriage contract as follows, that is to say Jane Randall as a legacy lent her by her deceased husband Thomas Randall

for and during her natural life and the said John Bulger is to have no concern right or title to the said legacy and the same is to remain at her disposal and management during her life as she had never been married to the said Bulger but as for her own rights properties and privileges she submits them to the care and protection of the said John Bulger during his and her natural life as she is allowed by the above agreement to have the management Thomas Randall's estate in her own disposal during her life she agrees to and with the said Bulger to have no right or title to any part of profits of the said John Bulger's estate after his death. In witness whereof the parties to these presents have hereunto set their hands and seals the day month and year first above written.
Signed sealed and delivered in the presence of us John Bulger
Augustine Sanford Jane Randall
Catey Randall (her mark)
At a Court held for Westmoreland County the 28th day July 1767 this indenture and the bond annexed were proved by the oath of Augustine Sanford and Catey Randall the witnesses thereto and ordered to be recorded. Teste

Page 484.
Lee to Lane Indenture
This indenture made the 28th day of July 1767 between Richard Lee of the Parish of Cople in the County of Westmoreland, Esq., surviving executor of the last will and testament of Willoughby Newton, gentlemen, deceased of the one part and Joseph Lane of the said parish and county, Gent., of the other part. Whereas Willoughby Newton by his last will and testament bearing date the 27th day of December 1766 amongst others, made the following declaration of his will; "it is my will and desire that all my lands in Loudoun County and Fairfax County not before devised or given away together with all my stocks of cattle, hogs and on those lands and all the rest of my estate in Westmoreland County or elsewhere not before given or devised be sold by my executors to the best advantage in money. I also desire that the land I bought of the Hon. Philip Ludwell Lee, Esq. Philip Ludwell Lee be sold for money in the money arising from such sales to be equally divided between my daughters Elizabeth Newton: Judith Brent, Catherine Lane, Lettice Lawson, Martha Berryman, Mary Newton and Sarah Berryman and my granddaughter Elizabeth Ashton and Ann Jackson that is after all my just debts be paid which my will and desire is that they will be first paid out of the money arising from such sales with the crops in the debts due me in the remainder to be divided as above, "and of his said will appointed the said Richard Lee and his son John Newton, late of the parish and county of Westmoreland aforesaid, Gent., deceased executors which the said John Newton dying in the lifetime of the said Willoughby Newton the said Willoughby Newton afterwards to with, on the 28th day of January in the present year made and annexed to his said will a codicil thereto in which the following devise; "I hereby give and devise my lands in Loudoun County mentioned in my said will and also the tract of land purchased by me of Philip Ludwell the, Esq. in the said County of Westmoreland to Richard Lee, Esq. my surviving executor mentioned in my same will to be sold in fee simple to the purchasers and the money arising by such sale to be applied as directs by my said last will," as by the said will and codicil relation being thereto had may appear. Now this indenture witnesseth that the said Richard Lee to comply with the will of the testator aforesaid for and in consideration of the sum of 156 pounds to the said Richard Lee in hand paid has sold to the said Joseph Lane the before mentioned tract of land in Westmoreland County which the said Willoughby Newton purchased of the Hon. Philip Ludwell Lee containing by estimation 150 acres. In witness whereof the parties to these presents have hereunto set their hands and seals the day in the year within written.
Sealed and delivered in the presence of us Richard Lee
At a court continued and held for Westmoreland County the 29th day of July 1767 this indenture and the receipt thereon endorsed were acknowledged by Richard Lee, Esq. party thereto and ordered to be recorded. Teste

Page 486.
Lane to Lee Indenture
This indenture made the 29th day of July 1767 between Joseph Lane of the Parish of Cople and County of Westmoreland, Gent., Of the one part and Richard Lee of the said parish and county,

Esq. of the other part. Witnesseth that Joseph Lane in consideration of 156 pounds has sold to Richard Lee all that tract of land lying in the County of Westmoreland containing by estimation 150 acres being the same land Willoughby Newton, Gent., Lately deceased purchased of Philip Ludwell the, Esq. and devise to the said Richard Lee who by deed bearing date the day before the day of eight of these presents convey the same to the said Joseph Lane. In witness whereof the parties to these presents have hereunto set their hands and seals the day and year first above written.
Sealed and delivered in presence of us Joseph Lane
At a court continued and held for Westmoreland County the 29th day of July 1767 this indenture and the receipt thereon endorsed were acknowledged by Joseph Lane party thereto and ordered to be recorded. Teste

Page 487.
Strother's Wife to Weedon Privy Examination
To William Berryman, John Martin and James Blair, Gent. Whereas William Strother and Winifred Strother his wife by their indenture of release bearing date the 13th day of June 1767 have sold and conveyed unto George Weedon the fee simple estate of 50 acres of land with the appurtenances lying in the Parish of Washington and County of Westmoreland and whereas the said Winifred Baker [sic Strother] cannot conveniently travel to record of Westmoreland County to make acknowledgment. Therefore, we do give unto you or any two or more of you power to receive the acknowledgment which the said Winifred Strother. Witness James Davenport, clerk of our said court the first day of June 1767.
Westmoreland Sct. Agreeable to the within commission we have taken the privy examination of Winifred Strother a party to the deed hereunto annexed as to the giving up all her right title property and interest to the land within mentioned who freely and willingly doth relinquished the same without compulsion. Given under our hands and seals this 21st day of August 1767
John Martin
William Berryman
At a Court held for Westmoreland County the 23rd day of August 1767 this commission for the privy examination of Winifred Strother the wife of William Strother and a certificate of the execution thereof being returned was ordered to be recorded. Test

Page 488.
Arrowsmith & Wife to Ashton Indenture
1767 between Thomas Arrowsmith and Mary Arrowsmith his wife of the Parish of Washington and County of Westmoreland of the one part and John Ashton of the said parish and county of the other part. Witnesseth that Thomas Arrowsmith in consideration of 80 pounds current money has sold unto John Ashton a parcel of land lying in the parish and county aforesaid containing by estimation 174 acres and bounded as follows; easterly by the land of Joseph Smith, southerly by Attopin Dam, westerly by the land of John Pierce and northerly by the land of James Dishman. In witness whereof the said Thomas Arrowsmith and Mary Arrowsmith his wife have hereunto set their hands and seals the day and year above written.
Signed sealed and delivered in the presence Thomas Arrowsmith
William Bernard Mary Arrowsmith (her mark)
Lawrence Washington
William Washington
At a Court held for Westmoreland County the 25th day of August 1767 this indenture was acknowledged by Thomas Arrowsmith and Mary Arrowsmith his wife parties thereto and ordered to be recorded, previous to which, the said Mary Arrowsmith being first privy examined as the law directs voluntarily relinquished her right of dower in the lands conveyed by the said indenture. Teste

Page 490.
William Spark Will
Jamaica Sct, In the name of God Amen, I William Spark of the Parish of St. Thomas in the East, in the County of Surrey and island of Jamaica being at this time possessed of as much sense and

judgment as I commonly have been, and have also a sound memory though but weak and infirm in body do make this my last will and testament in the following manner and form.
I do hereby give and bequeath unto Elizabeth Cooper of the aforesaid Parish of St. Thomas in the East two Negro coopers; Warwick cooper and Sampson cooper during the term of her natural life in this I give her as a small acknowledgment of her great kindness and care of me during my long sickness.
Item I hereby require and direct my executors to remit the sum of £50 unto my dear mother Margaret Duthie in the Parish of Arbuthnott in the County of Kincardine in Scotland out of the first money that may arise from the administration of my affairs and it is my earnest desire that this remittance be made within three months after my death but if my mother happens to die before me, I then give the above mentioned £50 and to my three sisters Jane Spark, Rebecca Spark and Mary Spark all of the County of Kincardine to be equally divided. I also give unto each of my said three sisters or their heirs the sum of £40 to be paid by my executors within three years after my death.
Item I give and bequeath unto my mother an annuity of £10 to be paid her yearly out of the residue of my interest or estate by my brother Alexander Spark, merchant in Westmoreland County in Virginia unto whom I do hereby give and devise all my estate or interest whether real or personal or of whatsoever kind or quality the same may be in Jamaica or elsewhere unto him the said Alexander Spark and to his heirs forever subject always to the payment of all my just and lawful debts and the bequeaths and legacies herein or hereby otherwise disposed of.
Item I nominate and appoint John Henry, David Fife and John Robertson both of the Parish of St. Thomas aforesaid, Gent., Together with my above-mentioned brother Alexander Spark of Virginia to be executors of this my will, and I give unto each of the two first named, the sum of 10 pistoles two by rings if they please, if not anything else they think.
In witness whereof I have hereunto set my hand this first day of January 1764. William Spark
At a court held for Westmoreland County the 25th day of August 1767 this last Will and Testament of William Spark: deceased was presented into Court by Alexander Spark one of the executors therein named and no witnesses being subscribed thereto, John Ballantine, Jr., Jeremiah Rust and Richard Parker severally made oath that they are well acquainted with the testator's handwriting and verily believe the said will and the name thereto subscribed to be the proper hand writing of the said testator and on motion of the said Alexander Spark who made oaths according to law and together with Richard Parker and Alexander Rose his securities entered into and acknowledged by with condition as the law directs, certificate is granted him for obtaining a probate, thereof in due form, liberty being reserved to John Henry, David Fife and John Robertson the other executors named in the said will to join in the probate thereof when they shall think fit. Teste

Page 491.
<u>Spark to Neale Indenture</u>
This indenture made the 25th day of August 1767 between Alexander Spark and Elizabeth Spark his wife of the County of Westmoreland of the one part and Richard Neale of the same County of the other part. Witnesseth that Alexander Spark and Elizabeth Spark his wife in consideration of 335 pounds lawful money of Virginia have sold to Richard Neale all that tract of land lying in the Parish of Cople in the County of Westmoreland containing 110 acres bounded as followeth; beginning at a small red oak standing near a branch which divides this land from the land of William Stewart Minor's and extending down the branch to the Great Swamp and up the said swamp to the junction of the Spring Branch and up the Spring Branch to a gum thence South West 86 poles to a small red Oak to the beginning which said tract was sold and conveyed to William Black by John Spence by indenture bearing date the 27th day of May 1751 and by the said William Black was sold and conveyed to Alexander Spark by indenture bearing date the 13th day of June 1767.
We the said Alexander Spark and Elizabeth Spark his wife for the consideration before mentioned do likewise bargain and sell unto Richard Neale another small tract of land lying in the parish and county aforesaid containing by estimation 17 acres beginning at a small gum tree standing by William Sturman's Spring Branch and running from thence along a row of marked trees along the line of William Stewart Minor to a branch on which was formerly a mill which belong to Dr. William Flood and at this time belonging to George Turberville and along the said branch to the junction of Sturman's Spring Branch and up the said branch to the beginning place. In witness whereof the

parties to these presents have hereunto set their hands and seals the day and year above written.

Sealed and delivered in presence of Alexander Spark
Elizabeth Spark

At a Court held for Westmoreland County the 25th day of August 1767 this indenture of bargain and sale and receipt were acknowledged by Alexander Spark and Elizabeth Spark his wife parties thereto and ordered to be recorded, previous to which the said Elizabeth Spark being first privily examined as the law directs voluntarily relinquished her right of dower in the lands conveyed by the said indenture. Teste

Page 493.

Spark to Neale Indenture

This indenture made the 25th day of July 1767 between Alexander Spark of the County of Westmoreland, merchant and Elizabeth Spark his wife of the one part and Richard Neale of the same County of the other part. Witnesseth that Alexander Spark and Elizabeth Spark his wife in consideration of 35 pounds current money of Virginia have sold to Richard Neale all that tract of land in the Parish of Cople in in the County of Westmoreland containing 100 acres and bounded as followeth; beginning at a chestnut tree standing near Solomon Redman's Mill Pond, thence along the said line to the main road, thence up the said road to the beginning which said tract was sold and conveyed to Samuel Walker by Valentine Sturman late of the said County of Westmoreland by indenture bearing date the eighth day of July 1752 and by the said Samuel Walker was sold and conveyed to the said Alexander Spark by indenture bearing date the 31st day of March 1767. In witness whereof the parties to these presents have hereunto set their hands and seals the day and year above written

Sealed and delivered in presence of Alexander Spark
Elizabeth Spark

At a Court held for Westmoreland County the 25th day of August 1767 this indenture of bargain and sale and receipt were acknowledged by Alexander Spark and Elizabeth Spark his wife parties thereto and ordered to be recorded, previous to which the said Elizabeth Spark being first privily examined as the law directs voluntarily relinquished her right of dower in the lands conveyed by the said indenture. Teste

Page 495.

Sanford to Sanford Indenture

This indenture made the 24th day of August 1767 between John Sanford of the Parish of Cople and County of Westmoreland of the one part and Willoughby Sanford of the aforesaid parish and county of the other part. Witnesseth that John Sanford in consideration of 2000 pounds crop tobacco has sold to Willoughby Sanford all his right title and interest to a dividend of land containing 30 acres lying in the Parish of Cople and County of Westmoreland and bounded as followeth; beginning at a marked persimmon on the land of the said John Sanford: from thence to a marked locus and then to a sassafras another marked tree and a corner in the land of the said John Sanford: from thence to a marked chestnut and along a line of marked trees to a corner white oak to the said John Sanford: Edward Ransdell and Edward Sanford: from thence along the line between the said John Sanford and Edward Sanford to the line of Richard Moxley (formerly the land belonging to Franklin Perry) so along the said Richard Moxley's line to a marked Locust stake corner between the said Richard Moxley, John Sanford in the said Willoughby Sanford, and from thence to the first mentioned beginning persimmon tree. In witness whereof the parties to these presents have interchangeably set their hands and seals the day month and year first above written

Signed sealed and delivered John Sanford
Augustine Sanford
Edward Muse, Jr.
Robert Sanford, Jr.

N.B. the above 30 acres of land (more or less) is sold by the said John Sanford out of the plantation which he now lives on.

At a court held for Westmoreland County the 25th day of August 1767 this indenture together with the memorandum of livery of seizen and receipt thereon endorsed were proved by the oaths of

Augustine Sanford, Edward Muse, Jr., and Robert Sanford, Jr., the witnesses thereto and ordered to be recorded Teste

Page 498.

Baley to Hall Lease

This indenture made the 15th day of August 1767 between William Baley of the County of Westmoreland and Parish of Cople of the one part and Jeremiah Hall of the same place, planter of the other part. Witnesseth that William Baley in consideration of the rents and covenants hereafter mentioned on the part of Jeremiah Hall has demised and to farm let unto him one tenement and tract of land containing 70 acres being part of the tract of land that was left to the said William Baley by William Baley, deceased, and bounded as follows; beginning at a pine and running a straight course to a white oak standing at the beginning of hedgerow of oaks, from thence running upon the entire of the said hedgerow next to William Flood's, from thence a straight course to a hickory and white oak, from thence running East to a pine and straight on to Flood's line and down the said line to a branch and from thence to the said branch to the pine at the beginning. To have and to hold the said tenement and tract of land to the said Jeremiah Hall during his natural life after the first day of September yielding and paying thereafter yearly and every year during the term unto William Baley the first day of March the full and just sum of 500 pounds of tobacco, or to be discharged in cash at two per pound or corn at 10 ½ pound per barrel. In witness whereof the parties before mentioned have set their hands and seals the day and year first above written.

Signed sealed and delivered in presence of us — William Baley
Presley Hall — Jeremiah Hall
Solomon Bennett
Samuel Beale
Jonathan Hockins
Ashton Hall

At a Court held for Westmoreland County the 29th day of September 1767 this indenture was proved by the oath of Presley Hall, Solomon Bennett and Jonathan Hockins, witnesses thereto and ordered to be recorded. Teste

Prepare of Page 500.

Lane & Wife to Edwards Indenture

This indenture made the 29th day of September 1767 between Joseph Lane of Cople Parish and County of Westmoreland and Martha Lane: relict of William Lane: deceased of the same parish and county of the one part and Thomas Edwards of the said parish and county of the other part. Witnesseth that Joseph Lane and Martha Lane for several good causes and considerations them thereunto moving and especially for the valuable consideration of 150 pounds current money of Virginia have sold to Thomas Edwards all that parcel or tenement of land containing 150 acres lying in the forest of Nominy in the aforesaid Parish of Cople and County of Westmoreland, being part of a tract formerly purchased by William Smith by William Carr by deed bearing date the 30th day of October 1695, and the said William Carr by his last will and testament gave and devise the same to his daughter Mary Carr which descended by inheritance to her son William Walker who conveyed the same by deed bearing date the third day of March 1737 to the above named William Lane and by him given to the said Joseph Lane as by deed of gift bearing date the 28th day of September 1756. In witness whereof the parties to these presents have interchangeably set their hands and fix their seals the day and year above written.

Sealed signed and delivered in the presence of — Joseph Lane
William Carr Tidwell — Martha Lane
Garland Moore
Reuben Jordan

At a Court held for Westmoreland County the 29th day of September 1767 this indenture together with a memorandum of livery of seizen and receipt thereon endorsed in a bond for performance of covenants were proved by the oaths of Reuben Jordan, William Carr Tidwell, and Garland Moore the witnesses thereto and ordered to be recorded. Test James Davenport, Cl Cur

Page 505.

Tebbs to Morgan Indenture

This indenture made the 25th day of August 1767 between Daniel Tebbs of Cople Parish and County of Westmoreland, planter of the one part and Daniel Morgan of the same Parish and County, overseer of the other part. Witnesseth that Daniel Tebbs in consideration of 80 pounds current money of Virginia and the rents and covenants herein after mentioned on the part of Daniel Morgan to be paid and performed hath demised and to farm let one tenement and tract of land containing 70 acres in Yeocomico Neck and the Parish of Cople and County of Westmoreland being the plantation whereon Catherine Jones formerly lived and whereupon Ashton Hall now liveth. Beginning at the edge of the Mash Pot on Daniel McCarty's line and extending along Jones' line a straight course to the road that leads to Yeocomico Warehouses where there is a locust post fixed, then down the said road to a chestnut stump, from thence a straight course by the church wall down to the run that runs from Steptoe's and Tebb's Mill, from thence down the said run the several courses and meanders to the said McCarty's line, and down the said line to the beginning. To have and to hold the said tenement and tract of land with the appurtenances to the said Daniel Morgan during the natural lives of said Daniel Morgan and Temperance Morgan or the longest liver of them yielding and paying unto Daniel Tebbs on the 25th day of December one ear of Indian corn; and engages to put a brick chimney to the now dwelling house and to plant and keep up an orchard of 1000 peach trees during the term of this lease and the said Daniel Tebbs to furnish the said Daniel Morgan and Temperance Morgan with hogshead and nail, timber and firewood (for the use of the said tenement) of any part of the said Tebbs land which he now rents to John Hodge. In witness whereof the said parties above mentioned have interchangeably set their hands and seals the day and year above Signed sealed and delivered in the presence of Daniel Tebbs

Joseph Lane Daniel Morgan

Augustine Sanford

Solomon Redman

At a Court held for Westmoreland County the 29th day of September 1767 this indenture and receipt thereon endorsed proved by the oaths of Joseph Lane, Augustine Sanford, and Solomon Redman witnesses thereto and ordered to be recorded. Teste

Page 503.

Spilman to Spilman Indenture

This indenture made the 24th day of November 1767 between John Spilman of the colony of King George and parish of Brunswick in the colony of Virginia, planter of the one part and Thomas Spilman of the Parish of Washington and County of Westmoreland and William Spilman of the same parish and county aforesaid of the other part, which John Spilman, Thomas Spilman and William Spilman are the three sons of William Spilman their late father, deceased. Witnesseth that John Spilman in consideration of 25 pounds current money of Virginia has sold to Thomas Spilman and William Spilman the undivided one third part of a tract of land containing 200 acres lying in the Parish of Washington and County of Westmoreland, being part of a tract formerly belonging to Robert Frank and on the North side of the main branch of Mattox Creek and bounded as followeth; beginning at a marked black oak and extending West to the line of William Piper to marked red oak, thence along the said Piper's line North by West to marked hickory, thence down to the main branch of the said creek and then along the said dam to the uppermost line, thence North to a black oak, thence East to a live oak in a small branch, finally South to the first station which said tract of land was given and devised to the said John Spilman, Thomas Spilman and William Spilman party hereto by the last will and testament of William Spilman, their father deceased. In witness whereof all the said parties have hereunto set their hands and seals the day and year first above written.

Sealed and delivered in the presence of us John Spilman

Robert Frank Thomas Spilman

James Frank William Spilman

Thomas Rollings [Rawlings]

At a court held for Westmoreland county the 24th day of November 1767 this indenture and receipt thereon endorsed was acknowledged by John Spilman party thereto and ordered to be recorded.

Teste James Davenport Cl Cur

Page 511.

Roach to Roach Indenture

This Indenture made the 28th day of September 1767 between John Roach, Sr., of the Parish of Washington and County of Westmoreland of the one part and Price Roach of the parish and county aforesaid, planter of the other part. Witnesseth that John Roach in consideration of 35 pounds current money of Virginia have sold to Price Roach all that tract of land being part in Washington Parish and county of Westmoreland and part in Hanover Parish and county of King George containing by estimation 100 acres and bounded as followeth; beginning at a marked corner tree of the land of James Cash standing on the north side of a main road that leads out of the ridge road to the Round Hill Church, thence northerly along the said Cash's line to another corner of the said Cash, thence westerly to the land of James Dishman: thence southerly along the said Dishman's line to the land of Elizabeth McCullock, thence along the said McCullock's line to the first beginning tree. In witness whereof the said John Roach have hereunto set his hand and seal this 28th day of September 1767.

Signed sealed and delivered in the presence of us John Roach (his mark)

Thomas Peach

George Kitchen

William Canfield (his mark)

At a court held for Westmoreland County the 24th day of November 1767 this indenture together with a memorandum of livery of seizen and receipt thereon endorsed were proved by the oaths of Thomas Peach, George Kitchen and William Canfield, Witnesses thereto and ordered to be recorded. Teste

Page 513.

Magalene Jackson's Will

In the name of God Amen, I Magalene Jackson of the Parish of Cople in the County of Westmoreland being in perfect sense and memory do make this my last will and testament in manner and form following.

Item I give and bequeath to my beloved son Samuel Rust a silver box valued at one pound five shillings.

Item I give and bequeath to my beloved son Julius Augustus Jackson all debts (due to me) in the eastern shore.

Item my Will is that my son Julius Augustus Jackson have a negro purchased by my executors about seven years of age the said Negroe of the female sex.

Item I give to my son Julius one-half dozen of silver spoons four large and two small ones.

Item I give and bequeath to my beloved son Thaddeus Jackson Negro man Cesar and Negro woman Nancy, also one-half dozen of silver spoons four large and two small ones.

Item I give and bequeath to my beloved son Christopher Maccabeus Jackson, Negro man Ben and Negro Woman Janey and one-half dozen of silver spoons four large and two small ones.

Item I give and bequeath unto my two sons above mentioned Viz Thaddeus Jackson & Christopher Maccabeus Jackson all my right and title of a joynture made to me by my husband Christopher Dominick Jackson before marriage amounting to 200 pounds current money of Virginia.

Item my will is that the remainder of my estate not yet given be divided between my two sons Thaddeus Jackson & Christopher Maccabeus Jackson in such sort that Thaddeus have twenty pounds above his equal part......

Lastly, I appoint my two sons Thaddeus Jackson & Christopher Maccabeus Jackson my executors of this my last will and testament. In Witness whereof I have hereunto set my hand and seal this 11th day of August 1766.

Signed sealed and delivered in presence of Magdalene Jackson

James Baley

George Lamkin

At a Court held for Westmoreland County the 24th day of November 1767 this will was proved according to law by the oath of James Baley and George Lamkin the witnesses thereto and ordered to be recorded and on the motion of Thaddeus Jackson one of the executors named in the said will who made oath according to law and together with Jeremiah Rust his security entered into and acknowledged their bond with conditioned as the law directs, certificate is granted him for obtaining a probate thereof in due form, liberty being reserved to Christopher Maccabeus Jackson the other executor named in said will to join in the probate thereof when he shall think fit. Teste

Page 514.
Jeffries to Hall Indenture
This indenture made the third day of October 1767 between Robert Jeffries of the County of Westmoreland in Parish of Cople the one part in Jeremiah Hall the same place, planter of the other part. Witnesseth that Robert Jeffries in consideration of the rents and covenants hereafter mentioned on the part of Jeremiah Hall to be paid and performed hath demised and to farm let by these presents a tenement and tract of land containing 159 acres lying in the County and parish aforesaid in being a tract of land that fell to the said Robert Jeffries by the decease of his brother Jeremiah Jeffries, deceased and bounded as followeth; beginning at a cornerstone that was formerly a corner between Jeffries, Earle and Skinner and from thence down to a run and down the said run to a creek and around the said creek westward to Rust's Mill and from thence to Mr. Samuel Rust line beginning at a pine and down the said line to the before mentioned cornerstone. To have and to hold the said tenement and tract of land with the appurtenances to Jeremiah Hall for and during his natural life after the 25th day of December next coming yielding and paying yearly unto the Robert Jeffries on the 25th day of December the full and just some of 2 bushels of corn. In witness whereof the parties above mentioned have set their hands and seals the day and year first above written.
Signed sealed and delivered in presence of us Robert Jeffries
Leasure Hall
Jonathan Hockins
John Harrison (his mark)
William Short
Jeremiah Spurling (his mark)
At a Court held for Westmoreland County the 24th day of November 1767 this indenture of lease was acknowledged by Robert Jeffries and Jeremiah Hall the parties thereto and ordered to be recorded. Teste

Page 516.
Doleman to Doleman Deed of Gift
I Thomas Doleman of the Parish of Cople in the County of Westmorland, bricklayer in consideration of the love good will and affection which I have and do bear towards my two sons William Doleman and Thomas Sturman Doleman of the same Parish and County aforesaid have given and granted by these presents unto my two sons all and singular my goods and chattels as followeth; one cow and two steers, 10 head of hogs, one bed and furniture, one pewter dish, six plates and two basons, some earthenware, one chest, one table, one box, three chairs and one bell metal skillet, and all other things which I am at this time possessed of to be equally divided between them. In witness whereof I have hereunto put my hand and seal this 23rd day of November 1767.
Signed sealed and delivered in presence of us Thomas Doleman
Augustine Sanford
Edward Muse, Jr.
At a Court held for Westmoreland County this 24th day of November 1767 this deed of gift was proved by the oath of Augustine Sanford in witness thereto and ordered to be recorded. Teste

Page 517.
Ransdell to Redman Indenture
This indenture made the 29th day of March 1768 between Edward Ransdell, Gent., Guardian to the orphans of Daniel Neale of the County of Westmoreland, deceased of the one part and Solomon Redman: millwright and carpenter of the aforesaid County of Westmoreland of the other part. Witnesseth that Edward Ransdell with the approbation of the court doth place and bond unto the

said Solomon Redman, John Neale an orphan of the said Daniel Neale, deceased to serve him the said Solomon Redman from the day and date of these presents until he shall arrive to the full age of 21 years and to teach him the truth part and trade of a millwright and carpenter. In witness whereof the parties to these presents have hereunto set their hands and seals the day month and year first above written

Signed sealed and delivered in the presence of us Edward Ransdell
Solomon Redman

At a court held for Westmoreland County the 29th day of March 1768 this indenture was acknowledged by the parties thereto and with the approbation of the court ordered to be recorded. Teste

Page 518.

William Hutcheson Will

In the name of God Amen, I William Hutcheson of the County of Westmorland being sick and weak of body but of a disposing sense and memory do make this my last will and testament in the manner following.

First, I give to my daughter Mary Hutcheson, Negro boy Garrett.

Secondly, all the rest of my estate of what kind soever, that is to say the land I bought of Robert Washington as also Negroes Jack and Beck, with all my personal estate of what sort shall be sold for cash by my executors they giving 18 months credit and the money arising from the said sale to be put interest only. My wife's dower which she is to do what she thinks proper with.

I appoint Jeremiah Kirk and James Degge to be my whole and sole executor to this my last will and testament. Witness whereof I have set my hand and seal this 14th day of April 1767

Signed sealed and delivered in presence of us William Hutcheson
William Berryman
Benjamin Stuart
Charles Murray

At a Court held for Westmoreland County the 29th day of March 1768 this will was proved according to law by the oath of William Berryman and Benjamin Stuart witnesses thereto and ordered to be recorded and on motion of Jeremiah Kirk the executors named in the said will who made oaths according to law and together with Benjamin Stuart and James Degge his securities entered into and acknowledged bond with conditioned as the law directs, certificate is granted him for obtaining a probate thereof in due form. Teste

(Page 567, Elizabeth Hutcheson renunciation of will)

Page 519.

Wickliffe to McCarty Indenture

This indenture made the 16th day of November 1767 between David Wickliffe and Jane Wickliffe his wife of the Parish of Washington and County of Westmoreland of the one part and Daniel McCarty of the same parish and county of the other part. Witnesseth that David Wickliffe in consideration of 537 pounds 10 shillings current money of Virginia has sold to Daniel McCarty all that tract of land lying upon the north side the mouth Popes Creek in the said Parish of Washington and County of Westmoreland containing 150 acres which is to be laid off agreeable to a certain deed from Henry Brooks to David Wickliffe and Robert Wickliffe dated 10 March 1655 and the remaining 50 acres agreeable to the will of the said Henry Brooks bearing date the 3 February 1662. In witness whereof the said David Wickliffe and Jane Wickliffe his wife have hereunto set their hands and seals the day and year above written.

Signed sealed and delivered in presence of David Wickliffe
John Martin Jane Wickliffe (her mark)
Charles Weeks
Benoney Williams
Richard Watts

To Benjamin Weeks, John Martin and Samuel Oldham, Gent. Whereas David Wickliffe and Jane Wickliffe his wife by their indenture of bargain and sale bearing date the 16th day of November 1767 have sold unto Daniel McCarty the fee simple estate of 150 acres of land with the appurtenances

lying in the Parish of Washington and County of Westmoreland and whereas the said Jane Wickliffe cannot conveniently travel to our quarter Westmoreland to make acknowledgment. Therefore, we do give unto you or any two of you power to receive the acknowledgment which the said Jane Wickliffe shall be willing to make. Witness James Davenport, clerk of our said court third day of November 1767.
Westmoreland Sct. According to the above commission to us directed we have taken the privy examination of Jane Wickliffe and she relinquished her right of dower to the above-mentioned land to the above-named Daniel McCarty with free consent without any manner of compulsion as witness our hands 16 November 1767.
John Martin
Benjamin Weeks
At a Court held for Westmoreland County the 29th day of March 1768 this bargain and sale and receipt thereon endorsed proved by the oath of Benjamin Weeks, John Martin, Charles Weeks and Benoney Williams witnesses thereto and together with the commission annexed for taking the acknowledgment and privy examination of Jane Wickliffe the wife of David Wickliffe and a certificate of the execution thereof ordered to be recorded. Teste

Page 522.
Smith Executor's to Baley Indenture
This indenture made the second day of January 176[8] between Samuel Smith, James Baley, Jr., Ann Smith, executors of Stephen Smith, deceased of the Parish of Cople and County of Westmoreland of the one part and John Baley of the same parish and county aforesaid of the other part. Witnesseth that Samuel Smith, James Baley, Jr., and Ann Smith in consideration of 14 pounds five shillings current money has sold unto John Baley all that tract of land containing 30 acres lying in the parish and county aforesaid; binding on the lands of James Baley, on the lands of Robert Moore, deceased and on the land of Samuel Smith. In witness whereof the parties to these presents interchangeably set their hands and seals the day and year first above written.
Signed sealed and delivered in presence of — Samuel Smith
William Moore — James Baley
John Moore — Anne Smith
John Mothershead (his mark)
Daniel Baley
At a Court held for Westmoreland County the 29th day of March 1768 this indenture together with the memorandum of livery of seizen and receipt thereon endorsed or proved by the oath of William Moore, John Moore and John Mothershead witnesses thereto and ordered to be recorded. Teste

Page 525.
Baley to Smith Indenture
This indenture made the second day of January 1768 between John Baley of the County of Westmoreland and Parish of Cople of the one part and Samuel Smith of the parish and county aforesaid of the other part. Witnesseth that John Baley in consideration of 14 pounds five shillings current money has sold unto Samuel Smith all that tract of land containing 30 acres lying in the county and parish aforesaid and bounded as followeth; on the land of James Baley, on the land of Robert Moore, deceased and on the land of Samuel Smith being a tract of land formerly given by Robert Smith, deceased to his son Stephen Smith, deceased. In witness whereof the parties to these presents have interchangeably set their hands and seals the day and year above written.
Signed sealed and delivered in presence of us — John Baley
William Moore
John Moore
John Mothershead (his mark)
Daniel Baley
At a Court held for Westmoreland County the 29th day of March 1768 this indenture together with the memorandum of livery of seizen and receipt thereon endorsed were proved by the oaths of William Moore, John Moore and John Mothershead witnesses thereto and ordered to be recorded. Teste

Page 528.

Marye to Johnston Bond

I James Marye of Orange County am held and firmly bound unto George Johnston of Washington County in the full and just some of 100 pounds current money of Virginia to which payment will and truly to be made. The condition of the above obligation is such that if James Marye will allow George Johnston to have quiet possession of his land on Mattox without any molestation or disturbance for the term of 10 years from the said James Marye unless the said Marye shall sell his land in that time and in that case the said George Johnston is to resign the land on having six months' notice and the said Johnston shall be paid for what buildings he shall make of the land if it is sold before the expiration of 10 years.

Witnesses — James Marye
Thomas Jett — November 10, 1766
Thomas Turner

At a Court held for Westmoreland County the 29th day of March 1768 this bond for performance of covenants was proved by the oath of Thomas Jett a witness thereto and ordered to be recorded. Teste

The condition of George Johnston's Bond to the Rev. James Marye is that the said Johnston is not to work more than six Negroes and overseer on the least land, to keep a sufficient quantity of stock thereon and that no waste should be committed on the land, that the peach orchard should be replanted with young trees where any are wanting.

In presence of — William Bernard
Lawrence Washington — December 29, 1766
Charles Weeks
Richard Bernard

At a Court held for Westmoreland County the 29th day of March 1768 this bond for performance of covenants was acknowledged by William Bernard, Gent., party thereto and ordered to be recorded. Teste

Page 530.

William Porter Will

I William Porter do make this my last will and testament as followeth.

I give to my son Edward Porter the plantation whereon I live to him and his heirs forever.

I give to my son William Porter my other plantation in the forest to him and his heirs forever.

I leave the piece of land I had from James Smith adjoining to Joseph Pierce's land to be sold by my executors to the highest bidder discharge my debts and all my other estate to be divided among my children; William Porter, Edward Porter: Ann Porter, Sarah Porter and Betty Porter equally to be divided share and share like to them and their heirs forever.

As witness my hand and seal this 27th day of December 1767

I leave Mr. William Pierce my whole executor [and William Stuart Packet executor (mm: this seems to be an error; Hutt was the executor not Pierce or Packet.]

Thomas Sanford, Jr. — William Porter (his mark)
Youell Sanford
Vincent Marmaduke

At a Court held for Westmoreland County the 29th day of March 1768 this will was proved according to law by the oath of Thomas Sanford and Vincent Marmaduke witnesses thereto and ordered to be recorded and on the motion of John Hutt and Gerrard Hutt who made oath according to law and together with Gerrard Hutt, Sr., their security entered into and acknowledged bond with condition as the law directs, certificate is granted them for obtaining letters of administration of the estate of the said decedent with the said will next in due form. Teste

Page 531.

Booth & Wife and Washington to Lane Indenture, Privy Examination and Bond

This indenture made 27th day of October 1767 between William Booth of the Parish of Cople and County of Westmoreland, Gent., and Elizabeth Booth his wife and Anne Washington of the Parish of Washington and said County of Westmoreland of the one part and Joseph Lane of the said parish Cople and County of Westmoreland, Gent., of the other part. Witnesseth that William Booth and Elizabeth Booth his wife and Ann Washington in consideration of 300 pounds current money of Virginia have sold unto Joseph Lane a parcel of land known by the name Peyton's Levels lying in Nominy Forrest in the Parish of Cople and County of Westmoreland containing by estimation 462 acres being half of the tract of land supposed to contain 850 acres which Col. Henry Ashton by his last will and testament bearing date the 26th day of February 1730 gave to his granddaughter Elizabeth Turberville who died without any lawful issue or without making a will, after whose death one half of which said 850 acres became vested in Grace Lee: daughter to the said Henry Ashton and wife to the Hon. Richard Lee, Esq., and the other half descended to the said Elizabeth Booth and Anne Washington (relic of Col. Augustine Washington, deceased) granddaughters to the said Henry Ashton as next heirs at law to the said Elizabeth Turberville and by the mutual consent and agreement of them the said Richard Lee, William Booth and Anne Washington the said tract of land was equally divided the 23rd day of September 1767 by Charles Weeks, surveyor of the County of Westmoreland as to allot the said Richard Lee in his right of his wife's Grace Lee's 462 acres adjoining his other tract of land Peyton's Level and the said William Booth in the right of his wife Elizabeth Booth and Anne Washington the first above mentioned 462 acres adjoining the lands of William Porter the heirs of Rev. Joseph Simpson, deceased, the said Joseph Lane, Gerrard Hutt and the said Richard Lee, beginning at [missing] which said 850 acres of land being the same more or less is part of a tract known by the name Peyton's Levels granted to Col. Valentine Peyton by patent bearing date the 22nd day of July 1662 and also all their right and title to the said 462 acres of land or to any part of the said tract of land granted to the said Valentine Peyton and given away by the said Henry Ashton's will. In witness whereof the first parties to these presents interchangeably set their hands and seals the day and year first above written.

Signed sealed and delivered in the presence of us — William Booth, Elizabeth Booth, Anne Washington

Ann Booth
Reuben Jordan
Allen McDonald
Philip Ludwell Lee
Francis Lightfoot Lee
George Turberville

Commission for Privy Examination of Elizabeth Booth, witness James Davenport, clerk of our said court the 9th day of December 1767. Executed the 22nd day of February 1768, John Augustine Washington, Thomas Chilton.

William Booth and Anne Washington performance bond to Joseph Lane

At a Court held for Westmoreland County the 29th day of March 1768 this indenture and receipt thereon endorsed and a bond for performance of covenants were acknowledged by William Booth and Anne Washington parties thereto and together with the commission annexed for taking the acknowledgment and privy examination of Elizabeth Booth the wife of William Booth and the certificate of the execution thereof, ordered to be recorded. Test

Page 536.

Ball to Rust Indenture

This indenture made the 16th day of October 1767 between Sarah Ball of the Parish of Cople and County of Westmoreland of the one part and John Rust and James Rust both of the said parish and county of the other part. Witnesseth that in consideration of 20 pounds current money of Virginia has sold unto John Rust and James Rust all that plantation and tract of land which formerly belonged to Robert King of the Parish of Cople and County of Westmoreland, deceased and by the said Robert King was devised to his two grandchildren Robert Ball and Gerrard Ball by his last will and testament bearing date the 25th day of September 1693 containing by estimation 200 acres lying in the parish and county aforesaid and bounded as followeth; by Potomack River, the lands of John Critcher, deceased, of William Tebbs: of James Steptoe, deceased, and commonly called and known by the name of Sandy Point in Yeocomico Neck. In witness whereof the parties to these presents have hereunto set their hands and seals the day and year first above written

Sealed and delivered in the presence of — Sarah Ball (her mark)

Thomas Claytor
Peter Rust
George Rust
Samuel McCave
At a court held for Westmoreland County the 29th day of March 1768 this indenture together with the memorandum of livery of seizen and receipt thereon endorsed were proved by the oath of Thomas Claytor, Peter Rust, and Samuel McCave witnesses thereto and ordered to be recorded. Teste

Page 538.
Rust to Cox Indenture
This indenture made the 6th day of February 1768 between Jeremiah Rust and Frances Rust his wife in consideration of 60 pounds current money of Virginia has sold to Fleet Cox all that tract of land which Jeremiah Rust: late of Westmoreland County did by his last will and testament give and devise to his wife Magdalene Rust for and during her life and after her decease he gave the said land to his son Jeremiah Rust being 100 acres more or less, the graveyard that is within a bunch of cedars where there is a vault only excepted, which land is bounded as followeth; bounded on the land that the said Cox purchased of Matthew Lamkin, and on the land of William Morton, and Samuel Walker: and on the land of the said Cox purchased of Samuel Rust, and on the land of William Gilbert: and on the land the said Cox purchased of Matthew Rust. In witness whereof the parties to these presents have interchangeably set their hands and seals the day and year first above written.
Signed sealed and delivered in presence of Jeremiah Rust
William Cox Frances Rust
William Morton
Ann Lamkin
Nicholas Bran (his mark)
At a Court held for Westmoreland County the 29th day of March 1768 this indenture together with the memorandum of livery of seizen and receipt endorsed were acknowledged by Jeremiah Rust and Frances Rust his wife, parties (she being first privy examined as the law directs) and ordered to be recorded. Teste

Page 541.
John Critcher's Will
In the name of God Amen, I John Critcher of the Parish of Cople in the County of Westmoreland being sick but of perfect sense and memory do make this my last will and testament in manner following.
Item I give to my loving wife Susannah Critcher, Negroes Forten, Nan and Jean during her natural life.
Item I give to my loving wife mullato boy John Spence.
Item I give to my son John Critcher the plantation whereon I now live and Negro Joan.
Item I give to my son Thomas Critcher, Negroes Great Tom and Little Nann.
Item I give to my son Joseph Critcher, Negroes Bray and Judea.
Item I give to my daughter Susannah Critcher Negroes Pegg and Sam.
Item my will and desire is that all the rest of my estate of what nature or kind soever be equally divided between my loving wife in my four children and I do appoint my loving wife Susannah Critcher and Joseph Garner, Sr., executors of this my last will and testament.
Witness my hand and seal this fourth day of September 1767
Signed and sealed in presence of John Critcher
Jeremiah Courtney
Joseph Garner
George Rust
At a Court held for Westmoreland County the 26th day of April 1768 this will was proved according to law by the oath of Jeremiah Courtney and George Rust witnesses thereto and ordered to be recorded, and on the motion of Susannah Critcher and Joseph Garner the executors therein named

who made oath thereto according to law and together with the said Jeremiah Courtney and George Rust their securities entered into and acknowledged bond with condition as the law directs, certificate is granted them for obtaining a probate thereof in due form. Teste

Page 542.
Davis to Hutt Deed
This indenture made the 21st day of April 1768 between Gerrard Davis and Ann Davis his wife of the Parish of Cople in the County of Westmoreland, planter of the one part and John Hutt of the aforesaid parish and county of the other part. Witnesseth that Gerrard Davis and Ann Davis his wife in consideration of 120 pounds current money have sold to John Hutt all that plantation in tract of land containing 150 acres in the Parish of Cople and County of Westmoreland being the land formerly belonging to John Wright, the said land adjoining to the land formerly belonging to Coleman Read and the land of Thomas Blundell's. In witness whereof the said parties first above mentioned to these presents have interchangeably set their hands and seals the day and year above written.
Signed sealed and delivered in presence of us Gerrard Davis
William Brown Ann Davis (her mark)
Reuben Freshwater
At a Court held for Westmoreland County the 26th day of April 1768 this indenture and the receipt endorsed were acknowledged by Gerrard Davis and Ann Davis his wife parties thereto (she being first privy examined as the law directs) and ordered to be recorded. Teste

Page 545.
Hutt to Rochester Indenture
This indenture made the 28th eighth day of October 1767 between Gerrard Hutt, Sr., and Mary Hutt his wife of the Parish of Cople and County of Westmoreland, Gent., Of the one part and John Rochester of the same Parish and County aforesaid, planter of the other part. Witnesseth that Gerrard Hutt and Mary Hutt his wife in consideration of 100 pounds current money of Virginia have sold to John Rochester all that tract of land lying in the Parish of Cople and County of Westmoreland containing by estimation 100 acres in binding as followeth; on the lands of the Hon. Robert Carter, on the lands of John Yeatman, and on the lands of the said John Rochester (it being the land whereon Jane Moore now liveth as a tenant) which said land was purchased by the said Gerrard Hutt of Daniel Remey, deceased. In witness whereof the first parties to these presents have interchangeably set their hands and seals the day and year first above written.
Signed sealed and delivered in presence of us Gerrard Hutt
Gerrard Hutt, Jr. Mary Hutt (her mark)
Sampson Moore (his mark)
James Moore (her mark)
At a Court held for Westmoreland County the 31st day of May 1768 this indenture was acknowledged by Gerrard Hutt and Mary Hutt his wife parties thereto (she being first privy examined as the law directs) and the receipt endorsed was also acknowledged by the said Gerrard Hutt and together with the said indenture ordered to be recorded. Teste

Page 547.
Jackson to Sandy Indenture
This indenture made the seventh day of May 1768 between Daniel Jackson, Sr., of the Parish of Cople and County of Westmoreland of the one part and Uriah Sandy of the same Parish and County aforesaid of the other part. Witnesseth that Daniel Jackson, Sr., in consideration of 25 pounds current money of Virginia has sold unto Uriah Sandy 50 acres of land whereon George Brown, deceased formerly did possess. Beginning at a marked hickory tree joining John Lawson, from thence to a poplar standing on the head of a little branch, a corner tree between Mr. John Lawson and Uriah Sandy, from thence to a chestnut a corner tree between William Fryer and Uriah Sandy: from thence to a dead red oak between William Fryer and Uriah Sandy and Mr. Daniel Jackson, a corner tree, from thence to a cedar tree standing on a little branch. In witness whereof the parties to these presents have hereunto interchangeably set their hands and seals the day and

year first above written.
Signed sealed and delivered in the presence of us Daniel Jackson (his mark)
William Brown
Charles Knight
John Sandy (his mark)
At a court held for Westmoreland County the 31st day of May 1768 this indenture in the memorandum of livery of seizen endorsed were acknowledged by Daniel Jackson, Sr., party thereto and ordered to be recorded. Teste

Page 550.
Williams to Jett & Bernard Indenture
This indenture made the 31st day of May 1768 between Francis Williams of the County of Westmoreland of the one part and Thomas Jett and William Bernard of the other part. Witnesseth that Francis Williams for the uses, intent and purposes hereafter mentioned has sold by these presents unto Thomas Jett and William Bernard the following lands, Negroes and effects to wit; one parcel of land in the Parish of Washington and County of Westmoreland containing 400 acres or thereabouts whereon Benjamin Settle now resides, 10 Negroes; Landon, Jemra, Jerry, Lucy, Lucy and her child Lewis, Cyrus, Ben, Milly, Winney and Lett, 22 head of cattle, two horses, five beds and furniture, six ewes and lambs, and all the household and kitchen furniture belonging to the said Francis Williams at his residence in the parish aforesaid. To have and to hold the said tract and premises together with the said Negroes and other effects above mentioned unto the said Thomas Jett and William Bernard in trust to be sold for the pavement of the demands of the creditors of the said Francis Williams who have levied attachments on the effects of the said Williams and who has accepted judgments according to the priority in the first place and for the payment of all his other creditors after adjustment of their several demands and to and for no other use intent or purpose whatsoever. In witness whereof the said Francis Williams hath hereunto set his hand and seal the day and year above mentioned. Francis Williams
At a Court held for Westmoreland County the 31st day of May 1768 this indenture was acknowledged by Francis Williams party thereto and ordered to be recorded. Teste

Page 551.
Brown to Carmichael Lease
this indenture made the 1st day of January 1768 between John Brown of the Parish of Washington in County of Westmoreland, planter the one part and George Carmichael of the aforesaid Parish in County. Witnesseth that John Brown in consideration of the annual rent of 5 pounds current money has farm let unto George Carmichael 60 acres of land bounded as follows; beginning at a dead willow, from thence running North East into the run, thence up the meanders of said run opposite to a small marked apple tree making a corner, from thence to a cedar bush, from thence to a broken top spanish oak, from thence to a black scrubby oak marking a corner, from thence to a red oak, from thence to the Green Swamp, and running down the meanders of the said run or swamp to Carmichael's line, from thence down the said line to a holly bush, from thence down the said line to a dead willow which is the beginning. It being part of a tract of land which fell to the said John Brown by the death of his father. To have and to hold the said 60 acres from the date of the date hereof during the term of 19 years yielding and paying to the said John Brown the before said rent duly and yearly. The said rent is to become due the first day of January 1775. In witness whereof the parties aforesaid have either to other to these presents interchangeably set their hands and seals this first day of January 1768.
Signed sealed and delivered in the presence of John Brown
Archibald Bryce
James Bowcock
Hugh Lietch
At a Court held for Westmoreland County the 31st day of May 1768 this indenture was acknowledged by John Brown party thereto and ordered to be recorded. Teste

.
Page 552.

Butler to Butler Deed of Gift

I Thomas Butler of the County of Westmoreland, planter this 28th day of November 1767 for diverse good causes and valuable considerations do give and bequeath unto my son Nathaniel Butler my manor plantation binding on the land I gave to my son Thomas Butler: and the land of my son William Butler: and the land of Richard Lowe: and the land of William Jeffries, and the lands of Elizabeth Rust which said land and plantation I do freely clearly and absolutely give to my son Nathaniel Butler to him and his heirs. In witness whereof I have hereunto set my hand and seal the day and year first above written.

Signed sealed and delivered in presence of us Thomas Butler
George Rust
George Curtis
Peter Mullins
Jeremiah Courtney

At a Court held for Westmoreland County the 31st day of May 1768 this deed of gift was proved by the oath of George Rust and Peter Mullins witnesses thereto and the same having been proved in March last by the oath of George Curtis another of the witnesses thereto is ordered to be recorded. Test

Page 552.
Bashaw to Nelson Indenture

This indenture made the 27th day of October 1767 between Warner Bashaw and Behethelem Warner his wife of the County of Westmorland, bricklayer of the one part and William Nelson of the Parish of Washington and County of Westmoreland of the other part. Witnesseth that Warner Bashaw and Behethelem Warner his wife in consideration of 60 pounds current money of Virginia have sold unto William Nelson a tract of land in the Parish of Washington and County of Westmoreland containing 60 acres which said tract was given to the said Warner Bashaw by his father Peter Bashaw as by his will on record may fully appear. In witness whereof the said Warner Bashaw and Behethelem Warner his wife hath hereunto set their hands and seals the day and year above written.

Signed sealed and acknowledged in presence of Warner Bashaw
John Nelson, Jr. Behethelem Warner
William Blagg
Thomas Jones

At a Court held for Westmoreland County the 31st day of May 1768 this indenture was acknowledged by Warner Bashaw and Behethelem Warner his wife parties thereto (she being first privily examined as the law directs) in the receipt endorsed was also acknowledged by the said Warner Bashaw in together with the said indenture ordered to be recorded

Page 554.
James White's Will

In the name of God Amen,
this 23rd day of January 1768, I James White of Washington Parish in Westmoreland County being in perfect sense and memory.
Item I give to Elizabeth Weedon 20 Shillings money and no more of my estate.
Item I give and bequeath to my son George White all my lands and all my other personal estate.
Lastly, I appoint my son George White my whole and sole executor of this my last will and testament. In witness whereof I have hereunto set my hand and seal the day and month first above written.

Signed sealed and delivered George White
John Baxter
George Wilkerson (his mark)
Mildred Wilkerson (her mark)

At a Court held for Westmoreland County the 31st day of May 1768 this will was proved according to law by the oath of John Baxter and George Wilkerson witnesses thereto and ordered to be recorded and on the motion of George White the executor therein named who made oath thereto according to law and together with John Baxter his security entered into and acknowledged bond with condition as the law directs, certificate is granted him for obtaining a probate thereof in due form. Test

Page 555.

Ashton to Wray Deed of Gift

by John Ashton, the younger of the Parish of Washington and County of Westmoreland in consideration of the natural love and affection which I have for my sister Mrs. Mary Wray of the town of Hampton have given her Negro wench Winney and her two children, Ben and Jenny. In witness whereof I have hereunto set my hand and seal this first day of April 1767.

Signed sealed and delivered in presence of John Ashton
William Bernard

At a Court held for Westmoreland County the 26th day of July 1768 this deed of gift was proved by the oath of William Bernard the witness thereto and ordered to be recorded. Teste

Page 555.

Arnold to Bryce Indenture

This indenture made the 25th day of June 1768 between Ann Arnold, relict of Weedon Arnold of Westmoreland County, Virginia of the one part and Archibald Bryce of the said County of the other part. Witnesseth that Ann Arnold in consideration of 144 pounds 10 shillings and 10 pence Virginia currency due from Ann Arnold to Andrew Thompson and Company, merchants in Glasgow for whom the said Archibald Bryce is factor and attorney in fact, and in consideration of 10 shillings to the said Arnold in hand paid she the said Arnold acknowledge bargained and sold transferred and confirmed by these presents unto Archibald Bryce six slaves; Lett, Athatah, Cornelius, Len, Ann, Henne, together with the issue of the four female slaves, five cows, five yearlings, three calves, two feather beds and furniture, six leather chairs, one desk, one table, three flag chairs, a trunk, a chest, one dozen and three plates, three dishes, three pots, one iron kettle, 8 sows, and 18 young hogs. To have and to hold the said slaves and other premises to the Archibald Bryce in trust that at any time after the first day of October 1769 sell and dispose of the said slaves and premises on one month's credit to the highest bidder taking from the purchasers bonds in good securities and to the end that the said Bryce may out of the purchase money or bonds taken for the same, detain so much or so much thereof as will be sufficient to discharge the debt and interest due to the said Thompson and Company and also to defray the charges of the said Bryce insured in the execution of the said trust and thereafter to assign the remaining bonds or money to the said Ann Arnold and the said Ann Arnold binds herself to the said Archibald Bryce the penal sum of 1000 pounds current money of Virginia to permit the said Archibald Bryce to sell and dispose of the premises and to concur in everything to give satisfaction to the purchasers. In testimony whereof the said Ann Arnold hath hereunto put her hand and seal the day and year above written.

Signed and sealed in presence of Ann Arnold
Daniel Fitzhugh
Robert Lovell, Jr.
John Lovell

At a court held for Westmoreland County the 26th day of July 1768 this indenture was proved by the oath of Daniel Fitzhugh and John Lovell witnesses thereto and ordered to be recorded. Test

Page 557.

Fryer to Lawson Indenture

This indenture made the 25th day of July 1768 between William Fryer of the County of Westmoreland and Parish of Cople of the one part and John Lawson of the County of Richmond of the other part. Witnesseth that William Fryer in consideration of 50 pounds lawful money of Virginia has sold to John Lawson all that tenement of land which he now possesses containing by estimation 90 one acres lying in Nominy Forrest in the County of Westmoreland and Parish of Cople whereof 30 acres was bequeathed to him by his grandfather George Brown by his last will and the remainder being 61 acres from a patent from the Hon. Thomas Lord Fairfax bearing date the 3rd day of September 1741 and according to a survey of Elias Davis is bounded as follows;

beginning at a locust stake in the line of George Brown and Elias Morris, deceased and Richard Sutton the elder, corner, thence along a line of the said Sutton's North 66° West 100 poles, crossing a branch of Cos Cos Creek to a small white oak sapling, thence down another line of the said Sutton, Southwest 41 poles to the land of Thomas Browning, deceased but now in possession of Andrew Hutchinson, thence along the said Thomas Browning's line, South 10° West 143 poles to a small poplar standing on the head of a small branch, thence along a line of George Brown and Elias Morris, deceased, 82 poles, crossing a branch of Rappahannock Creek to an old dead white oak corner tree to the land of George Brown and Elias Morris, deceased but now in possession of Daniel Jackson and the said William Fryer, thence along the said George Brown and Elias Morris' line North East 112 poles to the place it first began containing 61 acres, 1 rod and 10 perches. In witness whereof I have hereunto set my hand and seal the for these witnesses.

Signed sealed and delivered in presence of us William Fryer
James Muse
Beckwith Butler
William Templeman

At a Court held for Westmoreland County the 28th day of July 1768 this indenture was acknowledged by William Fryer party thereto and ordered to be recorded. Teste

Page 559.

Butler to Bayne Indenture

This indenture made the 11th day of December 1767 between Nathaniel Butler of the County of Westmoreland, planter of the one part and Matthew Bayne: Sr., of the same County, planter of the other part. Witnesseth that Nathaniel Butler in consideration of 90 pounds current money of Virginia has sold to Matthew Bayne: Sr., all that tract lying in the Parish of Washington and County of Westmoreland containing 180 acres and bounded as followeth; beginning at the mouth of a branch of the Beaverdam of Pope's at a hollow poplar which tree was spoken of in my father's will and so up the branch to a red oak standing on the southwest side, thence to a red oak by the roadside, thence along the road to a horse path that goes to the house belonging to Lawrence Butler, to a marked white oak standing in the said line, thence down the said line to the land of William Quisenbury unto the first beginning. In witness whereof the parties to these presents have hereunto set their hands and seals the day and year above written.

Sealed and delivered in presence of Nathaniel Butler
Edward Ransdell, Jr.
Richard Neale
William Bridger
Edward Muse
Matthew Bayne: Jr.

At a court held for Westmoreland County the 26th day of July 1768 this indenture was proved by the oaths of Richard Neale and William Bridger and Matthew Bayne: Jr. witnesses thereto and the receipt endorsed was also proved by the oaths of the said Neale and Bridges and together with the said indenture ordered to be recorded. Teste.

Page 560.

Turberville to Turberville Indenture

This indenture made the 29th day of March 1768 between George Turberville of the Parish of Cople and County of Westmoreland, Gent., of the one part and John Turberville of the same parish and county, Gent., of the other part. Witnesseth that George Turberville in consideration of 5 shillings has sold to John Turberville a tract of land in the Parish of Lunenburg and county of Richmond containing 81 acres, 1 rod and 6 poles which the said George Turberville purchased of William Black by deed of bargain and sale bearing date the 14th day of June 1766 and bounded as followeth; beginning at a small marked gum standing on the south side of a swamp and running South 32 ½° East 59 pole along a line of marked trees dividing this land from other lands belonging to the said George Turberville to a marked red oak corner tree thence along a row of irregular marked trees which being reduced to a straight line is South 8° West 59 pole to a marked red oak corner tree of this land in the aforesaid John Turberville's land, thence along another of the said

Turberville's lines South 14° West 80 pole to a marked red Oak corner to this land the said Turberville's land and that now held by Edmund Bulger, thence along the said Bulger's line being reduced straight is North 34° West 161 ½ poles to a small gun marked for a corner between the said Bulger and this land standing on the side of the above swamp, then up the several windings and meanders of the said swamp to the first beginning gum. In witness whereof the parties to these presents have hereunto interchangeably set their hands and seals the day and year first above written.

Sealed and delivered in presence of George Turberville

At a court continued and held for Westmoreland County the 27th day of July 1768 this indenture was acknowledged by George Turberville, Gent., party thereto and ordered to be recorded. Teste James Davenport Cl Cur

Page 562.

Rust to Morse Indenture

This indenture made the 27th day of June 1768 between Samuel Rust of the Parish of Cople and County of Westmoreland of the one part and Obediah Morse [Moss] of the same parish and county of the other part. Witnesseth that Samuel Rust in consideration of 20 pounds current money has sold to Obediah Morse all that tenement of land that the said Rust purchased of John Garner containing by estimation 30 acres being part of a tract of land granted by patent to William Walker in 1662 and being in the Parish of Cople and County of Westmoreland and bounded by the land of Samuel Rust, Southeast 175 poles to a corner near Mrs. Elizabeth Rust's Mill Pond, and from thence up the said mill pond side, 130 poles to a branch, from thence up the said branch and Valley and from the head of the said valley northerly to the beginning. In witness whereof the said Samuel Rust to these presents have set my hand and affixed my seal the day month and year first above written.

Sealed and delivered in the presence of us Samuel Rust

At a court continued and held for Westmoreland County the 27th day of July 1768 this indenture and the receipt endorsed were acknowledged by Samuel Rust party thereto and ordered to be recorded. Teste

Page 563.

Watts to Bankhead Indenture

This indenture made the 16th day of August 1768 between John Watts, Gent., Of the Parish of Washington and County of Westmoreland of the one part and James Bankhead, surgeon of the same parish and county of the other part. Witnesseth that John Watts in consideration of 1400 pounds current money has sold to James Bankhead the following tracts of land each of them situated and being on the north side of Mattox Creek in the Parish of Washington County of Westmoreland to wit;

1. One piece or parcel thereof on which said John Watts now resides containing 565 acres besides the marsh were marshes adjoining.
2. One other piece purchased by John Watts, the father of the said John Watts party thereto of John Bowcock adjoining northerly upon the before mentioned tract of land, containing 250 acres or thereabouts.
3. One other parcel of land also purchased of the said John Watts the father of John Triplett containing 300 acres commonly called the Barrens.
4. One other parcel of land situate in the White Oak Swamp containing 121 acres or thereabouts.

In witness whereof the said John Watts hath hereunto set his hand and seal the day and year above written.

Signed sealed and delivered in presence of John Watts

William Bernard

Lawrence Washington

William Robinson

At a court held for Westmoreland County the 30th day of August 1768 this indenture and the receipt underwritten were acknowledged by John Watts, Gent., party thereto and ordered to be recorded. Teste

Page 565.
Peach to Atwood Lease
This indenture made the 29th day of August 1768 between Thomas Peach of Washington Parish in the County of Westmoreland of the one part and John Atwood and Sarah Atwood his wife, planters of the same county and parish of the other part. Witnesseth that Thomas Peach in consideration of the annual rent of 40 shillings for the years 1768 and 1769 and 50 shillings for the years 1770, 1771 in 1772, and ever after 55 shillings yearly and the quit rents and taxes of 100 acres of land has farm let all that tenement of land lying in the aforesaid County and bounded as followeth; beginning at a marked red oak, a corner tree of the land of Capt. James Blair standing on the west side of a branch known by the name of Polly Branch running easterly a small course along the said Blair's line to a another corner of the said Blair's land, thence southerly another course along the said Blair's land to the land of Robert Frank's and Spillman's, thence easterly along the said Frank's and Spillman's land to a path commonly called Spillman's Path, thence northerly along the said path to the land of Gabriel Johnson: thence westerly to the first beginning tree of the land of the said Capt. James Blair it being a parcel of land the said Thomas Peach purchased of Col. John Triplett, Gent., containing by estimation 100 acres. To have and to hold unto the said John Atwood and Sarah Atwood lives yielding and paying to the said Thomas Peach the before said annual rent after the 25th day of December yearly; and the said John Atwood doth oblige himself to plant, tend and keep under a good fence, 50 apple trees and 150 peach trees within three years hereafter. In witness whereof the parties aforesaid have hereunto either to the other to these presents interchangeably set their hands and seals the day month and year first above written. John Atwood or his wife Sarah Atwood shall have liberty to give up this lease if they shall think proper to Thomas Peach his heirs assigns or administrators.

Signed sealed and delivered in presence of us — Thomas Peach
John Bailey — John Atwood
Stephen Bailey
Robert Frank, Sr.
Robert Frank, Jr.
Samuel Frank

At a court held for Westmoreland County the 30th day of August 1768 this indenture was acknowledged by Thomas Peach the lessor and ordered to be recorded. Teste

Page 567.
Hutcheson's Wife Renunciation of Will (refer to Page 518)
Gentleman, As I do not intend to stand to my husband William Hutcheson's will, desire that and order may be made that the gentleman that was appointed appraisers or any others may allot me and set apart my dower according to law. Given under my hand this 24th day of June 1768. Teste

William Berryman — Elizabeth Hutcheson (her mark)
Lovell Massey
Nathaniel Gray, Jr.
Spence Monroe
James Butler
Benjamin Berryman
Gerard Blackistone Causine

At a court held for Westmoreland County the 20th day of August 1768 this letter of renunciation of the will of William Hutcheson, deceased was proved by the oaths of Lovell Massey: Benjamin Berryman and Gerard Blackistone Causine witnesses thereto and ordered to be recorded. Teste

Page 568.
William Rowe's Will
In the name of God Amen, I William Rowe of Washington Parish in the County of Westmoreland do make this my last will and testament in the manner and form following;
First, I give to my daughter Jane Pope Rowe the following slaves; Daniel, Sam, Pegg, Lucy, Winney, Jack, Ben, Dick, Bess, Harry and Kate. Also the feather bed and furniture that stands in

the hall shed and she may have a horse and saddle purchased for her.
I give to my granddaughter Elizabeth Fox, Negro girl Milly.
I give my whole tract of land to my daughter Anjalellah [Angelica] Fox and to the heirs of her body.
Item I give all the rest of my slaves to my daughter Anjalellah [Angelica] Fox.
Tis my desire my wife may have one feather bed and furniture and the use any room in the house, provided she chooses it.
All the rest of my estate may be equally divided between my two daughters.
Tis my desire my estate may not be appraised, but that three honest men may be chosen to set apart and divide the personal estate after the legacies are paid.
I appoint my son in law Joseph Fox my whole and sole executor of this my last will and testament.
In witness whereof I have hereunto set my hand and seal this 12th day of May 1768.
Signed sealed and delivered in presence of William Rowe
James Degge
George Monroe
Jane Brown
At a court held for Westmoreland County the 27th day of September 1768 this will was proved according to law by James Degge and George Monroe witnesses thereto and ordered to be recorded and on the motion of Joseph Fox, the executor therein named who made oath thereto according to law and together with William Smith his security entered into and acknowledged bond with condition as law directs, certificate is granted him for obtaining a probate thereof in due form. Teste.

Page 569.
George Beard's Will
In the name of God Amen, I George Beard of the Parish of Washington in the county of Washington being very sick and weak in body but of perfect sense and memory.
I give and bequeath unto my beloved wife Marina Beard, my daughter Susanna Beard and my son George Beard all my personal estate to be equally divided between them when my son arrives to the age of 21 years and not before unless my wife should marry before the time mentioned.
Item I give and bequeath to my son George Beard all my land, and if he dies without heirs it should return to my daughter Susanna Beard.
Item my will and desire is that my beloved wife Marina Beard shall have the benefit of my whole estate both real and personal during her widowhood and that she keep the children with her and give them good education and after my debts are paid and my estate clear, then to let my mother Ann Hilton to have in goods the value of 50 shillings.
I do hereby make and ordain my beloved wife Marina Beard executrix and William Smith and William Hilton executors of this my last will and testament.
In witness whereof I have hereunto set my hand and seal this 12th day of September 1768.
Signed sealed and delivered in presence of George Beard (his mark)
John Beard
William South
John Lansdown (his mark)
At a court held for Westmoreland County the 27th day of September 1768 this will was proved according to law by the oaths of John Beard and John Landown witnesses thereto and ordered to be recorded and on the motion of William Smith, Marina Beard and William Hilton the executors and executrix in the said will named who made oath thereto according to law and together with George Monroe, William Wroe and Thomas Peach their securities entered into and acknowledged bond with condition as the law directs, certificate is granted them for obtaining a probate thereof in due form. Teste

Page 570.
Hurley to Martin Indenture
This Indenture made the 14th day of April 1768 between John Hurley of the Parish of Washington and County of Westmoreland son and heir of John Hurley and Ann his wife of the one part and John Martin of the same parish and county of the other hand. Witnesseth that John Hurley in

consideration of 30 pounds current money has sold to John Martin all that parcel of land lying on the north side of Mattox Creek in the Parish of Washington and County of Westmoreland containing 33 acres, the same being in the possession of the said John Martin and Daniel Fitzhugh. In witness whereof the said John Hurley have hereunto set his hand and seal the day and year above written.

Signed sealed and delivered in presence of John Hurley
John Ashton
Benjamin Berryman
Woffendall Kendall
James Dishman

At a court held for Westmoreland County the 27th day of September 1768 this indenture and the receipt endorsed were proved by the oaths of James Dishman a witness whereto and the same having been before proved by the oaths of two other of the witnesses thereto and ordered to be recorded. Teste

www.ingramcontent.com/pod-product-compliance
Lightning Source LLC
LaVergne TN
LVHW061245100826
845148LV00008B/1030

* 9 7 8 0 7 8 8 4 2 9 5 7 6 *